CAMDEN TOWN

Oberstufe

Arbeitsheft zu den Pflichtmaterialien

Erarbeitet von

Anne-Kathrin Böker
Ilka Kratz
Jana Oldendörp
Alexander Woltin

Abkürzungen:

AE	American English
BE	British English
e.g.	exempli gratia (Latin) = for example
i.e.	id est (Latin) = that is
infml.	informal
pl.	plural
sb	somebody
sth	something

Webcodes
Auf manchen Seiten findest du Webcodes, die dich zu zusätzlichen Materialien im Internet führen. Gib dazu einfach den Code auf www.westermann.de/webcode ins Suchfeld ein.

Filmauszüge
Je nach Abspielgerät und verwendeter Software kann es vorkommen, dass die Zeitangaben zu den Filmauszügen nicht exakt mit den im Kapitel angegebenen übereinstimmen.

Frankenstein
Die Verweise zu *Frankenstein* beziehen sich auf die Ausgabe: Mary Shelley, *Frankenstein*, Westermann 2020, ISBN: 978-3-425-73623-5.

Hamlet
Die Verweise zu *Hamlet* beziehen sich auf die Ausgabe: William Shakespeare, *Hamlet*, Westermann 2021, ISBN: 978-3-425-73068-4

Verweise auf *Skills pages* und *Workshops*
Die Verweise auf *Skills pages* und *Workshops* beziehen sich auf das Schülerbuch *Camden Town Oberstufe Qualifikationsphase Niedersachsen*, ISBN: 978-3-425-73642-6.

westermann GRUPPE

© 2021 Westermann Bildungsmedienverlag GmbH, Georg-Westermann-Allee 66, 38104 Braunschweig
www.westermann.de

Druck A² / Jahr 2021
Alle Drucke der Serie A sind im Unterricht parallel verwendbar.

Redaktion: Nicola Birkner, Thorsten Schimming, Linda Knief
Umschlaggestaltung: Gingco.Net Werbeagentur GmbH & Co. KG, Braunschweig
Layout: Visuelle Lebensfreude, Hannover; thom bahr GRAFIK
Druck und Bindung: Westermann Druck Zwickau GmbH, Crimmitschauer Straße 43, 08058 Zwickau

ISBN 978-3-425-**73652**-5

			Abiturvorgaben/Themen
Part 1	**Frankenstein**		
6	Novel	Pre-reading While reading Post-reading	Roman: Mary Shelley, *Frankenstein*
21	Topic	**Ethics of science**	Ethics of science Science and technology: chances and risks Beliefs, values and norms in society Visions of the future
27		**The role of nature**	Questions of human identity
29		**Questions of (human) identity**	Questions of human identity Individual and society Visions of the future
Part 2	**The postcolonial experience**		
32	Topic	**Facts and figures about the British Empire**	Postcolonial experience Britishness
33		**Two views of colonialism**	Postcolonial experience
35		**Immigration to Britain**	Postcolonial experience Questions of belonging and identity
37		**Refugees in the 20th and 21st century**	Postcolonial experience Questions of belonging and identity
38	Short story	**The third and final continent** (1999) Pre-reading While reading Post-reading	Postcolonial experience Questions of belonging and identity Ethnic, cultural and linguistic diversity Beliefs, values and norms in society
49		**The escape** (2009) Pre-reading While reading Post-reading	Postcolonial experience Questions of belonging and identity Ethnic, cultural and linguistic diversity Beliefs, values and norms in society
63		**Loose change** (2005) Pre-reading While reading Post-reading	Postcolonial experience Questions of belonging and identity Ethnic, cultural and linguistic diversity Beliefs, values and norms in society Britishness
71		**The rain missed my face and fell straight to my shoes** (2005) Pre-reading While reading Post-reading	Postcolonial experience Questions of belonging and identity Ethnic, cultural and linguistic diversity Beliefs, values and norms in society Migration effects on the world of work
79		**She shall not be moved** (2005) Pre-reading While reading Post-reading	Postcolonial experience Ethnic, cultural and linguistic diversity Beliefs, values and norms in society Britishness
	Post-reading	**The short stories**	Postcolonial experience Questions of belonging and identity

Contents

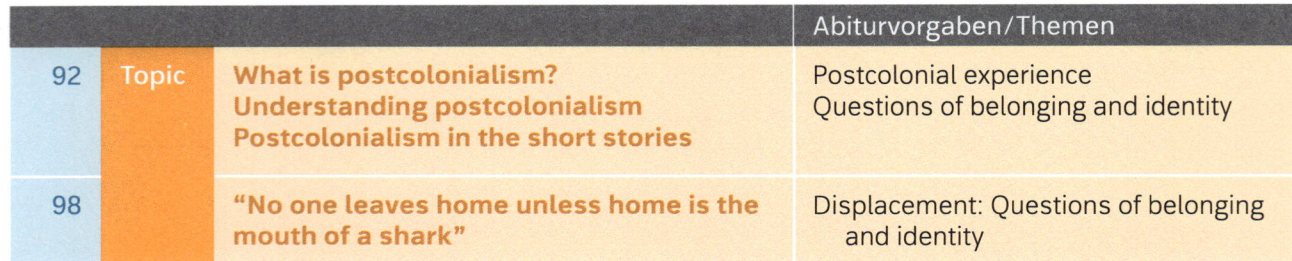

			Abiturvorgaben/Themen
92	Topic	**What is postcolonialism?** **Understanding postcolonialism** **Postcolonialism in the short stories**	Postcolonial experience Questions of belonging and identity
98		**"No one leaves home unless home is the mouth of a shark"**	Displacement: Questions of belonging and identity

Part 3 Ethnic and cultural diversity: Gran Torino

100	Topic	**American core beliefs and cultures**	Cultural clashes
106	Film	**Gran Torino** *Pre-viewing* Detroit in numbers and figures Getting closer to the "Gran Torino" Revisiting cinematography	Cultural clashes The American experience Beliefs, values and norms in society Ethnic, cultural and linguistic diversity
116		*While viewing* (Un)wanted birthday presents for Walt A tender breeze blows Walt and Sue – a culture clash? Racism – now and then Walt Kowalski – an angry white male?	Cultural clashes Ethnic, cultural and linguistic diversity Identity The American experience
127		*Post-viewing* Is Walt a hero? Dealing with the film as a whole	Cultural clashes Individual and society Beliefs, values and norms in society
130	Topic	**Violence: Gang culture** **The omnipresence of violence in "Gran Torino"**	The role of gang culture and violence Beliefs, values and norms in society Cultural clashes
136		**Gang culture in film**	The role of gang culture and violence

Part 4 Hamlet

141	Play	Pre-reading While reading Post-reading	Shakespeare: The world that made him Drama: Auszüge aus: William Shakespeare, *Hamlet*
168	Topic	**Fate vs. free will**	Fate vs. free will
171		**Fate vs. free will in *Hamlet***	Fate vs. free will
173		**The role(s) of women**	The role(s) of women
174		**The role(s) of women in *Hamlet***	The role(s) of women
176		**Questions of morality**	Questions of morality

Liebe Schülerin, lieber Schüler,

mit diesem Arbeitsheft kannst du dich ideal auf das Abitur vorbereiten. Du beschäftigst dich mit dem Film und allen Texten, die für das Abitur vorgeschrieben sind, und außerdem mit weiteren abiturrelevanten Themen. Für das schriftliche Abitur 2023 müssen die folgenden Materialien unter den genannten inhaltlichen Gesichtspunkten behandelt werden:

Roman:
Mary Shelley, *Frankenstein* (1831)
→ verbindliche Unterrichtsaspekte:
- ethics of science
- the role of nature
- questions of (human) identity

Film:
Gran Torino (Clint Eastwood, 2008)
→ verbindliche Unterrichtsaspekte:
- ethnic and cultural diversity: cultural clashes
- the role of gang culture and violence

Drama:
Auszüge aus: William Shakespeare, *Hamlet*
→ verbindliche Unterrichtsaspekte:
- fate vs. free will
- the role(s) of women
- questions of morality

Short stories (Allgemein bildende Schulen):
Jhumpa Lahiri, *The third and final continent* (1999)
Andrea Levy, *Loose change* (2005)
Shereen Pandit, *She shall not be moved* (2005)
Qaisra Shahraz, *The escape* (2009)
→ verbindliche Unterrichtsaspekte:
- postcolonial experience
- displacement: questions of belonging and identity

Short stories (Berufliche Gymnasien):
Saeed Taji Farouky, *The rain missed my face and fell straight to my shoes* (2005)
Jhumpa Lahiri, *The third and final continent* (1999)
Andrea Levy, *Loose change* (2005)
Qaisra Shahraz, *The escape* (2009)
→ verbindliche Unterrichtsaspekte:
- postcolonial experience
- displacement: questions of belonging and identity

Aufbau des Arbeitshefts

In **Part 1**: *Frankenstein* und **Part 4**: *Hamlet* erfolgen zunächst eine inhaltliche Sicherung und allgemeine Bearbeitung der jeweiligen Materialien. Auf speziell ausgewiesenen *Topic*-Seiten werden die verbindlichen Unterrichtsaspekte generell eingeführt, bevor sie im Kontext der jeweiligen Lektüre noch einmal vertieft werden. Wo es sich anbietet, werden auch weitere Themen aus dem Lehrplan (Kerncurriculum) aufgegriffen.

In **Part 2**: *Postcolonial Short Stories* und **Part 3**: *Gran Torino* werden zunächst auf *Topic*-Seiten für die Erarbeitung relevante thematische Aspekte behandelt, und dann wird in die Arbeit mit den Pflichtmaterialien eingestiegen. Die thematischen Aspekte werden auf zusätzlichen *Topic*-Seiten wieder aufgegriffen und vertieft.

An vielen Stellen findest du Verweise auf *Skills pages* und *Workshops* im Schülerbuch *Camden Town Oberstufe Qualifikationsphase* (ISBN: 978-3-425-73642-6). Die *Skills pages* geben dir Hilfestellungen zu wichtigen Aufgabenformaten. In den *Workshops* werden bestimmte Kompetenzen intensiv trainiert. Im Schülerbuch werden außerdem weitere Aspekte der Themen dieses Arbeitsheftes behandelt.

Pre-reading

1

You are going to read the novel *Frankenstein* by Mary Shelley (1831).
Create a mind-map. Note down what you already know about *Frankenstein*.

2

Describe the following pictures. Do some research on their background. Based on the pictures speculate on the plot of *Frankenstein*.

University of Ingolstadt

Film still starring Boris Karloff in *Frankenstein*, cf. p. 18

Figure of Prometheus

Frederic Edwin: Arctic Landscape

_____

_____

_____

_____

_____

_____

_____

3

Read the information about some of the characters involved and try to predict what their roles in the plot might be:

• **Victor Frankenstein** – a scientist striving for progress by starting an unorthodox scientific experiment

_____

• **Elizabeth Lavenza** – a beautiful young woman and the adopted sister of Victor Frankenstein

_____

• **Professor Waldman** – a natural scientist at Ingolstadt University

_____

• **Captain Robert Walton** – an Arctic voyager who set out to explore the North Pole

_____

• **The De Laceys** – an impoverished but devoted French family

_____

Language support

The story might revolve around …
I expect a story about …
I expect the novel to be full of personal tragedy/murder/science …
I would imagine that the character/story …

4

Use the internet to find out the key events of Mary Shelley's life.

5 → **S8:** How to improve your text
Write a short biography of her for a website on female English literature.

While reading

PART ONE

Info

Keeping a reading journal will help you follow and keep track of aspects of a novel such as the plot, the characters and the setting. Your notes will make it easier for you to understand the structure of the novel and the issues it deals with. Initial responses to the text or questions can be noted down, as well as the corresponding lines to help you find the relevant chapters and quotations more quickly. As the novel has a non-linear structure, you can also note down time markers for your orientation. You should take notes in the simple present tense.

6

Now start reading the novel. While reading the book, fill in the appropriate table of your reading journal. Take notes on what you consider to be most important in each section.

The Letters		
Characters	Main events	Your notes
Robert Walton *Margaret Saville* *…*	— *Robert Walton is headed on a dangerous voyage to the North Pole as the captain of the ship.* — *Walton tells his sister of the preparations leading up to his undertaking.* — *Walton wants to discover a northern passage to the Pacific and set foot on undiscovered territory.*	

Chapters I–VIII		
Characters	Main events	Your notes

Chapters IX-XVI		
Characters	Main events	Your notes

Chapters XVII–XXIV		
Characters	Main events	Your notes

PART TWO: THE LETTERS

7

a) Outline facts about Walton, his undertaking and the setting of the plot (time and place).

_____

_____

b) Sum up Walton's drive for scientific investigation.

_____

_____

c) Describe Victor Frankenstein's physical and psychological condition as shown in Walton's letters. Provide evidence from the novel.

_____

_____

_____

_____

_____

8

Describe Walton's feelings towards his guest Frankenstein. Use some of the nouns from the box. Justify your answer with proof from the text.

adaptability | hope | pity | envy | optimism | friendship | excitement | admiration | respect | wonder | curiosity | love | happiness

_____

_____

_____

_____

9

Frankenstein addresses Walton by saying: "Have you drunk also of the intoxicating draught? Hear me – let me reveal my tale, and you will dash the cup from your lips!" (p. 24). Speculate on what Frankenstein might be talking about.

10

Analyse how nature and landscape are used in the letters to create suspense for the upcoming story. Work in a group of four. Use a placemat to come up with ideas. Discuss your findings in your group.

> **The usage of nature and landscape in the letters in order to create suspense for the upcoming story**

PART THREE: CHAPTERS I–VIII

11

a) Sum up what Victor Frankenstein recounts about his family background.

b) Draw a family tree of the members of the Frankenstein family.

c) Outline key events of Victor Frankenstein's formal education.

_____

_____

_____

12

Use the internet to find out information about natural philosophy, Cornelius Agrippa, Paracelsus and Albertus Magnus. With the information found create a profile of each personality. Refer to their date and place of birth, their approach to natural philosophy, their research and criticism of their work.

a) Explain why Frankenstein is fascinated by these ancient scholars.

_____

_____

_____

b) At Ingolstadt University one of the teachers, Mr. Krempe, scolds Frankenstein for sticking to outdated scientific beliefs by saying: "My dear sir, you must begin your studies entirely anew." (p. 41). Comment on Frankenstein's reaction to this incident.

_____

_____

_____

13 CHOOSE → **Workshop:** Analysing characters

State why Frankenstein feels encouraged in his scientific purpose by his teacher Mr. Waldman.

OR

State what Frankenstein's criteria for choosing his mentors suggests about his character.

14

Explain the role that death plays in Victor Frankenstein's life.

_____

_____

_____

15 CHOOSE

Frankenstein tries to create a beautiful creature and is upset when it ends up being hideous when brought to life. Describe his reaction to his creature using text references. Explain the effect the creature has on him.
OR
Comment on Frankenstein's decision to run from his own creature after having finished it.
Note: Until 1832 the dissection of human bodies was regarded as desecration and was therefore illegal.

16 Group work
a) Sum up what the reader gets to know about Justine Moritz (Chapter VI and following).
b) Examine whether or not Justine has a telling name which predicts her development and fate.
c) Discuss why Frankenstein decides not to speak up for Justine but rather decides to keep his creation a secret.

Info

Telling Name
Some authors deliberately choose character names that reveal some of their character's traits.

17 Group work → **Workshop:** Analysing characters
Read Chapters I–VIII again carefully. Work in a group of four. Choose one of the following characters and note what you have learned about them. Collect information for your task from these chapters only. Provide references from the text. Present your results to your group members and add the missing information.

Characters in *Frankenstein*	Text references
Walton	
Clerval	
Justine	
Elizabeth	

PART FOUR: CHAPTERS IX-XVI

18

Decide whether these statements are true or false. Tick the correct box. Provide evidence for each statement.

	true	false	evidence
1. Frankenstein's creature felt confused because of all the new sensations of life.			
2. Frankenstein's health suffers as a result of his massive sense of guilt.			
3. Elizabeth isn't much changed by the tragedy of William's death but stays faithful and strong for her family.			
4. Nature contributes to Frankenstein's mental healing process.			
5. The creature is thankful to Victor Frankenstein for giving it life.			
6. Although Victor Frankenstein takes pity on his creature, he cannot bring himself to promise it a female companion.			
7. The creature longs for human company after leaving Frankenstein.			
8. The De Laceys teach the creature how to speak, read and write.			
9. The creature compares its fate to that of Adam and Eve in the Bible.			
10. The rejection of the De Laceys leads the creature to hatred and murder.			

19 → **Workshop:** Analysing atmosphere   → **Workshop:** Analysing characters

Examine how landscape and nature are used in these chapters in relation to Frankenstein. How does the way they are described reflect his feelings, actions and state of mind? Reread pp. 89-90 (Chapter X).

_____

_____

_____

_____

FRANKENSTEIN AND CLERVAL'S FRIENDSHIP

20 Group work

Discuss:

• What is important in a friendship?
• Is it ok to keep a secret from your friend?
• Does a good friend always have to be faithful?

21

Describe and analyse Frankenstein and Clerval's friendship. Reread pp. 55-57 and pp. 146-149.

_____

_____

_____

22

Discuss the following quote:

a) "How can I move thee? Will no entreaties cause thee to turn a favourable eye upon thy creature, who implores thy goodness and compassion? Believe me, Frankenstein: I was benevolent; my soul glowed with love and humanity; but am I not alone, miserably alone? You, my creator, abhor me; what hope can I gather from your fellow creatures, who owe me nothing? they spurn and hate me." (p. 92)
What do you think of the creature's claims? Can you relate to the creature's frustrations?

b) Evaluate what Victor Frankenstein owes his creature as its maker.

23

Frankenstein and the creature have an argument about whether or not Frankenstein will create a female companion for the creature.
Sum up and compare their arguments for and against a female companion. (Chapter XVII)

Victor Frankenstein: _____

_____

_____

The creature: _____

_____

_____

24

Frankenstein reflects upon his creature's demands: "After a long pause of reflection, I concluded that the justice due to both to him and my fellow creatures demanded of me that I should comply with his request." (p. 136). Discuss in class.

25 → **S8:** How to improve your text

"Frankenstein's rejection of the creature is due to the fact that he doesn't give it a name, causing a lack of identity." Write a comment on this statement saying whether you agree or disagree with it, taking into account the nouns Frankenstein uses to address or talk about his creature.

_____

_____

_____

_____

26

a) Frankenstein says: "I felt as if I were placed under a ban – as if I had no right to claim their sympathies – as if never more might I enjoy companionship with them. Yet even thus I loved them to adoration; and to save them, I resolved to dedicate myself to my most abhorred task. The prospect of such an occupation made every other circumstance of existence pass before me like a dream, and that thought only had to me the reality of life." (p. 137). Explain the context of this account.

b) Read the information given in the box. Analyse whether or not Victor Frankenstein is a reliable narrator. Give proof from the text.   → **Workshop:** Analysing narrative perspective

Info

Unreliable narrator

An **unreliable narrator** is usually a first-person narrator and character within the story whose narration and perception are not completely credible due to the character's affected mental condition or maturity. As a result, this narrator has a distorted view of events, gives illogical or contradicting information and speaks with a bias or even lies. Accordingly, a **reliable narrator** is considered a credible storyteller being fully aware of the circumstances around him. His perception of the world is trustworthy and coherent.

Reliable and unreliable narration has been widely debated within literary scholarship since some literary critics argue that there is no such thing as a reliable first-person narrator at all. According to them, every literary character is affected by his or her past experiences and perception in the telling of a story. However, generally most first-person narrators attempt to give the most accurate and therefore reliable version of the events told in the story. One reason for creating an unreliable narrator is to make the reader reconsider their point of view and create dramatic suspense by making the truth unclear.

_____

_____

_____

PART FIVE: CHAPTERS XVII-XXIV

27

Match the sentence parts. Write the numbers 1-7 in the boxes.

Henry Clerval		dies of grief as a result of recent events.
The creature breaks into the room		dies of natural causes on Walton's ship.
After he left the magistrate		was the creature's most recent victim.
At Frankenstein's trial		and kills Elizabeth.
Frankenstein		tells Walton to travel to the far north and commits suicide.
The creature		Frankenstein decides to hunt the creature and kill it.
Frankenstein's father		witnesses can prove that he was on the Orkney Islands at the time Clerval was found dead.

28

a) Describe the landscape as depicted in these chapters. How does the setting mirror the characters and events?

b) Describe the use of light and darkness as shown in the last part of the novel.

_____

_____

_____

29

Analyse the language the creature uses to address Frankenstein. What strikes you as interesting?

30 → **Workshop:** Analysing characters → **S8:** How to improve your text

a) Look at the list of adjectives that can be used in a characterization. Look up unknown words in a dictionary.

innocent | caring | cruel | destructive | worried | miserable | envious | obsessed | dissatisfied | ugly
desperate | anxious | impulsive | furious | impatient | frightening | ruthless | manipulative | sad | unfriendly
lonely | sensitive | sophisticated | fragile | wild | intelligent | friendly | strange | pessimistic | crazy

b) Choose five adjectives that you think characterize the creature best.
c) Justify your ideas with examples from the novel.
d) Using the chosen adjectives and the information given in these chapters, write a characterization of the creature.

31 CHOOSE

Compare the characters of Frankenstein and Walton. Are they both driven by obsession?
OR
Walton and Frankenstein are both men of science seeking personal reward and satisfaction. Analyse what this reveals about gender roles in 18th century England.

32 → **S2:** Creative Writing

After seeing Frankenstein dead on the ship, the creature floats away into the darkness on an ice raft intending to kill itself. Write the creature's interior monologue after having left its creator.

_____

_____

_____

_____

33 Pair work

Comment on the ending of the novel.

34

Discuss the question of responsibility in the novel: Who would you hold responsible for the tragedy in the novel (Victor Frankenstein, the creature, society)? Justify your point of view.

35

Create a comic strip: Re-tell the death of Frankenstein in six cartoon sketches with captions or speech bubbles. Focus on the following events:
- Frankenstein in his cabin
- Frankenstein making Walton promise to kill the creature once he found it
- Walton weeping over Frankenstein's death
- the first personal encounter between the creature and Walton
- the last encounter between the creature and Frankenstein
- the disappearance of the monster

Post-reading

36

Discuss the thematic focus of the novel. Is it a novel of science/human nature/prejudice/identity/ friendship/...? Find arguments for and against the different options.

37

a) Think: Make a list of five themes you consider central to your understanding of the novel.
b) Pair: Explain your choices to your partner and agree on five major themes.
c) Share: Discuss your results in a small group and agree on five themes, giving reasons for your choices by presenting examples from the novel.

38

Now that you have read the novel, think about its subheading "The Modern Prometheus".
a) Use the internet to find out about the mystical figure Prometheus.
b) **Group work** Discuss why Shelley chose this complement to the book title.
c) Compare the fate of Frankenstein with that of ancient Prometheus.

Heinrich Füger:
Prometheus is giving fire to man, 1817

39 Group work

Discuss why Robert Walton was chosen to frame the novel. How would the story and the reader's perception be different if the story was continually told by Frankenstein himself?
OR How would the story and the reader's perception be different if the story was continually told by the creature itself?

40

Most people do not realize that Frankenstein is the name of the scientist and creator of the monster, but not the monster itself. Speculate on possible reasons why the creature has often been mistakenly called "Frankenstein".

41

Brainstorm in class which media products relating to *Frankenstein* you have encountered so far.

FRANKENSTEIN – THE FILM: PRE-VIEWING

42

The 1931 film is one of the most iconic films of all time, setting the standard for a new genre called "horror" in Hollywood.
a) Describe the poster.
b) Predict what the creature might be like in the movie.

WHILE VIEWING

43

Watch the movie. Answer the following questions:
a) What is Victor Frankenstein like in the movie?
b) How does he bring the creature to life?
c) How is the creature depicted in the movie in terms of appearance and behaviour?
d) What happens to the frame story?

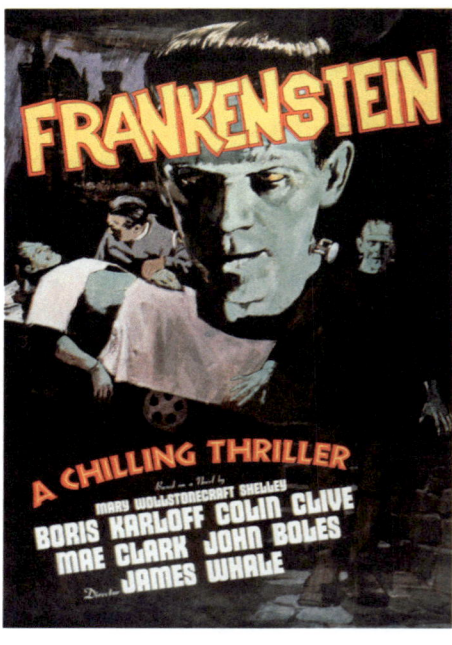

POST-VIEWING

44

a) Compare your predictions to the actual depiction in the film.

b) Discuss whether you feel more sympathy for the creature in the film or in the novel.

45

Novel or film? Discuss which of the two versions you prefer. Justify your opinion.

LANGUAGE AND GENDER ROLES REVISITED

46

Looking at language: Figurative language corresponds to language which uses figures of speech, such as metaphors, personifications, similes, symbolisms etc. in order to make writing more visual and effective.

a) Look up more examples of figurative language and their definitions.

b) Mary Shelley uses a lot of figurative language in her novel, such as:

simile: "But the appearance of my father was to me like that of my good angel, and I gradually recovered my health." (p. 164)

metaphor: "My strength was gone. I was a mere skeleton (...)." (p. 166)

Find more examples of figurative language in the novel and explain their meaning in class.

47

From what you have already found out about Mary Shelley's biographical background, explain why she wrote *Frankenstein* and what influenced the development of her idea.

_____

_____

_____

_____

_____

48

Think about gender roles and discuss the presentation of women in the novel. Use the following statement as a starting point: "There are some women that are main characters, but the roles they play are often passively docile and supportive. For the most part they act as tools for men."

49

Frankenstein was originally published anonymously, and some critics speculated that Mary Shelley's husband, Percy, wrote it. Draw conclusions about the role of women at that time.

50

Go back to the mind-map you drew before reading the novel.
Correct and add missing information.

51

Frankenstein is considered to be one of the world's most famous horror stories.

a) Read and sum up the definition of a horror story as given below.

_____

_____

_____

_____

_____

_____

b) Examine whether the given definition applies to *Frankenstein* by giving examples from the novel.

_____

_____

_____

_____

_____

_____

Info

A **horror story** is a story in which the focus is on creating a feeling of fear. Such tales are of ancient origin and form a substantial part of the body of folk literature. They can feature supernatural elements such as ghosts, witches, or vampires, or they can address more realistic psychological fears. In Western literature the literary cultivation of fear and curiosity for its own sake began to emerge in the 18th-century pre-Romantic era with the Gothic novel. The genre was invented by Horace Walpole, whose *Castle of Otranto* (1765) may be said to have founded the horror story as a legitimate literary form.

Mary Wollstonecraft Shelley introduced pseudoscience into the genre in her famous novel *Frankenstein* (1818), about the creation of a monster that ultimately destroys its creator. [...]

[...] In the Romantic era the German storyteller E.T.A. Hoffmann and the American Edgar Allan Poe raised the horror story to a level far above mere entertainment through their skillful intermingling of reason and madness, eerie atmosphere and everyday reality. They invested their spectres, doubles, and haunted houses with a psychological symbolism that gave their tales a haunting credibility. The Gothic influence persisted throughout the 19th century in such works as Sheridan Le Fanu's **The House by the Churchyard** and **Green Tea,** Wilkie Collins's **The Moonstone**, and Bram Stoker's vampire tale **Dracula**. The influence was revived in the 20th century by science-fiction and fantasy writers such as Mervyn Peake in his **Gormenghast** series. Other masters of the horror tale are Ambrose Bierce, Arthur Machen, Algernon Blackwood, H. P. Lovecraft, and Stephen King. [...]

Ethics of Science

1 **Group work**

a) Think: Read the article below. Sum up its most relevant aspects concerning the ethics of science.

b) Pair: Compare your results with your partner.

c) Share your results in class.

The role of ethics in science

Ethics are a set of moral obligations that define right and wrong in our practices and decisions. Many professions have a formalized system of ethical practices that help guide professionals in the field. For example, doctors commonly
5 take the Hippocratic Oath, which, among other things, states that doctors "do no harm" to their patients. Engineers follow an ethical guide that states that they "hold paramount[1] the safety, health, and welfare of the public." Within these professions, as well as within science, the principles become
10 so ingrained[2] that practitioners rarely have to think about adhering[3] to the ethic – it's part of the way they practice. And a breach of ethics is considered very serious, punishable at least within the profession (by revocation of a license, for example) and sometimes by the law as well.
15 Scientific ethics calls for honesty and integrity in all stages of scientific practice, from reporting results regardless to properly attributing collaborators. This system of ethics guides the practice of science, from data collection to publication and beyond. As in other professions, the scientific
20 ethic is deeply integrated into the way scientists work, and they are aware that the reliability of their work and scientific knowledge in general depends upon adhering to that ethic. Many of the ethical principles in science relate to the production of unbiased[4] scientific knowledge, which is critical
25 when others try to build upon or extend research findings. The open publication of data, peer review, replication, and collaboration required by the scientific ethic all help to keep science moving forward by validating research findings and confirming or raising questions about results (...).
30 Some breaches of the ethical standards, such as fabrication of data, are dealt with by the scientific community through means similar to ethical breaches in other disciplines – removal from a job, for example. But less obvious challenges to the ethical standard occur more frequently, such as
35 giving a scientific competitor a negative peer review. These incidents are more like parking in a no-parking zone – they are against the rules and can be unfair, but they often go unpunished. Sometimes scientists simply make mistakes that may appear to be ethical breaches, such as improperly
40 citing a source or giving a misleading reference. And like any other group that shares goals and ideals, the scientific community works together to deal with all of these incidents as best as they can – in some cases with more success than others.

Ethical standards in science

45 Scientists have long maintained an informal system of ethics and guidelines for conducting research, but documented ethical guidelines did not develop until the mid-twentieth century, after a series of well-publicized ethical breaches and war crimes. Scientific ethics now
50 refers to a standard of conduct for scientists that is generally delineated into two broad categories (...). First, standards of methods and process address the design, procedures, data analysis, interpretation, and reporting of research efforts. Second, standards of topics and
55 findings address the use of human and animal subjects in research and the ethical implications of certain research findings. Together, these ethical standards help guide scientific research and ensure that research efforts (and researchers) abide by several core principles (...),
60 including:

1. Honesty in reporting of scientific data

2. Careful transcription and analysis of scientific results to avoid error

3. Independent analysis and interpretation of results that is based on data and not on the influence of external sources

4. Open sharing of methods, data, and interpretations through publication and presentation

5. Sufficient validation of results through replication and collaboration with peers

6. Proper crediting of sources of information, data, and ideas

7. Moral obligations to society in general, and, in some disciplines, responsibility in weighing the rights of human and animal subjects

---

Annotations

[1] to **hold paramount** = to consider sth as very important   [2] **ingrained** = fixed   [3] **adhering** = following (the)   [4] **unbiased** = neutral

Mediation

2 → **Workshop:** Mediation → **S19:** How to improve your mediation skills

You are taking part in an ERASMUS project on the ethics of science in the 21st century which deals with the ethical dimension of genetic engineering. You found the following article online and want to use it for an upcoming presentation. Read the article and do further research if neccessary. Present your findings to your fellow students. Emphasize risks and opportunities concerning genetic engineering of food.

Pro und Contra von „Frankenfood"

Internationale Experten beraten über Position zu
Grüner Gentechnik
Von Volkart Wildermuth

Umwelt. – „Frankenfood", so nennen Kritiker Produkte der grünen Gentechnik – also genetisch veränderter Pflanzen. Während in Europa vor allem Risiken der Gentechnik auf dem Acker diskutiert werden, steigen weltweit die
5 Anbauflächen genetisch veränderter Pflanzen immer weiter. Die Forschergemeinschaft sucht bis Dezember nach einem gemeinsamen Standpunkt.
Europa fürchtet grüne Gentechnik weit mehr als der Rest der Welt. (AP)

10 Sie kamen aus der Schweiz und aus Südafrika, aus China und den USA, aus Frankreich und Deutschland – ein Dutzend Pflanzenexperten aus aller Welt. Ihre Aufgabe: kurz und knapp die Position der Wissenschaft zur grünen Gentechnik zusammenzufassen. Nun gibt es schon seit
15 Jahren eine umfangreiche Diskussion unter Forschern, doch Professor Bernd Müller Röber vom Max-Planck-Institut für Molekulare Pflanzenphysiologie in Golm bei Potsdam ist dennoch davon überzeugt, dass eine erneute Stellungnahme notwendig ist.
20 „Wir als Wissenschaftler erleben leider immer wieder, dass in der Öffentlichkeit immer noch fehlerhaft über die Technologie diskutiert wird, mit viel Unwissen auch. Das kann uns nicht zufrieden stellen, zumal wir Kenntnisse haben, gerade in den letzten Jahren,
25 die eindeutig belegen, dass gentechnisch veränderte Pflanzen durchaus sehr positive Effekte in der Landwirtschaft haben können."
Davon aber würden die Medien weit seltener berichten als über die wenigen Studien, die Gefahren der genetisch
30 veränderten Pflanzen zeigen. Einer, der ihren Nutzen aus erster Hand kennt, ist Professor Yufa Peng von der Chinesischen Akademie für Agrarwissenschaften in Peking.
„Viele Kleinbauern pflanzen insektenresistente
35 Baumwolle an. Dabei steigt ihr Einkommen deutlich an, zusätzlich verbessert sich auch ihre Lebensqualität und Gesundheit, weil sie weniger chemische Insektenvernichtungsmittel versprühen."
Die Zahl der Vergiftungen ist deshalb messbar

40 zurückgegangen. In der dritten Welt wird die Forschung nicht von den Großkonzernen dominiert, hier gibt es in vielen Ländern öffentliche Institute, die die Gentechnik gezielt für die nationalen Bedürfnisse nutzen. Am Agrarforschungszentrum in Kairo wird an einer breiten
45 Palette genetisch veränderten Pflanzen gearbeitet, erläutert selbstbewusst Dr. Ismail Abdel Hamid.
„Wir arbeiten an unseren eigenen Nutzpflanzen, mit unseren eigenen Händen, mit unseren eigenen Forschern und wir haben Erfolg. Feldversuche zeigen,
50 dass diese Pflanzen zum Beispiel vor Viren geschützt sind, und dass sie im Vergleich zu den konventionellen Sorten höhere Erträge und eine bessere Qualität bieten. Man muss an den nationalen Problemen arbeiten, dann hat man auch Erfolg."
55 Die Bedenken der Europäer kann er nicht nachvollziehen. „Europa ist eine einsame Insel, isoliert durch diese Furcht. Hier glaubt man, dass die Gentechnik Monster erzeugen wird. Wir in Ägypten haben diese Ängste nicht. Wir arbeiten an Gesetzen zur Biosicherheit, die
60 sicherstellen, dass die genetisch veränderten Pflanzen so sicher wie konventionelle Sorten sind."
Die Bedenken der Europäer behindern den Einsatz der grünen Gentechnik in der Dritten Welt. Dabei sind Nahrungsmittel aus genetisch veränderten Pflanzen
65 besonders sicher, meint Professor Klaus Ammann, bis vor kurzem Direktor des Botanischen Gartens Bern, nach intensivem Studium der wissenschaftlichen Literatur.
„Es ist so, dass schlicht und einfach diese Gentech-Nahrungsmittel die sichereren sind als die normalen

Nahrungsmittel, weil man genau gewusst hat, was getestet werden soll und die ganz wenigen, raren Fälle, wo man gesehen hat, das sind Allergene oder sonstige Probleme, die hat man eben eliminieren können."

Bei der Einführung der ganz natürlichen Kiwi kam es in Europa dagegen zu Todesfällen durch Allergien. Auch die negativen Umweltauswirkungen der Gen-Tech-Pflanzen halten die Wissenschaftler in Berlin für völlig übertrieben. In dem Entwurf für die Erklärung des internationalen Forums der Akademien der Wissenschaften sollen Regierungen und Umweltorganisationen aufgefordert werden, ihren Kampf gegen die genetisch veränderten Pflanzen einzustellen. Ein wenig überraschendes Fazit, schließlich haben in Berlin vor allem Pflanzenforscher miteinander diskutiert. Kritiker waren nicht geladen. Die Debatte geht also sicher weiter. Es wird interessant sein zu sehen, mit welchen wissenschaftlichen Studien Greenpeace oder Friends of the Earth dem in Berlin gefundenen Konsens der Akademien der Wissenschaften antworten wollen.

no i don't see any problems with genetically modified food

3 → **S17:** How to work with cartoons

Describe the cartoon.

4

Analyse its message and its reference to the novel.

5

Comment on the message.

ETHICS OF SCIENCE IN *FRANKENSTEIN*

6 CHOOSE

Sum up the personal satisfaction Frankenstein expects from creating a new human.

OR

Describe how science is portrayed in *Frankenstein*.

7

Explain the unintended consequences of Frankenstein's scientific experiment.

8 CHOOSE

Discuss the moral relevance of the novel. Is it ethical that Frankenstein rejects his creature, leading to a cascade of calamities?

OR

Comment on the dilemma of scientific inquiry as depicted in the novel.

9

Read the article.

'Frankenstein' Reflects the Hopes and Fears of Every Scientific Era
The novel is usually considered a cautionary tale for science, but its cultural legacy is much more complicated.

Philipp Ball   April 20, 2017

Victor Frankenstein becoming disgusted at his creation. Illustration from the frontispiece of the 1831 edition. Steel engraving to the revised edition of *Frankenstein* by Mary Shelley, published by Colburn and Bentley, London 1831. The novel was first published in 1818.

The bicentennial[1] of Frankenstein started early. While Mary Shelley's momentous[2] novel was published anonymously in 1818, the commemorations began last year to mark the dark and stormy night on Lake Geneva
5 when she (then still Mary Godwin, having eloped with her married lover Percy Shelley) conceived what she called her "hideous progeny[3]."

In May, MIT Press will publish a new edition of the original text, "annotated for scientists, engineers, and creators of
10 all kinds." As well as the explanatory and expository notes throughout the book, there are accompanying essays by historians and other writers that discuss *Frankenstein*'s relevance and implications for science and invention today.

15 It's a smart idea, but treating *Frankenstein* as a meditation on the responsibilities of the scientist, and the dangers of ignoring them, is bound to give only a partial view of Shelley's novel. It's not just a book about science. Moreover, focusing on Shelley's text doesn't explore
20 the scope of the Frankenstein myth itself, including its message for scientists.

This is one of those stories everyone knows even without having read the original: Man makes monster; monster runs amok; monster kills man. It may come as a surprise
25 to discover that the creator, not the creature, is called Frankenstein, and that the original creature was not the shambling, grunting, green-faced hunk played by Boris Karloff in the 1931 movie but an articulate soul who meditates on John Milton's *Paradise Lost*. Such
30 misconceptions might do little justice to Shelley, but as the critic Chris Baldick has written, "That series of adaptations, allusions, accretions, analogues, parodies, and plain misreadings with follows upon Mary Shelley's novel is not just a supplementary component of the myth;
35 it *is* the myth."

In any case, the essays in the MIT edition have surprisingly little to say about the reproductive and biomedical technologies of our age, such as assisted conception, tissue engineering, stem-cell research,
40 cloning, genetic manipulation, and "synthetic human entities with embryo-like features" — the remarkable potential "organisms" with a Frankensteinian name.

That feels like a missed opportunity. *Frankenstein* is still frequently the first point of reference for media reports
45 of such cutting-edge developments, just as it was when human IVF (In-Vitro-Fertilisation) became a viable technique in the early 1970s. The "Franken" label is now a lazy journalistic cliché for a technology you should distrust, or at least regard as "weird": Frankenfoods, Frankenbugs.
50 The "wisdom of repugnance[4]," the phrase coined by the U.S. bioethicist Leon Kass and which informed the decision of the George W. Bush administration to pose drastic restrictions on federally funded stem-cell research in 2001, harked back directly to Mary Shelley's novel.

55 Let's be in no doubt: *Frankenstein* is one of the most extraordinary achievements in English literature. It's not flawlessly written, the construction is sometimes awkward – yet it is a profound and unsettling vision, deeply informed about the science and philosophy of
60 its day. That it was written not by an established and experienced author but by a teenager at a very difficult period in her life feels almost miraculous. It's in fact those troubled circumstances and those flaws that have helped the book to persist, to keep on stimulating debate, and
65 to continue attracting adaptations and variations – some good, many bad, some plain execrable[5].

It's too often suggested — some of the commentaries in the MIT edition repeat the idea — that *Frankenstein* is a warning about a hubristic, overreaching science that
70 unleashes forces it cannot control. "Victor's error is failing to think harder about the potential repercussions of his work," writes the bioethicist Josephine Johnston. To Mary Shelley's biographer Anne Mellor, the novel "portrays the penalties of violating Nature." This makes it sound as

though the attempt to create an "artificial person" from scavenged[6] body parts was always going to end badly: that it was a crazy, doomed project from the start.

But Mary Shelley takes some pains to show that the real problem is not what Victor Frankenstein made, but how he reacted to it. "Now that I had finished," he says, "the beauty of the dream vanished, and breathless horror and disgust filled my heart." He rejects the "hideous wretch" he has created, but nothing about that seems inevitable. What would have happened if Victor had instead lived up to his responsibilities by choosing to nurture his creature? One might answer that the result would have been a pretty dull and short novel. But I'm not so sure. Imagine the story of Victor struggling to have the creature accepted by a society that shunned it as vile and unnatural. We would then be reading a book about social prejudice and our preconceptions of nature — indeed, about the kind of prospect one can easily imagine for a human born by cloning today (if such as thing were scientifically possible and ethically permissible). The moral and philosophical landscape it might have explored would be no less rich.

That Victor did not do this — that he spurned[7] his creation the moment he had made it, merely because he judged it ugly — means that, to my mind, the conclusion we should reach is the one that the speculative-fiction author Elizabeth Bear articulates in the new volume. It is for Victor's "failure of empathy and his moral cowardice," Bear says – for his overweening egotism and narcissism – that we should think ill of him, and not because of what he discovered or created.

Mary Shelley, however, gives her readers mixed messages. What she *shows* us is a man behaving badly, but what she seems to *tell* us is that he is tragic and sympathetic. All of her characters think so well of "poor, dear Victor" that we're given pause. Even Robert Walton, the ship's captain who finds Victor pursuing his creature in the Arctic and whose letters describing that encounter begin and end the book, sees in him a noble, pitiable figure, "amiable and attractive" despite his wrecked and emaciated[8] state. Frankenstein's only critic is his creature.

This could be seen as a rather exquisite piece of authorial artifice, an early example of the unreliable narrator. It seems more likely to me that Shelley herself wasn't clear what to make of Victor. In her revised edition of 1831, she emphasized the Faustian aspect of the tale, writing in her introduction that she wanted to show how "supremely frightful would be the effect of any human endeavour to mock the stupendous mechanism of the Creator of the world." In other words, it was preordained that the creature would be hideous, and inevitable that its creator would recoil "horror-stricken". That wasn't then a character failing of Victor's.

This idea invites the interpretation that Mellor offers in the new edition: "Nature prevents Victor from constructing a normal human being: His unnatural method of reproduction spawns an unnatural being, a freak."

She sees this as a feminist interpretation (Nature being, in her view, feminine and inviolable), I feel that to the extent that Shelley's book supports a feminist reading, it is not this, and to the extent that one might draw this interpretation, it is not a feminist one. To condemn Victor for violating "Mother Nature" with his "unnatural being" seems plain disturbing in the 21st century. Certainly it bears out the complaint of the British biologist J. B. S. Haldane in 1924:

There is no great invention, from fire to flying, which has not been hailed as an insult to some god. But if every physical and chemical invention is a blasphemy, every biological invention is a perversion.

By accepting that Victor's work is inherently perverted and bound to end hideously, Mellor's accusation leaves us wondering what exactly is meant by "unnatural." Which real-life interventions are guaranteed to produce a freak? Might that be so with IVF, as its early detractors insisted? Is it the case for so-called "three-parent babies" made by mitochondrial transplantation, a misleading term apparently invented for the very purpose of insisting on its unnaturalness? Would the first human clone be the next "unnatural freak," if ever that technology becomes possible and desirable? "Unnatural" is not a neutral description but a morally laden term, and dangerous for that reason: Its use threatens to prejudice or shut down discussion before it begins.

There's something of this rush to judgment also in the commentary of Charles Robinson, the *Frankenstein* scholar who introduces the new annotated text. Speaking about the evils released from Pandora's box by Prometheus's brother Epimetheus in Greek myth — Shelley subtitled her novel "The Modern Prometheus" — Robinson says that such terrible consequences of careless tampering are reflected in "the pesticide DDT, the atom bomb, Three Mile Island, Chernobyl," and the British government's allowing a stem-cell scientist to perform genome editing "despite objections that ethical issues were being ignored." But each of these modern developments in fact involved a complex and case-specific chain of events, and incurs a delicate balance of pros and cons. Some, such as the Chernobyl nuclear accident, had rather little to do with the intrinsic ethics of the underlying technology, but were a consequence of particular political and bureaucratic decisions. To imply that they unambiguously show a lack of foresight (Epimetheus's name means "afterthought") or indeed of responsibility on the part of the scientists whose work made them possible would be to cheapen the discourse and to evade the real issues.

The decision on genome editing, meanwhile — presumably this refers to the granting of a license by the U.K. Human Fertilization and Embryology Authority for gene-editing of very early stage, non-viable embryos — supports medical research that might, among other things, help to reduce rates of miscarriage. Such work will never be free of ethical objections raised by those opposed to all research on human embryos. Without a doubt, *Frankenstein* asks challenging questions about research like this that touches on interventions in human life. But to suggest that it warns us to abjure[9] such work doesn't do Mary Shelley justice.

What, then, does the story of Victor Frankenstein's doomed and misguided quest have to tell us about modern science in general, and technological intervention in life in particular? I think that, to find an answer, we needn't try too hard to discern Shelley's own intentions. Her text arose not out of a conscious desire to tell a moral tale — not, at any rate, one about science — but literally out of a nightmare. In her preface to the 1831 edition she described how the "ghastly image" of a "pale student of unhallowed arts kneeling beside the thing he had put together" came to her as she tried to sleep after listening to conversations between Byron and Percy Shelley deep into the night, concerning the "principle of life."

That retrospective account surely included some embellishment[10], but it seems fair to accept Shelley's assertion that "my imagination, unbidden, possessed and guided me." The impact and enduring fascination of her novel depend on the author not having worked too hard to impose a meaning on the "ghastly image" she dreamed, to resolve the conflicts that it evoked in her, or to maintain a consistent attitude as she reworked her book.

So we can draw Luddite conclusions if that's what we look for, just as we can read into the text Shelley's fears about childbirth, her frustration and anger at her father's rejection, political worries about the destructive potential of the inchoate mob, or an examination of male terror of female sexual and procreative independence. But it surely matters at least as much now not just what *Frankenstein* is about but what the Frankenstein myth is about — what as a culture we have made of this wonderful, undisciplined book, whether that is Hollywood's insistence that the artificial being be a stiff-limbed quasi-robotic mute or more contemporary efforts to tell a story that is sympathetic to the creature's point of view. *Frankenstein*, after all, was never intended as an instruction manual to the bioethicist or the engineer. It is better seen as a catalyst, even an *agent provocateur*, that lures us into disclosing what we truly hope and fear.

The ambiguity of the book is an essential feature of myth, and all modern myths come from a similar fertile lack of authorial control. That isn't a failing. Everyone loves a well-crafted story, but those crafted partly by the unconscious and delivered to us misshapen and unfinished hold a particular potential to be reanimated, time after time, to fit and to dramatize the anxieties of the age. Like Victor, we make Frankenstein in our own image.

Annotations

[1] **bicentennial** = the novel appeared 200 years ago
[2] **momentous** = very important
[3] **hideous progeny** = horrible child
[4] **repugnance** = aversion
[5] **execrable** = horrible

[6] **scavenged** = gathered together
[7] **spurned** = rejected
[8] **emaciated** = weakened
[9] to **abjure sth** = to take sth back
[10] **embellishment** = exaggeration

10

Outline the main statements of the article.

11

Speculate on why *Frankenstein* is still often used as the first point of reference for media reporters concerning the reproductive and biomedical technologies of our age.

12

Discuss *Frankenstein*'s relevance and implications for science and invention today.

13

a) Read the following statements on the subject of science. Choose the one that appeals to you as most likely.
b) Explain what the quotation means to you.
c) Milling around: Find three other students that have chosen different positions and tell each other why you have chosen yours.

     a. It is the government's responsibility to regulate and control science. All research that is legal should be seen as ethically justifiable.
     b. Scientists should have complete freedom in their research, no matter what the issue is.
     c. It is morally reprehensible for humans to create life for their own purposes.
     d. Creating life is only justifiable in order to cure diseases and promote medical research.

The role of nature

1 → **S15:** How to describe pictures

a) Describe the painting. What is your first reaction when you see it?

b) Compare the painting to the frame story depicted in *Frankenstein*.

c) Analyse what the painting might convey about the spirit of the early 19th century.

Caspar David Friedrich: The Arctic Ocean, 1823/24

2 → **S10:** How to work with poetry

Read John Keats' poem.

a) Sum up how nature is presented in Keats' poem.

b) Analyse how Keats conveys the theme of rebirth through death.

c) Discuss the overall message of the poem.

To Autumn (1820)
by John Keats

John Keats, 1795-1821

Annotations
[1] **thatch-eves** = *Dachziegel*
[2] **gourd** = *Kürbis*
[3] **clammy** = close
[4] **granary** = floor of a storehouse for grain
[5] **winnowing** = cleaning
[6] **swath** = *Schwaden*
[7] **gleaner** = sharecropper, *Ährenleser*
[8] **wailful** = lamenting

Season of mists and mellow fruitfulness
Close bosom-friend of the maturing sun
Conspiring with him how to load and bless
With fruit the vines that round the thatch-eves[1] run;
5 To bend with apples the moss'd cottage-trees,
And fill all fruit with ripeness to the core;
To swell the gourd[2], and plump the hazel shells
With a sweet kernel; to set budding more,
And still more, later flowers for the bees,
10 Until they think warm days will never cease,
For Summer has o'er-brimm'd their clammy[3] cells.

Who hath not seen thee oft amid thy store?
Sometimes whoever seeks abroad may find
Thee sitting careless on a granary[4] floor,
15 Thy hair soft-lifted by the winnowing[5] wind;
Or on a half-reap'd furrow sound asleep,
Drows'd with the fume of poppies, while thy hook
Spares the next swath[6] and all its twined flowers:
And sometimes like a gleaner[7] thou dost keep
20 Steady thy laden head across a brook;
Or by a cider-press, with patient look,
Thou watchest the last oozings hours by hours.

Where are the songs of Spring? Ay, where are they?
Think not of them, thou hast thy music too,–
25 While barred clouds bloom the soft-dying day,
And touch the stubble-plains with rosy hue;
Then in a wailful[8] choir the small gnats mourn
Among the river sallows, borne aloft
Or sinking as the light wind lives or dies;
30 And full-grown lambs loud bleat from hilly bourn;
Hedge-crickets sing; and now with soft treble
The red-breast whistles from a garden-croft;
And gathering swallows twitter in the skies.

3

Read the text on Romanticism.

Info

Romanticism: an attitude or intellectual orientation that characterized many works of literature, painting, music, architecture, criticism, and historiography in Western civilization over a period from the late 18th to the mid-19th century. Romanticism can be seen as a rejection of the precepts[1] of order, calm, harmony, balance, idealization, and rationality that typified Classicism in general and late 18th-century Neoclassicism in particular. It was also to some extent a reaction against the Enlightenment and against 18th-century rationalism and physical materialism in general. Romanticism emphasized the individual, the subjective, the irrational, the imaginative, the personal, the spontaneous, the emotional, the visionary, and the transcendental. Among the characteristic attitudes of Romanticism were the following: a deepened appreciation of the beauties of nature; a general exaltation of emotion over reason and of the senses over intellect; a turning in upon the self and a heightened examination of human personality and its moods and mental potentialities; a preoccupation with the genius, the hero, and the exceptional figure in general, and a focus on his passions and inner struggles; a new view of the artist as a supremely individual creator, whose creative spirit is more important than strict adherence to formal rules and traditional procedures; an emphasis upon imagination as a gateway to transcendent experience and spiritual truth; an obsessive interest in folk culture, national and ethnic cultural origins, and the medieval era; and a predilection[2] for the exotic, the remote, the mysterious, the weird, the occult, the monstrous, the diseased, and even the satanic.

Annotations

[1] **precept** = dogma   [2] **predilection** = preference

a) Outline the most important aspects and ideas that Romanticism emphasizes.

_____

_____

_____

b) Explain what nature meant to the Romantics.

_____

_____

c) Discuss the question of whether "To Autumn" can be considered a typical Romantic piece of literature.

ROMANTICISM AND NATURE IN *FRANKENSTEIN*

4

a) Outline how the major themes and ideas of Romanticism are represented and explored in Mary Shelley's *Frankenstein.*

b) Frankenstein confesses: "When happy, inanimate nature had the power of bestowing on me the most delightful sensations. A serene sky and verdant fields filled me with ecstasy." (p. 64)
Comment on this statement with regards to the principles of Romanticism.

c) Group work CHOOSE Discuss one of the statements:
Frankenstein's manipulation of nature conflicts with an otherwise Romantic celebration of nature.
OR
Frankenstein can be considered a novel about the Romantic striving against the customary limitations placed on our existence.

Questions of (human) identity

1

Discuss in class: What makes a human being? What does it mean to be human?

2

Bill Gates answers the question "What does it mean to be human?" for the Big History Project video contest.
a) Watch the video and sum up his answer to this question. **Webcode** WES-73652-01
b) Compare his answer with your own results.
c) **Group work** Create your own video for the contest (maximum two minutes). Present your video in class.

3

a) Do research on the topic of transhumanism. Use the links given in the Webcode. **Webcode** WES-73652-02
b) Define the term "transhumanism".

4

a) Do a survey: Think about the statements on transhumanism below and decide whether you agree or
   disagree. Then ask two or three classmates if they would accept or reject the statements.
b) Analyse the results of your survey by counting how many of the questions were answered with "yes".

Are you ready for the future of transhumanism?

a. Transhumans will be better leaders in politics and business.

b. I would use technology components to improve my physical abilities.

c. Transhumans will be superior to humans.

d. For me, a relationship with a transhuman would be possible.

e. I would use technology components to enhance my senses.

f. Transhumanism is fair although it enhances abilities artificially.

g. Serving humans is not the only purpose of transhumanism.

h. Transhuman technology that extends human life-span is a part
   of evolution.

i. I look up to transhumans because they are like super-humans to me.

j. Extending life-span through transhuman technology is human.

k. Humans and transhumans should have equal rights.

l. I would use technological components to help me professionally.

m. I would have no problem working alongside transhumans.

n. I would use technological components to improve mentally.

5

Discuss the chances and risks of transhumanism.

WHAT DOES IT MEAN TO BE HUMAN IN *FRANKENSTEIN*?

6

Sum up how Frankenstein brings his creature to life.

7

Examine whether you would consider the creature a "monster" or a "human being". Explain your decision with character descriptions from the text.

8

Comment on the fact that the only person to address the creature with sympathy is blind.

_____

_____

_____

_____

9

Read the text.

The theme of isolation in *Frankenstein* raises many questions about the role of community and its importance. Many characters in the novel find themselves in isolated positions, and a few suffer grave consequences because of it. Characters suffer from both physical and emotional isolation, although, as in the case of the monster, isolation is not always self-inflicted. Victor Frankenstein, on the other hand, chooses to isolate himself from his family, his peers,
5 and even the monster he created. Throughout the novel, we see isolation manifested in multiple ways in multiple characters. Mary Shelley makes this theme apparent in the very beginning of the novel by using setting and nature. The remote Arctic is her choice for an introductory setting. It is not surprising that Shelley would choose to make this a theme in her debut novel; isolation and abandonment were characteristic of many Romantic texts. Samuel Taylor Coleridge, an early Romantic poet, also chose to use nature as a way to engage isolation in his poem, "The Rime of the
10 Ancient Mariner" by showing the mariner unnecessarily killing an albatross. The mariner's punishment for killing the albatross is watching his crew die in front of him. Coleridge depicts the mariner as a perpetual loner as a result of his choices, and shows that he is eternally cursed because of this. In *Frankenstein*, horrible things happen when a character is isolated from others. When Victor's knowledge and ambition are unchecked by his peers, a monster is created. When Elizabeth is left alone on her wedding night, the monster attacks. When society abandons the monster, he
15 becomes enraged and malicious. These instances prove that the destructive power lies not in the monster or his creator, but in solitude. Shelley uses this theme and its manifestation in her characters to pose questions about community, knowledge, and its role in society. Is unbridled[1] knowledge always dangerous, or is there a middle ground? Should one abandon his or her pursuits if they are driving him or her away from a community? Is it possible for someone to be more intellectually advanced than his or her peers and still maintain a sense of community with them? Mary Shelley
20 challenges her audience to answer these questions and more about isolation. (...)

Impact in/for *Frankenstein*
Isolation serves an important function in Shelley's novel. A thorough understanding of this theme is important to the text because it develops characters, exposes its consequences, and generates challenging questions about the role of isolation and community in our everyday lives. Isolation touches the lives of every character in Frankenstein in some
25 way. The most obvious are Victor and the monster, but through them, isolation seeps into everyone else's lives in the forms of death and destruction. Shelley makes it clear that there are two different types of isolation: self-inflicted and societal. We see self-inflicted isolation manifested in Victor; he detaches from his world and the people he loves and, as a result, everyone suffers tremendously. Rejection from society is demonstrated in the monster's life. Again and again, he is turned away from love and companionship, which is what he has longed for since he was first brought to

^{Annotations}
[1] **unbridled** = uncontrolled
[2] **deterrent** = sth that stops you from doing sth

30 life. Eventually, he resorts to sinister actions to avenge his miserable life. The persistent power of alienation also shows the power of a strong community. Is community the only deterrent[2] to unchecked knowledge? Would Victor have proceeded with his scientific research if he had had a community of peers to audit his ambition? The entire novel is based on Victor's laboratory circumstances, but why do these circumstances occur? While Victor's ambition and pride are definitely what cause the creation of the monster, his isolation
35 is the channel through which they come to fruition. Similarly, the monster's exclusion from society is the catalyst for his horrific actions.

10

Sum up the key statements.

11

Explain the terms "self-inflicted" and "societal destruction" as presented in the text, using suitable examples from the novel.

12

"The monster was doomed to disaster from the very start due to a lack of acceptance by society." Discuss in class.

THE CREATURE'S IDENTITY

13

What is your personal view of identity? Write an acrostic poem using the letters as initials or placing them in the middle of a word or sentence.

I	_____
D	
E	
N	_____
T	
I	_____
T	
Y	_____

14

Discuss the influences education and socialization have on one's identity.

15

Read the question asked on gradesaver.com concerning the monster's identity and Steve's answer to it. How would you answer this question? Do you agree with Steve's opinion? Justify your answer using suitable references from the novel.

> Do you think that the creature has always been a monster? Human beings were scared of the creature ever since it was born. Did the creature become a monster because it was not accepted by humans? Or were the creature's intentions noble at first and then changed by society? Even at the end, after all the crimes, he still feels bad for Victor. What makes him a monster?
> Asked by Carole B #463663 on 05/30/2016 9:35 AM, Last updated by steve a #183822 on 05/30/2016 11:12 AM.

> Answered by steve a #183822 on 05/30/2016 11:12 AM
> I definitely think the creature was made into a monster. Victor created him and then left him right away. He did not have a teacher, human love, or anyone to care for him. Imagine if he had gained acceptance by anyone in society … he may have had a chance. I've always felt bad for the creature … he was alone, he caused fear, and that same fear made him afraid. And then he became upset … felt like it was wasn't fair – and he was right! Remember that the creature was more empathetic than the creator in the end!

Facts and figures about the British Empire

1

a) Read the information in the box below.

b) Write down four questions about the text to test your partner's knowledge.

The British Empire

At its peak in the 19th century, the British Empire had expanded its territory to cover about 25% of the world's landmass. It was the largest empire in history. Britain was the 'metropolis' and its colonies the 'periphery'. Britain's language, literature, and culture were regarded as superior to those of the colonized. By 1970 however, most of Britain's colonies had been given political independence. The lives of the people of the colonies and those of their ancestors had been formed by the colonial experience. They now had to start to find their own ways of expressing their political, economic and cultural freedom. Thus, writers from the former colonies emerged, who explored ways of expressing their individuality through their literary works and who showed the world the point of view of the colonized.

Salman Rushdie called this phenomenon "the Empire writes back with a vengeance" in an article published in 1982, where he pointed out that where English literature had once been exported throughout the world, now writing from the former colonies was being imported to Britain. Postcolonialism or postcolonial studies is the consideration of the relationship between the colonizer and the colonized, the effects or consequences of colonialism on the people and the changing nature of British society itself. The terms 'other' ('otherness') and 'hybrid' ('hybricity') are often used in this context. 'Other' describes the colonized as different, alien, non-Western with reference to the colonizers. For example, an Indian man might be characterised as primitive and naive in a fictitious text through the eyes of a British observer or narrator. The concept of hybridity refers to mixing cultural, political and literary levels, e. g. when an author uses a mix of storytelling techniques or different languages from the country of the colonizer and the colonized.

THE BRITISH EMPIRE: "THE SUN NEVER SETS ON THE BRITISH EMPIRE."

2

a) Look at the map below and list the countries that belonged to the British Empire. For a larger image, use the webcode. **Webcode** WES-73652-03

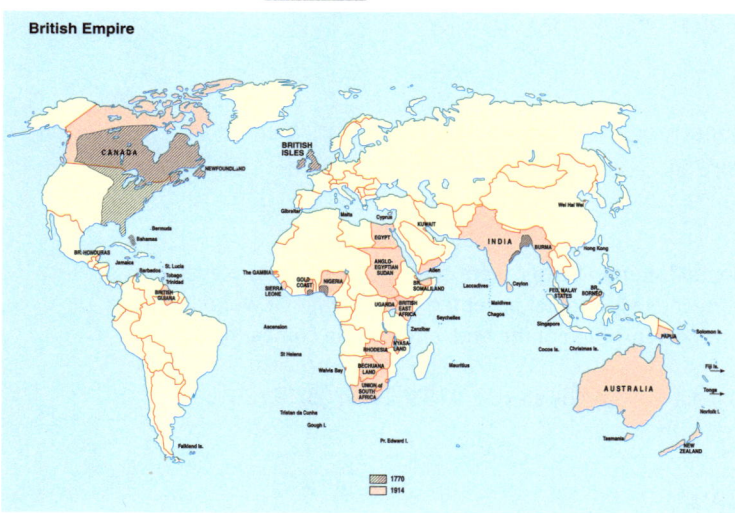

British Empire

b) Milling around: Give a two-minute talk on one of the following countries that belonged to the British Empire, in which you outline the country's colonial past. Refer to the beginning and end of colonialism in that country.

Canada | India | Australia | Nigeria | Egypt | Burma | Ireland | Sudan | Kenya | Malaya | Jamaica | Cyprus | Hong Kong

c) Explain the quote "The sun never sets on the British Empire." with reference to the map and the talks you have listened to.

Two views of colonialism

3 Pair work

Partner A: Research William Shakespeare's play "The Tempest" (1611) and then read the extract: Prospero and his daughter Miranda are stranded on Caliban's island. Caliban has been made a servant to Prospero.

William Shakespeare, 1564–1616

Act I, Scene 2

CALIBAN
   I must eat my dinner.
This island's mine, by Sycorax my mother,
Which thou takest from me. When thou camest first,
5 Thou strok'st me and made much of me, wouldst give me
Water with berries in 't, and teach me how
To name the bigger light, and how the less,
That burn by day and night. And then I loved thee
And showed thee all the qualities o' th' isle,
10 The fresh springs, brine pits, barren place and fertile.
Cursed be I that did so! All the charms
Of Sycorax, toads, beetles, bats, light on you!
For I am all the subjects that you have,
Which first was mine own king. And here you sty me
15 In this hard rock, whiles you do keep from me
The rest o' th' island.

PROSPERO
   Thou most lying slave,
Whom stripes may move, not kindness! I have used thee,
20 Filth as thou art, with human care, and lodged thee
In mine own cell till thou didst seek to violate
The honour of my child.

CALIBAN
Oh ho, oh ho! Would't had been done!
25 Thou didst prevent me. I had peopled else
This isle with Calibans.

MIRANDA
   Abhorrèd slave,
Which any print of goodness wilt not take,
30 Being capable of all ill! I pitied thee,
Took pains to make thee speak, taught thee each hour
One thing or other. When thou didst not, savage,
Know thine own meaning, but wouldst gabble like
A thing most brutish, I endowed thy purposes
35 With words that made them known. But thy vile race,
Though thou didst learn, had that in 't which good natures
Could not abide to be with. Therefore wast thou
Deservedly confined into this rock,
Who hadst deserved more than a prison.

40 **CALIBAN**
You taught me language, and my profit on 't
Is I know how to curse. The red plague rid you
For learning me your language!

Annotations

Sycorax = a witch and mother to Caliban
thou = you (informal; *du*)

to **stroke** = to touch gently

bigger light = sun
the less = the moon
thee = you (informal; *dich*)

brine = very salty water

to **sty** = to keep in a sty

to **lodge sb** = to house sb
till = until
didst seek = sought

Would't = I wish it
to **people** = to fill a place with people; Caliban suggests that he would have reproduced his own offspring if Prospero had let him.

abhorred = hateful

a) Decide if the statements are right or wrong. Explain your choice by giving line references.

	Statement	Evidence	Right	Wrong
0	Caliban was treated nicely at the beginning.	l. 5: "strok'st me"	✓	
1	Prospero has taught Caliban the names of the stars and planets.			
2	Caliban is free to go where he likes.			
3	Prospero regards Caliban as his equal.			
4	Prospero took care of him at first.			
5	Caliban taught Miranda his language.			
6	Miranda considers Caliban good-natured.			
7	Caliban complains that Miranda only taught him how to curse.			

b) List the things Caliban accuses Prospero and Miranda of.
c) Analyse Prospero and Miranda's attitude towards Caliban by examining their language.
d) Explain how this extract can be used as an example of the relationship between the colonizers and the colonized.

Partner B

Read the extract taken from George Orwell's first novel *Burmese Days* (1934), in which he portrays British colonial rule. John Flory, an Englishman who has spent most of his adult life in the Raj (the rule by the British Crown in India from 1858-1947) and works for a timber company, talks to his friend Dr. Veraswami, an Indian doctor.

George Orwell, 1903–1950

"Well, doctor," said Flory – the doctor had meanwhile thrust[1] him into a long chair, pulled out the leg-rests so that he could lie down, and put cigarettes and beer within reach. "Well, doctor, and how are things? How's the British Empire? Sick of the palsy[2] as usual?"
"Aha, Mr Flory, she is very low, very low! Grave complications setting in. Septicaemia, peritonitis[3]
5 and paralysis of the ganglia[4]. We shall have to call in the specialists, I fear. Aha!"
It was a joke between the two men to pretend that the British Empire was an aged female patient of the doctor's. The doctor had enjoyed this joke for two years without growing tired of it. "Ah, doctor," said Flory, supine[5] in the long chair, "what a joy to be here after that bloody Club. When I come to your house I feel like a Nonconformist minister dodging up to town and going home with a tart[6]. Such a glorious holiday from THEM"– he motioned
10 with one heel in the direction of the Club –"from my beloved fellow Empire-builders. British prestige, the white man's burden, the pukka sahib sans peur et sans reproche[7] – you know. Such a relief to be out of the stink of it for a little while." "My friend, my friend, now come, come, please! That is outrageous. You must not say such things of honourable English gentlemen! (...)." "But when they got on to that story about the old havildar[8] – you know, the dear old havildar who said that if the British left India there wouldn't be a rupee or a virgin between – you know;
15 well, I couldn't stand it any longer. It's time that old havildar was put on the retired list. He's been saying the same thing ever since the Jubilee in eighty-seven." The doctor grew agitated, as he always did when Flory criticized the Club members. He was standing with his plump white-clad behind balanced against the veranda rail[9], and sometimes gesticulating. When searching for a word he would nip his black thumb and forefinger together, as though to capture an idea floating in the air. "But truly, truly, Mr. Flory, you must not speak so! Why is it that always you
20 are abusing the pukka sahibs, as you call them? They are the salt of the earth. Consider the great things they have done – consider the great administrators who have made British India what it is. Consider Clive, Warren Hastings, Dalhousie, Curzon[10]. They were such men – I quote your immortal Shakespeare – as, take them for all in all, we shall not look upon their like again!" "Well, do you want to look upon their like again? I don't." "And consider how noble a type is the English gentleman! Their glorious loyalty to one another! The public school spirit! Even those of them
25 whose manner is unfortunate – some Englishmen are arrogant, I concede – have the great, sterling qualities[11] that we Orientals lack. Beneath their rough exterior, their hearts are of gold."

"Of gilt[12], shall we say? There's a kind of spurious[13] good-fellowship between the English and this country. It's a tradition to booze together and swap meals and pretend to be friends, though we all hate each other like poison." (...) The doctor shook his head. "Really, Mr Flory, I know not what it is that has made you so cynical. It is so most
30 unsuitable! You – an English gentleman of high gifts and character – to be uttering seditious[14] opinions that are worthy of the Burmese Patriot!" "Seditious?" Flory said. "I'M not seditious. I don't want the Burmans to drive us out of this country. God forbid! I'm here to make money, like everyone else. All I object to is the slimy white man's burden humbug. The pukka sahib pose. It's so boring. Even those bloody fools at the Club might be better company if we weren't all of us living a lie the whole time." "But, my dear friend, what lie are you living?" "Why, of course, the
35 lie that we're here to uplift our poor black brothers instead of to rob them. I suppose it's a natural enough lie. But it corrupts us, it corrupts us in ways you can't imagine. There's an everlasting sense of being a sneak[15] and a liar that torments us and drives us to justify ourselves night and day. It's at the bottom of half our beastliness to the natives. We Anglo-Indians could be almost bearable if we'd only admit that we're thieves and go on thieving without any humbug."

Annotations

[1] to **thrust oneself** = to throw oneself
[2] **palsy** = immobility
[3] **septicamia, peritonitis** = illnesses
[4] **ganglia** = nervous system
[5] **supine** = stretched out
[6] **tart** (offensive) = sex worker

[7] **sans peur et sans reproche** = without fear and reproach
[8] **havildar** = *einheimischer Sergeant der Britisch-Indischen Armee*
[9] **rail** = *Geländer*
[10] **Clive ... Curzon** = English governors in India

[11] **sterling qualities** = qualities like strength and reliability
[12] **gilt** = *vergoldet*
[13] **spurious** = not genuine
[14] **seditious** = here: non-patriotic
[15] **sneak** = mean person

4

a) Outline the major arguments of the two men's discussion.
b) Compare the two men's attitudes towards the British.
c) **Pair work** Examine the two men's relationship.
   Tell each other about your findings. Then talk about what picture of the colonizer and the colonized is created in the two texts.

British Army Recruiting Poster

Immigration to Britain

After World War II a worldwide process of decolonization set in, in which Britain granted its colonies independence. In the aftermath England has become a country of immigration for the people from its former colonies, the Commonwealth.

5

Read the text about immigration to Britain. The passages have all been jumbled up.
Put them into the correct chronological order.

1	2	3	4	5	6	7	8	9	10
c)									

a) Immigration from the West Indies was encouraged by the British Nationality Act of 1948, which gave all Commonwealth citizens free entry into Britain, and by a tough new US immigration law introduced in 1952, which restricted entry into the USA. The symbolic starting point of this mass migration to the 'mother country' was the journey of the SS Empire Windrush from Kingston, Jamaica, to Tilbury, Essex, in June 1948. On board were almost 500 West Indians intent on starting new lives in Britain.

b) The Race Relations Amendment Act of 2000 was introduced as a result of the Stephen Lawrence Inquiry of 1999. This was held in response to the campaigning of the black community following the flawed investigation of the murder of black teenager Stephen Lawrence in 1993. The inquiry's report acknowledged the existence of 'institutional racism' in the police and other organisations. The Scarman Report, produced as a result of unrest in Brixton, south London and other urban areas in 1981, also called for reform.

c) When the Second World War ended in 1945, it was quickly recognised that the reconstruction of the British economy required a large influx of immigrant labour. The Royal Commission on Population reported in 1949 that immigrants of 'good stock' would be welcomed 'without reserve', and potential newcomers from the Caribbean and elsewhere soon became aware of the pressing needs of the labour market in the UK.

d) Since the 1960s Britain has developed a substantial body of race relations legislation. Various Race Relations Acts (1965, 1968, 1976 and 2000) have provided a statutory basis for stamping out racial discrimination in employment and other areas. To reinforce this legislation, organisations such as the Commission for Racial Equality (created as part of the 1976 Race Relations Act) have tried to ensure that the principle of racial equality is put into practice.

e) The majority of immigrants from the Indian subcontinent arrived in Britain during the 1950s and 1960s. Although often lumped together as one group by white Britons, these newcomers, in fact, came from a variety of backgrounds. They included Hindus from the Gujarat region of western India, Sikhs from the eastern Punjab region, and Muslims both from the west part of Pakistan and from East Pakistan, which became Bangladesh in 1971.

f) In the 21st century, Britain is a multi-racial society. The huge contributions made by the various immigrant communities to Britain's economic and social development since the Second World War are now widely recognised. Their role in creating a more diverse and tolerant society is indisputable.

g) The appeal for new workers was, however, aimed primarily at white Europeans, who had dominated immigration to Britain during the century before the Second World War and still played an important role after 1945. Even in the 1970s, the Irish remained the largest immigrant community in Britain. In the years immediately after the war, new arrivals came from all over Europe. These included a small number of German prisoners of war, a larger number of refugees from the Communist regimes in Eastern Europe and the Soviet Union (130,000 Poles arrived during the first few years after the war, and 14,000 Hungarians after the failure of the 1956 uprising in Hungary), substantial numbers of Irish and Italian labourers, and a wide variety of displaced persons from refugee camps throughout Europe.

h) Assessing how these immigrants have been welcomed in Britain since the 1950s is a complicated task. There was, and still is, a minority of hardcore racists, with policies based on the idea of 'keeping Britain white' and banning all immigration. Groups such as the British National Party (BNP) have remained on the extremist fringe of British politics. It is also true that black and Asian immigrants faced various degrees of hostility and racial prejudice in postwar Britain. Surveys conducted in the mid-1960s, for example, revealed that four out of five British people felt that 'too many immigrants had been let into the country'.

i) Postwar immigration also attracted, for the first time, large numbers of workers and their families from outside Europe – mainly from the Caribbean and from India and Pakistan (the two separate states created by 'partition' after Britain relinquished its Indian empire in 1947). During the 1950s in particular, Britain's non-white immigrant population increased rapidly in size.

j) This view has expressed itself relatively rarely in racist violence – the flashpoints in Britain during the past 50 years have largely been confined to poor areas where local white and black communities compete for scarce jobs and housing. But it has frequently been represented by more casual and insidious forms of racism. Anti-immigrant feelings have also been inflamed, both directly and indirectly, by agitation for tighter immigration controls – usually proposed when there is not an acute labour shortage.

West Indian immigrants in the customs hall at Southampton, 27th May 1956

Refugees in the 20th and 21st century

Apart from immigrants from its former colonies, Britain has also taken in refugees from outside the Commonwealth.

6

a) Learn from the examples in the box below why refugees came to Britain after World War Two.
b) **Group work (4-5)**: Choose one example from the box below and find out background information.
c) Prepare a two-minute talk and present it to your group members.

- Hungarians after the Soviet invasion in 1956
- Greek and Turkish Cypriots in the 1960s and 1970s fleeing civil war
- Asians expelled from Kenya and Uganda in 1968 and 1972
- Chileans and other Latin Americans following military coups in the 1970s
- Iranians following the 1979 Revolution
- Afghans fleeing invasions and civil wars from the late 1970s until the present
- Vietnamese 'boat people' in the 1980s
- Sri Lankan Tamils during the civil war from the 1980s onwards
- Turkish Kurds and Somalis as a result of civil conflict in the 1990s
- Bosnians, Serbs, Croats and Kosovans escaping conflict in former Yugoslavia in the 1990s
- Eritreans escaping violent government repression, particularly since 2000
- Syrians, Iraqis and Libyans uprooted by foreign invasion and civil war in the 2000s

A TIMELINE

7

a) Scan the texts from task 5 and 6 for historical facts and draw a timeline to show when and why immigrants have come to Britain.
b) **Pair work** Talk to your partner: What do you find striking?

The third and final continent: A short story (1999)

PRE-READING

Moving abroad

a) Imagine you move abroad. Take notes on how you experience the first few weeks. What do you have to do? How would you adjust to your new surroundings?

b) Exchange your ideas with a partner. Talk about differences and similarities.

Info

Indian customs and traditions

custom: an accepted way of behaving or of doing things in a society, e. g. giving presents at Christmas, getting married young; sth that you do habitually	**belief:** sth that you believe, especially as part of your religion
tradition: a transmission of customs and beliefs over time from one generation to the next	**values:** beliefs about what is right and wrong and what is important in life

2
Look at the photos and describe what aspects of Indian life they show.

COMPREHENSION

3 **Group work**

Find out about Indian customs and traditions in regard to the aspects portrayed in the photos. Each student reports back on one topic to the other group members.

a) Discuss in your group what you find most striking about your findings and explain why.

b) Step into an Indian person's shoes: What would this person find striking about the topics from task a) in Germany?

The third and final continent

by Jhumpa Lahiri

I left India in 1964 with a certificate in commerce and the equivalent, in those days, of ten dollars to my name[1]. For three weeks I sailed on the S.S. Roma, an Italian cargo vessel, in a cabin next to the
5 ship's engine, across the Arabian Sea, the Red Sea, the Mediterranean, and finally to England. I lived in London, in Finsbury Park, in a house occupied entirely by penniless Bengali[2] bachelors like myself, at least a dozen and sometimes more, all struggling
10 to educate and establish ourselves abroad.

I attended lectures at L.S.E.[3] and worked at the university library to get by. We lived three or four to a room, shared a single, icy toilet, and took turns cooking pots of egg curry[4], which we ate with
15 our hands on a table covered with newspapers. Apart from our jobs we had few responsibilities. On weekends we lounged barefoot in drawstring pajamas, drinking tea and smoking Rothmans, or set out to watch cricket at Lord's[5]. Some weekends
20 the house was crammed[6] with still more Bengalis, to whom we had introduced ourselves at the greengrocer, or on the Tube, and we made yet more egg curry, and played Mukesh[7] on a Grundig reel-to-reel[8], and soaked our dirty dishes in the bathtub.
25 Every now and then someone in the house moved out, to live with a woman whom his family back in Calcutta[9] had determined he was to wed[10]. In 1969, when I was thirty-six years old, my own marriage

was arranged. Around the same time, I was offered
30 a full-time job in America, in the processing department[11] of a library at M.I.T[12]. The salary was generous enough to support a wife, and I was honored to be hired by a world-famous university, and so I obtained a green card[13], and prepared to
35 travel farther still.

By then I had enough money to go by plane. I flew first to Calcutta, to attend my wedding, and a week later to Boston, to begin my new job. During the flight I read "The Student Guide to North America",
40 for although I was no longer a student, I was on a budget[14] all the same. I learned that Americans drove on the right side of the road, not the left, and that they called a lift an elevator and an engaged phone busy. "The pace of life in North America is
45 different from Britain, as you will soon discover," the guidebook informed me. "Everybody feels he must get to the top. Don't expect an English cup of tea." As the plane began its descent over Boston Harbor, the pilot announced the weather and the
50 time, and that President Nixon had declared a national holiday: two American men had landed on the moon. Several passengers cheered. "God bless America!" one of them hollered.[15] Across the aisle[16], I saw a woman praying.

55 I spent my first night at the Y.M.C.A. in Central Square, Cambridge, an inexpensive accommodation

Annotations

[1] **ten dollars to my name** = ten dollars in a bank account

[2] **Bengali** = from Bangladesh or West Bengal in eastern India

[3] **L.S.E.** = London School of Economics

[4] **egg curry** = a traditional Indian curry

[5] **Lord's** = Cricket Ground in west London

[6] **crammed** = to be packed with

[7] **Mukesh** = Mukesh Chand Mathur (1923-76) was one of the most popular playback singers of the Hindi film industry

[8] **Grundig reel-to-reel** = a tape recorder manufactured by the German brand Grundig

[9] **Calcutta** = since 2001 Kolkata, capital of the Indian state of West Bengal

[10] **to wed** = to marry

[11] **processing department** = *Bearbeitungsabteilung*

[12] **M.I.T.** = The Massachusetts Institute of Technology

[13] **green card** = a document that legally allows sb from another country to live and work in the US

[14] **to be on a budget** = to have a limited amount of money

[15] **to holler** = to shout loudly

[16] **aisle** = a passage between rows of seats

Annotations

17 **cot** = a fold-out bed or camp bed
18 **bare** = not covered by anything
19 to **prolong** = continuing for a long time
20 to **blare** = to make a loud unpleasant noise
21 to **herald** = to be a sign that sth is going to happen
22 **S.S. Roma** = name of the cargo vessel, cf l.3
23 to **report to your job** = to tell sb that you have arrived for work
24 **chore** = task
25 **resident** = a person who lives or stays in a particular place
26 **stifling** = making you unable to breathe because it is too hot or there is no fresh air
27 **resolve** = to make a firm decision to do sth
28 **classified section** = information arranged in groups according to subjects
29 **housing office** = an office that owns houses or flats and helps people to rent or buy them at a low price
30 **occupancy** = the act of living in a place
31 to **sort through** = to look through sth in order to find sth
32 **paisa** = an Indian coin
33 **clamorous** = loud
34 **tentatively** = hesitantly
35 **Listerine** = product name of an American mouthwash
36 **perpendicular** = forming an angle of 90° with another line
37 **trim** = edging
38 **forsythia** = a twisted mass of forsythia, (a bush with small yellow flowers in the early spring)
39 to **be plastered** = to be covered
40 to **peer up** = to look up
41 **ruffles** = *Rüschen*
42 **pallid** = pale
43 **knuckles** = joint in the finger that connects the finger to the hand
44 to **batter** = to damage
45 **crease** = wrinkle
46 **chapped** = cracked

recommended by my guidebook which was within walking distance of M.I.T. The room contained a cot[17], a desk, and a small wooden cross on one
60 wall. A sign on the door said that cooking was strictly forbidden. A bare[18] window overlooked Massachusetts Avenue. Car horns, shrill and prolonged[19], blared[20] one after another. Sirens and flashing lights heralded[21] endless emergencies,
65 and a succession of buses rumbled past, their doors opening and closing with a powerful hiss, throughout the night. The noise was constantly distracting, at times suffocating. I felt it deep in my ribs, just as I had felt the furious drone of the engine
70 on the S.S. Roma[22]. But there was no ship's deck to escape to, no glittering ocean to thrill my soul, no breeze to cool my face, no one to talk to. I was too tired to pace the gloomy corridors of the Y.M.C.A. in my pajamas. Instead I sat at the desk and stared
75 out the window. In the morning I reported to my job[23] at the Dewey Library, a beige fortlike building by Memorial Drive. I also opened a bank account, rented a post-office box, and bought a plastic bowl and a spoon. I went to a supermarket called
80 Purity Supreme, wandering up and down the aisles, comparing prices with those in England. In the end I bought a carton of milk and a box of cornflakes. This was my first meal in America. Even the simple chore[24] of buying milk was new to me; in London
85 we'd had bottles delivered each morning to our door. In a week I had adjusted, more or less. I ate cornflakes and milk morning and night, and bought some bananas for variety, slicing them into the bowl with the edge of my spoon. I left my carton of
90 milk on the shaded part of the windowsill, as I had seen other resi-dents[25] at the Y.M.C.A. do. To pass the time in the evenings I read the Boston Globe downstairs, in a spacious room with stained-glass windows. I read every article and advertisement, so
95 that I would grow familiar with things, and when my eyes grew tired I slept. Only I did not sleep well. Each night I had to keep the window wide open; it was the only source of air in the stifling[26] room, and the noise was intolerable. I would lie on the cot with
100 my fingers pressed into my ears, but when I drifted off to sleep my hands fell away, and the noise of the traffic would wake me up again. Pigeon feathers drifted onto the windowsill, and one evening, when I poured milk over my cornflakes, I saw that it
105 had soured. Nevertheless I resolved[27] to stay at the Y.M.C.A. for six weeks, until my wife's passport and green card were ready. Once she arrived I would have to rent a proper apartment, and from time to time I studied the classified section[28] of the newspaper, or
110 stopped in at the housing office[29] at M.I.T. during my lunch break to see what was available. It was in this manner that I discovered a room for immediate occupancy[30], in a house on a quiet street, the listing said, for eight dollars per week. I dialled the number
115 from a pay telephone, sorting through[31] the coins, with which I was still unfamiliar, smaller and lighter than shillings, heavier and brighter than paisas[32]. "Who is speaking?" a woman demanded. Her voice was bold and clamorous[33].
120 "Yes, good afternoon, Madam. I am calling about the room for rent."
"Harvard or Tech?"
"I beg your pardon?"
"Are you from Harvard or Tech?" Gathering that
125 Tech referred to the Massachusetts Institute of Technology, I replied, "I work at Dewey Library," adding tentatively[34], "at Tech."
"I only rent rooms to boys from Harvard or Tech!"
"Yes, Madam."
130 I was given an address and an appointment for seven o'clock that evening. Thirty minutes before the hour I set out, my guidebook in my pocket, my breath fresh with Listerine[35]. I turned down a street shaded with trees, perpendicular[36] to Massachusetts
135 Avenue. In spite of the heat I wore a coat and tie, regarding the event as I would any other interview; I had never lived in the home of a person who was not Indian. The house, surrounded by a chain-link fence, was off-white with dark-brown trim[37], with
140 a tangle of forsythia[38] bushes plastered[39] against its front and sides. When I pressed the bell, the woman with whom I had spoken on the phone hollered from what seemed to be just the other side of the door, "One minute, please!"
145 Several minutes later the door was opened by a tiny, extremely old woman. A mass of snowy hair was arranged like a small sack on top of her head. As I stepped into the house she sat down on a wooden bench positioned at the bottom of a narrow carpeted
150 staircase. Once she was settled on the bench, in a small pool of light, she peered up[40] at me, giving me her undivided attention. She wore a long black skirt that spread like a stiff tent to the floor, and a starched white shirt edged with ruffles[41] at the throat
155 and cuffs. Her hands, folded together in her lap, had long pallid[42] fingers, with swollen knuckles[43] and tough yellow nails. Age had battered[44] her features so that she almost resembled a man, with sharp, shrunken eyes and prominent creases[45] on either
160 side of her nose. Her lips, chapped[46] and faded, had nearly disappeared, and her eyebrows were missing altogether. Nevertheless she looked fierce.
"Lock up!" she commanded. She shouted even though I stood only a few feet away. "Fasten the
165 chain and firmly press that button on the knob! This is the first thing you shall do when you enter, is that clear?"
I locked the door as directed and examined the

house. Next to the bench was a small round table, its legs fully concealed, much like the woman's, by a skirt of lace⁴⁷. The table held a lamp, a transistor radio, a leather change purse with a silver clasp⁴⁸, and a telephone. A thick wooden cane was propped against one side. There was a parlor⁴⁹ to my right, lined with bookcases and filled with shabby claw-footed furniture. In the corner of the parlor I saw a grand piano with its top down, piled with papers. The piano's bench was missing; it seemed to be the one on which the woman was sitting. Somewhere in the house a clock chimed seven times.

"You're punctual!" the woman proclaimed. "I expect you shall be so with the rent!"

"I have a letter, Madam." In my jacket pocket was a letter from M.I.T. confirming my employment, which I had brought along to prove that I was indeed from Tech.

She stared at the letter, then handed it back to me carefully, gripping it with her fingers as if it were a plate heaped with food. She did not wear glasses, and I wondered if she'd read a word of it. "The last boy was always late! Still owes me eight dollars! Harvard boys aren't what they used to be! Only Harvard and Tech in this house! How's Tech, boy?"

"It is very well."

"You checked the lock?"

"Yes, Madam."

She unclasped her fingers, slapped the space beside her on the bench with one hand, and told me to sit down. For a moment she was silent. Then she intoned⁵⁰, as if she alone possessed this knowledge: "There is an American flag on the moon!"

"Yes, Madam." Until then I had not thought very much about the moon shot. It was in the newspaper, of course, article upon article. The astronauts had landed on the shores of the Sea of Tranquility⁵¹, I had read, travelling farther than anyone in the history of civilization. For a few hours they explored the moon's surface. They gathered rocks in their pockets, described their surroundings (a magnificent desolation, according to one astronaut), spoke by phone to the President, and planted a flag in lunar⁵² soil. The voyage was hailed as man's most awesome achievement.

The woman bellowed, "A flag on the moon, boy! I heard it on the radio! Isn't that splendid⁵³?"

"Yes, Madam."

But she was not satisfied with my reply. Instead she commanded, "Say 'Splendid!'"

I was both baffled⁵⁴ and somewhat insulted by the request. It reminded me of the way I was taught multiplication tables as a child, repeating after the master, sitting cross-legged on the floor of my one-room Tollygunge⁵⁵ school. It also reminded me of my wedding, when I had repeated endless Sanskrit⁵⁶

verses after the priest, verses I barely understood, which joined me to my wife. I said nothing.

"Say 'Splendid!'" the woman bellowed once again.

"Splendid," I murmured. I had to repeat the word a second time at the top of my lungs, so she could hear. I was reluctant to raise my voice to an elderly woman, but she did not appear to be offended. If anything the reply pleased her, because her next command was:

"Go see the room!"

I rose from the bench and mounted the narrow staircase. There were five doors, two on either side of an equally narrow hallway, and one at the opposite end. Only one door was open. The room contained a twin bed under a sloping ceiling, a brown oval rug, a basin with an exposed pipe, and a chest of drawers. One door led to a closet⁵⁷, another to a toilet and a tub. The window was open; net curtains stirred in the breeze. I lifted them away and inspected the view: a small back yard, with a few fruit trees and an empty clothesline. I was satisfied. When I returned to the foyer the woman picked up the leather change purse on the table, opened the clasp, fished about with her fingers, and produced a key on a thin wire hoop⁵⁸. She informed me that there was a kitchen at the back of the house, accessible through the parlor. I was welcome to use the stove as long as I left it as I found it. Sheets and towels were provided, but keeping them clean was my own responsibility. The rent was due Friday mornings on the ledge⁵⁹ above the piano keys. "And no lady visitors!"

"I am a married man, Madam." It was the first time I had announced this fact to anyone.

But she had not heard. "No lady visitors!" she insisted. She introduced herself as Mrs. Croft.

My wife's name was Mala. The marriage had been arranged by my older brother and his wife. I regarded the proposition with neither objection nor enthusiasm. It was a duty expected of me, as it was expected of every man. She was the daughter of a schoolteacher in Beleghata⁶⁰. I was told that she could cook, knit, embroider⁶¹, sketch landscapes, and recite poems by Tagore⁶², but these talents could not make up for the fact that she did not possess a fair complexion, and so a string⁶³ of men had rejected her to her face. She was twenty-seven, an age when her parents had begun to fear that she would never marry, and so they were willing to ship their only child halfway across the world in order to save her from spinsterhood⁶⁴.

For five nights we shared a bed. Each of those nights, after applying cold cream and braiding her hair, she turned from me and wept; she missed her parents. Although I would be leaving the country in a few days, custom dictated that she was now a part

Annotations
⁴⁷ **lace** = decorative cloth; *Spitze*
⁴⁸ **clasp** = fastening device
⁴⁹ **parlor** = a room for sitting and entertaining visitors
⁵⁰ to **intone** = to say sth slowly and seriously
⁵¹ **Sea of Tranquility** = the landing site for the first manned landing on the Moon on July 20, 1969
⁵² **lunar** = connected with the moon
⁵³ **splendid** = old-fashioned: used to show that you approve of sth or are pleased
⁵⁴ **baffled** = confused
⁵⁵ **Tollygunge** = an area of South Kolkata, in West Bengal, India. It is famous for its Bengali film industry, known as Tollywood. It is named after the British Colonel William Tolly.
⁵⁶ **Sanskrit** = an ancient language of India in which the Hindu holy texts are written and on which many modern languages are based
⁵⁷ **closet** = a small storage room
⁵⁸ **hoop** = ring
⁵⁹ **ledge** = a narrow flat shelf fixed to a wall
⁶⁰ **Beleghata** = a poor to middle class residential area in Kolkata
⁶¹ **embroider** = to decorate cloth, *sticken*
⁶² **Tagore** = Rabindranath Tagore (1861–1941), a poet, musician, and artist from the Indian subcontinent. He was awarded the Nobel Prize in Literature in 1913.
⁶³ **string** = a series of people
⁶⁴ **spinsterhood** = for women: the state of staying unmarried

of my household, and for the next six weeks she was to live with my brother and his wife, cooking, cleaning, serving tea and sweets to guests. I did nothing to console her. I lay on my own side of the
285 bed, reading my guidebook by flashlight. At times I thought of the tiny room on the other side of the wall which had belonged to my mother. Now the room was practically empty; the wooden pallet on which she'd once slept was piled with trunks and
290 old bedding. Nearly six years ago, before leaving for London, I had watched her die on that bed, had found her playing with her excrement in her final days. Before we cremated her I had cleaned each of her fingernails with a hairpin, and then, because
295 my brother could not bear it, I had assumed the role of eldest son, and had touched the flame to her temple⁶⁵, to release her tormented soul to heaven.

The next morning I moved into Mrs. Croft's house. When I unlocked the door I saw that she was
300 sitting on the piano bench, on the same side as the previous evening. She wore the same black skirt, the same starched white blouse, and had her hands folded together the same way in her lap. She looked so much the same that I wondered if she'd spent the
305 whole night on the bench. I put my suitcase upstairs and then headed off to work. That evening when I came home from the university, she was still there. "Sit down, boy!" She slapped the space beside her.

I perched⁶⁶ on the bench. I had a bag of groceries
310 with me – more milk, more cornflakes, and more bananas, for my inspection of the kitchen earlier in the day had revealed no spare pots or pans. There were only two saucepans in the refrigerator, both containing some orange broth, and a copper kettle
315 on the stove.

"Good evening, Madam."

She asked me if I had checked the lock. I told her I had.

For a moment she was silent. Then suddenly she
320 declared, with the equal measures of disbelief and delight as the night before, "There's an American flag on the moon, boy!"

"Yes, Madam."

"A flag on the moon! Isn't that splendid?"

325 I nodded, dreading what I knew was coming. "Yes, Madam."

"Say 'Splendid!'"

This time I paused, looking to either side in case anyone was there to overhear me, though I knew
330 perfectly well that the house was empty. I felt like an idiot. But it was a small enough thing to ask. "Splendid!" I cried out.

Within days it became our routine. In the mornings when I left for the library Mrs. Croft was either
335 hidden away in her bedroom, on the other side of the staircase, or sitting on the bench, oblivious⁶⁷

of my presence, listening to the news or classical music on the radio. But each evening when I returned the same thing happened: she slapped the
340 bench, ordered me to sit down, declared that there was a flag on the moon, and declared that it was splendid. I said it was splendid, too, and then we sat in silence. As awkward as it was, and as endless as it felt to me then, the nightly encounter lasted
345 only about ten minutes; inevitably she would drift off to sleep, her head falling abruptly toward her chest, leaving me free to retire to my room. By then, of course, there was no flag standing on the moon. The astronauts, I read in the paper, had seen it fall
350 before they flew back to Earth. But I did not have the heart to tell her.

Friday morning, when my first week's rent was due, I went to the piano in the parlor to place my money on the ledge. The piano keys were dull⁶⁸ and
355 discolored. When I pressed one, it made no sound at all. I had put eight dollar bills in an envelope and written Mrs. Croft's name on the front of it. I was not in the habit of leaving money unmarked and unattended. From where I stood I could see the
360 profile of her tent-shaped skirt in the hall. It seemed unnecessary to make her get up and walk all the way to the piano. I never saw her walking about, and assumed, from the cane propped⁶⁹ against the round table, that she did so with difficulty. When
365 I approached the bench she peered up at me and demanded:

"What is your business?"

"The rent, Madam."

"On the ledge above the piano keys!"

370 "I have it here." I extended the envelope toward her, but her fingers, folded together in her lap, did not budge⁷⁰. I bowed slightly and lowered the envelope, so that it hovered just above her hands. After a moment she accepted it, and nodded her
375 head. That night when I came home, she did not slap the bench, but out of habit I sat beside her as usual. She asked me if I had checked the lock, but she mentioned nothing about the flag on the moon. Instead she said:

380 "It was very kind of you!"

"I beg your pardon, Madam?"

"Very kind of you!"

She was still holding the envelope in her hands.

On Sunday there was a knock on my door. An
385 elderly woman introduced herself: she was Mrs. Croft's daughter, Helen. She walked into the room and looked at each of the walls as if for signs of change, glancing at the shirts that hung in the closet, the neckties draped over the doorknob, the
390 box of cornflakes on the chest of drawers, the dirty bowl and spoon in the basin. She was short and thickwaisted, with cropped⁷¹ silver hair and bright

pink lipstick. She wore a sleeveless summer dress, a necklace of white plastic beads, and spectacles on
395 a chain that hung like a swing against her chest. The backs of her legs were mapped with dark-blue veins, and her upper arms sagged[72] like the flesh of a roasted eggplant. She told me she lived in Arlington, a town farther up Massachusetts Avenue. "I come
400 once a week to bring Mother groceries. Has she sent you packing yet?"

"It is very well, Madam."

"Some of the boys run screaming. But I think she likes you. You're the first boarder she's ever referred
405 to as a gentleman."

She looked at me, noticing my bare feet. (I still felt strange wearing shoes indoors, and always removed them before entering my room.) "Are you new to Boston?"

410 "New to America, Madam." "From?" She raised her eyebrows.

"I am from Calcutta, India."

"Is that right? We had a Brazilian fellow, about a year ago. You'll find Cambridge a very international
415 city."

I nodded, and began to wonder how long our conversation would last. But at that moment we heard Mrs. Croft's electrifying voice rising up the stairs.

420 "You are to come downstairs immediately!"

"What is it?" Helen cried back.

"Immediately!" I put on my shoes. Helen sighed.

I followed Helen down the staircase. She seemed to be in no hurry, and complained at one point that she
425 had a bad knee. "Have you been walking without your cane?" Helen called out. "You know you're not supposed to walk without that cane." She paused, resting her hand on the bannister[73], and looked back at me. "She slips sometimes."

430 For the first time Mrs. Croft seemed vulnerable. I pictured her on the floor in front of the bench, flat on her back, staring at the ceiling, her feet pointing in opposite directions. But when we reached the bottom of the staircase she was sitting there as
435 usual, her hands folded together in her lap. Two grocery bags were at her feet. She did not slap the bench, or ask us to sit down. She glared.

"What is it, Mother?"

"It's improper[74]!"

440 "What's improper?"

"It is improper for a lady and gentleman who are not married to one another to hold a private conversation without a chaperone[75]!"

Helen said she was sixty-eight years old, old enough
445 to be my mother, but Mrs. Croft insisted that Helen and I speak to each other downstairs, in the parlor. She added that it was also improper for a lady of Helen's station[76] to reveal her age, and to wear a dress so high above the ankle.

450 "For your information, Mother, it's 1969. What would you do if you actually left the house one day and saw a girl in a miniskirt?"

Mrs. Croft sniffed. "I'd have her arrested."

Helen shook her head and picked up one of the
455 grocery bags. I picked up the other one, and followed her through the parlor and into the kitchen. The bags were filled with cans of soup, which Helen opened up one by one with a few cranks[77] of a can opener. She tossed the old soup into the sink, rinsed
460 the saucepans under the tap, filled them with soup from the newly opened cans, and put them back in the refrigerator. "A few years ago she could still open the cans herself," Helen said. "She hates that I do it for her now. But the piano killed her hands."

465 She put on her spectacles, glanced at the cupboards, and spotted my tea bags. "Shall we have a cup?"

I filled the kettle on the stove. "I beg your pardon, Madam. The piano?"

"She used to give lessons. For forty years. It was
470 how she raised us after my father died." Helen put her hands on her hips, staring at the open refrigerator. She reached into the back, pulled out a wrapped stick of butter, frowned, and tossed it into the garbage. "That ought to do it," she said, and put
475 the unopened cans of soup in the cupboard. I sat at the table and watched as Helen washed the dirty dishes, tied up the garbage bag, and poured boiling water into two cups. She handed one to me without milk, and sat down at the table.

480 "Excuse me, Madam, but is it enough?"

Helen took a sip of her tea. Her lipstick left a smiling pink stain on the rim of the cup. "Is what enough?"

"The soup in the pans. Is it enough food for Mrs. Croft?"

485 "She won't eat anything else. She stopped eating solids[78] after she turned one hundred. That was, let's see, three years ago."

I was mortified[79]. I had assumed Mrs. Croft was in her eighties, perhaps as old as ninety. I had never
490 known a person who had lived for over a century. That this person was a widow who lived alone mortified me further still. Widowhood had driven my own mother insane. My father, who worked as a clerk at the General Post Office of Calcutta, died
495 of encephalitis[80] when I was sixteen. My mother refused to adjust to life without him; instead she sank deeper into a world of darkness from which neither I, nor my brother, nor concerned relatives, nor psychiatric clinics on Rash Behari Avenue[81]
500 could save her. What pained me most was to see her so unguarded, to hear her burp[82] after meals or expel gas in front of company without the slightest embarrassment. After my father's death my brother abandoned his schooling and began to work in the

Annotations

[72] to **sag** = to be hanging, to be no longer firm
[73] **bannister** = *Treppengeländer*
[74] **improper** = indecent
[75] **chaperone** = here: in the past an older woman who on social occasions took care of a young unmarried woman
[76] **station** = social position
[77] **cranks** = here: *Kurbeldrehung*
[78] **solids** = here: *feste Nahrung*
[79] **mortified** = ashamed, embarrassed
[80] **encephalitis** = a condition in which the brain becomes swollen
[81] **Rash Behari Avenue** = one of the most prominent and important east-west avenues of Kolkata with expensive shops. It is named after Sir Rash Behari Ghosh who was an Indian politician, lawyer and social worker.
[82] to **burp** = to let out air from the stomach through the mouth, making a noise

43

Annotations

83 **jute mill** = a factory that produces jute

84 **abacus** = a frame with small balls which slide along wires. It is used as a toy or tool for counting.

85 **vigorous** = energetic

86 **imperious** = expecting people to obey you and treating them as if they are not as important as you

87 **chaste** = not expressing sexual feelings

88 **bangle** = a piece of jewellery in the form of a large ring of gold, silver, etc. worn loosely around the wrist

89 **vermillion powder** = bright red powder made from the powdered mineral cinnabar *(Zinnober).* Hindu women use it along the hair parting line known as Sindoor, to signify that they are married.

90 to **conjure up** = to make sth appear as a picture in your mind

91 **Sari** = a long piece of cloth that is wrapped around the body and worn as the main piece of clothing by Indian women

92 to **drag** = to pull sth with effort and difficulty

93 **stroller** = buggy, pushchair

94 **boarder** = a person who pays money to live in sb else's house

95 **a small red circle** = A bindi is a red coloured dot worn on the forehead by Hindu women to show that they are married. It has many other meanings, too.

505 jute mill[83] he would eventually manage, in order to keep the household running. And so it was my job to sit by my mother's feet and study for my exams as she counted and recounted the bracelets on her arm as if they were the beads of an abacus[84]. We
510 tried to keep an eye on her. Once she had wandered half naked to the tram depot before we were able to bring her inside again.

"I am happy to warm Mrs. Croft's soup in the evenings," I suggested. "It is no trouble."
515 Helen looked at her watch, stood up, and poured the rest of her tea into the sink. "I wouldn't if I were you. That's the sort of thing that would kill her altogether."

That evening, when Helen had gone and Mrs. Croft
520 and I were alone again, I began to worry. Now that I knew how very old she was, I worried that something would happen to her in the middle of the night, or when I was out during the day. As vigorous[85] as her voice was, and imperious[86] as she
525 seemed, I knew that even a scratch or a cough could kill a person that old; each day she lived, I knew, was something of a miracle. Helen didn't seem concerned. She came and went, bringing soup for Mrs. Croft, one Sunday after the next.

530 In this manner the six weeks of that summer passed. I came home each evening, after my hours at the library, and spent a few minutes on the piano bench with Mrs. Croft. Some evenings I sat beside her long after she had drifted off to sleep, still in awe of how
535 many years she had spent on this earth. At times I tried to picture the world she had been born into, in 1866 – a world, I imagined, filled with women in long black skirts, and chaste[87] conversations in the parlor. Now, when I looked at her hands with their swollen
540 knuckles folded together in her lap, I imagined them smooth and slim, striking the piano keys. At times I came downstairs before going to sleep, to make sure she was sitting upright on the bench, or was safe in her bedroom. On Fridays I put the rent in her hands.
545 There was nothing I could do for her beyond these simple gestures. I was not her son, and, apart from those eight dollars, I owed her nothing.

At the end of August, Mala's passport and green card were ready. I received a telegram with her
550 flight information; my brother's house in Calcutta had no telephone. Around that time I also received a letter from her, written only a few days after we had parted. There was no salutation; addressing me by name would have assumed an intimacy we had
555 not yet discovered. It contained only a few lines. "I write in English in preparation for the journey. Here I am very much lonely. I sit very cold there. Is there snow. Yours, Mala."

I was not touched by her words. We had spent only
560 a handful of days in each other's company. And yet we were bound together; for six weeks she had

worn an iron bangle[88] on her wrist, and applied vermillion powder[89] to the part in her hair, to signify to the world that she was a bride. In those six weeks
565 I regarded her arrival as I would the arrival of a coming month, or season—something inevitable, but meaningless at the time. So little did I know her that, while details of her face sometimes rose to my memory, I could not conjure up[90] the whole of it.
570 A few days after receiving the letter, as I was walking to work in the morning, I saw an Indian woman on Massachusetts Avenue, wearing a sari[91] with its free end nearly dragging[92] on the footpath, and pushing a child in a stroller[93]. An American woman with a
575 small black dog on a leash was walking to one side of her. Suddenly the dog began barking. I watched as the Indian woman, startled, stopped in her path, at which point the dog leaped up and seized the end of the sari between its teeth. The American woman
580 scolded the dog, appeared to apologize, and walked quickly away, leaving the Indian woman to fix her sari, and quiet her crying child. She did not see me standing there, and eventually she continued on her way. Such a mishap, I realized that morning, would
585 soon be my concern. It was my duty to take care of Mala, to welcome her and protect her. I would have to buy her first pair of snow boots, her first winter coat. I would have to tell her which streets to avoid, which way the traffic came, tell her to wear her sari
590 so that the free end did not drag on the footpath. A five-mile separation from her parents, I recalled with some irritation, had caused her to weep.

Unlike Mala, I was used to it all by then: used to cornflakes and milk, used to Helen's visits, used to
595 sitting on the bench with Mrs. Croft. The only thing I was not used to was Mala. Nevertheless I did what I had to do. I went to the housing office at M.I.T. and found a furnished apartment a few blocks away, with a double bed and a private kitchen and bath,
600 for forty dollars a week. One last Friday I handed Mrs. Croft eight dollar bills in an envelope, brought my suitcase downstairs, and informed her that I was moving. She put my key into her change purse. The last thing she asked me to do was hand her the
605 cane propped against the table, so that she could walk to the door and lock it behind me. "Goodbye, then," she said, and retreated back into the house. I did not expect any display of emotion, but I was disappointed all the same. I was only a boarder[94],
610 a man who paid her a bit of money and passed in and out of her home for six weeks. Compared with a century, it was no time at all.

At the airport I recognized Mala immediately. The free end of her sari did not drag on the floor, but was
615 draped in a sign of bridal modesty over her head, just as it had draped my mother until the day my father died. Her thin brown arms were stacked with gold bracelets, a small red circle[95] was painted on

her forehead, and the edges of her feet were tinted⁹⁶
with a decorative red dye⁹⁷. I did not embrace her,
or kiss her, or take her hand. Instead I asked her,
speaking Bengali for the first time in America, if
she was hungry.
She hesitated, then nodded yes.
I told her I had prepared some egg curry at home.
"What did they give you to eat on the plane?"
"I didn't eat."
"All the way from Calcutta?" "The menu said oxtail
soup."
"But surely there were other items."
"The thought of eating an ox's tail made me lose
my appetite."
When we arrived home, Mala opened up one of
her suitcases, and presented me with two pullover
sweaters, both made with bright-blue wool, which
she had knitted in the course of our separation,
one with a V-neck, the other covered with cables. I
tried them on; both were tight under the arms. She
had also brought me two new pairs of drawstring
pajamas, a letter from my brother, and a packet of
loose Darjeeling tea. I had no present for her apart
from the egg curry. We sat at a bare table, staring at
our plates. We ate with our hands, another thing I
had not yet done in America.
"The house is nice," she said. "Also the egg curry."
With her left hand she held the end of her sari to
her chest, so it would not slip off her head.
"I don't know many recipes."
She nodded, peeling the skin off each of her potatoes
before eating them. At one point the sari slipped to
her shoulders. She readjusted it at once.
"There is no need to cover your head," I said. "I don't
mind. It doesn't matter here."
She kept it covered anyway.
I waited to get used to her, to her presence at my
side, at my table and in my bed, but a week later we
were still strangers. I still was not used to coming
home to an apartment that smelled of steamed rice,
and finding that the basin in the bathroom was
always wiped clean, our two toothbrushes lying
side by side, a cake of Pears soap⁹⁸ residing in the
soap dish. I was not used to the fragrance of the
coconut oil she rubbed every other night into her
scalp, or the delicate sound her bracelets made as
she moved about the apartment. In the mornings she
was always awake before I was. The first morning
when I came into the kitchen she had heated up the
leftovers and set a plate with a spoonful of salt on
its edge, assuming I would eat rice for breakfast,
as most Bengali husbands did. I told her cereal
would do, and the next morning when I came into
the kitchen she had already poured the cornflakes
into my bowl. One morning she walked with me to
M.I.T., where I gave her a short tour of the campus.
The next morning before I left for work she asked

me for a few dollars. I parted with them reluctantly,
but I knew that this, too, was now normal. When I
came home from work there was a potato peeler in
the kitchen drawer, and a tablecloth on the table, and
chicken curry made with fresh garlic and ginger on
the stove. After dinner I read the newspaper, while
Mala sat at the kitchen table, working on a cardigan
for herself with more of the blue wool, or writing
letters home.
On Friday, I suggested going out. Mala set down her
knitting and disappeared into the bathroom. When
she emerged I regretted the suggestion; she had put
on a silk sari and extra bracelets, and coiled her hair
with a flattering side part on top of her head. She
was prepared as if for a party, or at the very least for
the cinema, but I had no such destination in mind.
The evening was balmy⁹⁹. We walked several blocks
down Massachusetts Avenue, looking into the
windows of restaurants and shops. Then, without
thinking, I led her down the quiet street where for
so many nights I had walked alone.
"This is where I lived before you came," I said,
stopping at Mrs. Croft's chain-link fence.
"In such a big house?"
"I had a small room upstairs. At the back."
"Who else lives there?"
"A very old woman."
"With her family?"
"Alone."
"But who takes care of her?" I opened the gate.
"For the most part she takes care of herself."
I wondered if Mrs. Croft would remember me; I
wondered if she had a new boarder to sit with her
each evening. When I pressed the bell I expected
the same long wait as that day of our first meeting,
when I did not have a key. But this time the door was
opened almost immediately, by Helen. Mrs. Croft
was not sitting on the bench. The bench was gone.
"Hello there," Helen said, smiling with her bright
pink lips at Mala. "Mother's in the parlor. Will you
be visiting awhile¹⁰⁰?"
"As you wish, Madam." "Then I think I'll run to the
store, if you don't mind. She had a little accident.
We can't leave her alone these days, not even for a
minute."
I locked the door after Helen and walked into the
parlor. Mrs. Croft was lying flat on her back, her
head on a peach-colored cushion, a thin white
quilt spread over her body. Her hands were folded
together on her chest. When she saw me she pointed
at the sofa, and told me to sit down. I took my place
as directed, but Mala wandered over to the piano
and sat on the bench, which was now positioned
where it belonged.
"I broke my hip!" Mrs. Croft announced, as if no
time had passed.
"Oh dear, Madam."

Annotations
⁹⁶ **tinted** = coloured
⁹⁷ **dye** = a substance that is used to change the colour of sth
⁹⁸ **Pears Soap** = Pears soap is a brand of soap first produced and sold by Andrew Pears in 1807 in England. It was the world's first mass-market translucent soap and is available in India.
⁹⁹ **balmy** = mild
¹⁰⁰ **awhile** = for a short time

45

Annotations

101 **sedately** = calmly, quietly

102 **conductor** = a person who is in charge of a train and controls the tickets

103 to **scrutinize** = to examine or to look closely

104 **placid** = calm

105 **disdain** = the feeling that somebody is not good enough to deserve your respect or attention

106 **of sorts** = for a short time

107 **Prudential Building** = The Prudential Building, also known as The Prudential Tower, is a huge skyscraper in Boston, Massachusetts. At the time of its completion in 1964 it was the highest building in the world.

108 **The Globe** = the oldest and largest daily newspaper founded in Boston, Massachusetts in 1872. It has won the Pulitzer Prize several times.

109 **Social Security** = a system in the US in which people pay money regularly to the government when they are working and receive payments from the government when they are unable to work, especially when they are sick or too old to work.

110 to **hurl** = to throw sb/sth in a particular direction

"I fell off the bench!"

"I am so sorry, Madam."

735 "It was the middle of the night! Do you know what I did, boy?"

I shook my head.

"I called the police!"

She stared up at the ceiling and grinned sedately[101], 740 exposing a crowded row of long grey teeth. "What do you say to that, boy?"

As stunned as I was, I knew what I had to say. With no hesitation at all, I cried out, "Splendid!"

Mala laughed then. Her voice was full of kindness, 745 her eyes bright with amusement. I had never heard her laugh before, and it was loud enough so that Mrs. Croft heard, too. She turned to Mala and glared. "Who is she, boy?"

"She is my wife, Madam."

750 Mrs. Croft pressed her head at an angle against the cushion to get a better look. "Can you play the piano?"

"No, Madam," Mala replied.

"Then stand up!"

755 Mala rose to her feet, adjusting the end of her sari over her head and holding it to her chest, and, for the first time since her arrival, I felt sympathy. I remembered my first days in London, learning how to take the Tube to Russell Square, riding an 760 escalator for the first time, unable to understand that when the man cried "piper" it meant "paper," unable to decipher, for a whole year, that the conductor[102] said "Mind the gap" as the train pulled away from each station. Like me, Mala had travelled 765 far from home, not knowing where she was going, or what she would find, for no reason other than to be my wife. As strange as it seemed, I knew in my heart that one day her death would affect me, and stranger still, that mine would affect her. I wanted 770 somehow to explain this to Mrs. Croft, who was still scrutinizing[103] Mala from top to toe with what seemed to be placid[104] disdain[105]. I wondered if Mrs. Croft had ever seen a woman in a sari, with a dot painted on her forehead and bracelets stacked on 775 her wrists. I wondered what she would object to. I wondered if she could see the red dye still vivid on Mala's feet, all but obscured by the bottom edge of her sari. At last Mrs. Croft declared, with the equal measures of disbelief and delight I knew well:

780 "She is a perfect lady!"

Now it was I who laughed. I did so quietly, and Mrs. Croft did not hear me. But Mala had heard, and, for the first time, we looked at each other and smiled. I like to think of that moment in Mrs. Croft's parlor as 785 the moment when the distance between Mala and me began to lessen. Although we were not yet fully in love, I like to think of the months that followed as a honeymoon of sorts[106]. Together we explored the city and met other Bengalis, some of whom are 790 still friends today. We discovered that a man named Bill sold fresh fish on Prospect Street, and that a shop in Harvard Square called Cardullo's sold bay leaves and cloves. In the evenings we walked to the Charles River to watch sailboats drift across the 795 water, or had ice-cream cones in Harvard Yard. We bought a camera with which to document our life together, and I took pictures of her posing in front of the Prudential Building[107], so that she could send them to her parents. At night we kissed, shy at first 800 but quickly bold, and discovered pleasure and solace in each other's arms. I told her about my voyage on the S.S. Roma, and about Finsbury Park and the Y.M.C.A., and my evenings on the bench with Mrs. Croft. When I told her stories about my mother, she 805 wept. It was Mala who consoled me when, reading the Globe[108] one evening, I came across Mrs. Croft's obituary. I had not thought of her in several months – by then those six weeks of the summer were already a remote interlude in my past – but when I learned of 810 her death I was stricken, so much so that when Mala looked up from her knitting she found me staring at the wall, unable to speak. Mrs. Croft's was the first death I mourned in America, for hers was the first life I had admired; she had left this world at last, 815 ancient and alone, never to return.

As for me, I have not strayed much farther. Mala and I live in a town about twenty miles from Boston, on a tree-lined street much like Mrs. Croft's, in a house we own, with room for guests, and a garden that 820 saves us from buying tomatoes in summer. We are American citizens now, so that we can collect Social Security[109] when it is time. Though we visit Calcutta every few years, we have decided to grow old here. I work in a small college library. We have a son who 825 attends Harvard University. Mala no longer drapes the end of her sari over her head, or weeps at night for her parents, but occasionally she weeps for our son. So we drive to Cambridge to visit him, or bring him home for a weekend, so that he can eat rice with 830 us with his hands, and speak in Bengali, things we sometimes worry he will no longer do after we die.

Whenever we make that drive, I always take Massachusetts Avenue, in spite of the traffic. I barely recognize the buildings now, but each time I am 835 there I return instantly to those six weeks as if they were only the other day, and I slow down and point to Mrs. Croft's street, saying to my son, Here was my first home in America, where I lived with a woman who was a hundred and three. "Remember?"

840 Mala says, and smiles, amazed, as I am, that there was ever a time that we were strangers. My son always expresses his astonishment, not at Mrs. Croft's age but at how little I paid in rent, a fact nearly as inconceivable to him as a flag on the moon was to 845 a woman born in 1866. In my son's eyes I see the ambition that had first hurled[110] me across the world.

In a few years he will graduate[111] and pave his own way[112], alone and unprotected. But I remind myself that he has a father who is still living, a mother who 850 is happy and strong. Whenever he is discouraged, I tell him that if I can survive on three continents, then there is no obstacle he cannot conquer. While the astronauts, heroes forever, spent mere hours on the moon, I have remained in this new world for nearly thirty years. I 855 know that my achievement is quite ordinary. I am not the only man to seek his fortune far from home, and certainly I am not the first. Still, there are times I am bewildered by each mile I have travelled, each meal I have eaten, 860 each person I have known, each room in which I have slept. As ordinary as it all appears, there are times when it is beyond my imagination.

Annotations
[111] to **graduate** = to get a degree from a university or a college
[112] to **pave the way** = to create a situation in which sb will be able to do sth

WHILE READING

The narrator

4

a) While you read the short story collect information about the narrator's life in England, America and India. Make a table.

	England	America	India
housing			
job			
living conditions			

b) Explain what attitude towards his own life and his achievements the narrator shows and what role the moon landing plays for him. (p. 42, ll. 330 ff.; p. 46, ll. 843 f.)
c) Analyse the narrator's attitude towards the customs and traditions of his home country. (pp. 41 f., 44 f., 46)
d) Explain why the narrator is "mortified". (p. 43, ll. 488 ff.)

Mrs. Croft

5

a) Collect information about Mrs. Croft's life. Then find out what major/historical events Mrs. Croft must have experienced in her lifetime and show them all in a timeline.

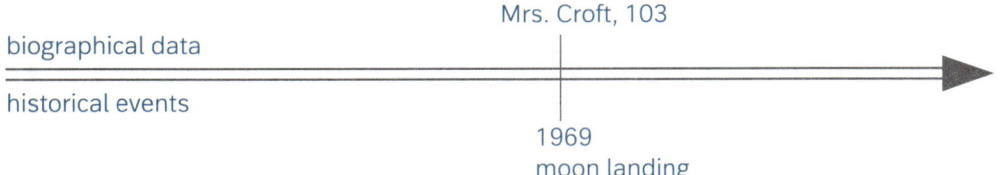

Mrs. Croft, 103

biographical data

historical events

1969
moon landing

b) Explain what the narrator means when he says: "I did not expect any display of emotion, but I was disappointed all the same. I was only a boarder, a man who paid her a bit of money and passed in and out of her home for six weeks. Compared with a century, it was no time at all." (p. 44, ll. 608 ff.)
c) Write Mrs. Croft's obituary using the information from tasks a) and b).

The narrator and his landlady

6

a) Describe the relationship between the narrator and Mrs. Croft.
b) Analyse the development of the narrator's marriage with Mala. What role does Mrs. Croft play?

Mala

7

a) Collect information about the narrator's wife and describe her.
b) Explain what the conversation between Mala and the narrator reveals about their understanding of how an old person should live. (p. 45, ll. 702 ff.)
c) Write one of her letters to her family back in India. Consider how she feels and what she expects from life in America and her husband. (p. 44/45)

POST-READING
The narration

8

a) Explain why the author has called her short story "The third and final continent".

b) Show what narrative perspective the author has chosen and explain how it contributes to the overall idea of the short story.   → **Workshop:** Analysing narrative perspective

c) Analyse the importance of the various repetitions in the short story.

9

a) Read the text below and collect arguments for and against arranged marriages that are mentioned.

Arranged marriage

In the western world people usually choose their own marriage partner but this is not the way for all cultures living in western society. Arranged marriages still happen. For example many Indian families who have
5 settled outside India still uphold this tradition. Often the most important aspect is the bond between the two families, rather than the relationship between the couple being married. Property or land with the aim of securing social status sometimes secures marriage agreements.
10 Supporters of the custom say that divorce rates are lower than among western society because parents are better able to choose a suitable partner for their children. The counter argument suggests that the pressure of society as a whole and from the two families concerned keep the
15 marriage together whether it is successful or not. Divorce therefore is not an option.

Is your family planning an arranged marriage for you?
Many Indian families who have settled outside of
20 India still uphold the tradition of arranged marriage. Being part of two cultures can be hard. Young people

born in Britain but from an Indian family can find this particularly difficult if their modern western lifestyles clash with their parents' hopes and wishes. Many young
25 Indian people living in Britain know that one day they will agree to an arranged marriage. To deny their parents this would be a sign of deep disrespect. Many families are able to discuss the issue and reach compromises that are suitable for everyone, such as the son or daughter
30 agreeing to meet prospective partners but insisting on a say in the final choice. Family and friends can be informed once the match is agreed and and soon meetings will be organised. You will be matched in terms of education, experience and caste – a social class
35 associated with the Hindu religion. Ideally your partner will be someone with whom you can share interests and who will encourage your independence. As with any relationship, friendship is the key. Good communication from the beginning will help to ensure that yours is a
40 lasting and beneficial partnership. It is also important to make a clear distinction between arranged marriages that are consensual and marriages that are arranged without the consent of the individuals involved. These are sometimes called Forced Marriages and are against
45 the law in this country.

b) CHOOSE

Group work Discuss the statement in your group.

"In England you marry the women you love. In India we love the women we marry. You fall out of love after marriage. We fall in love after marriage."

(Mark Tully quoting a Delhi village headman in his book *Ram Chander's Story*, 1995)   **OR**

Group work A radio station runs a special programme on "US immigrants living in two worlds". The narrator and his wife are interviewed by a journalist about their life in America, their traditions and values. Conduct the podcast interview.

10   → **S8:** How to improve your text

Writing a student guide: The narrator reads "The Student Guide to North America" on his flight to America to be prepared for the American way of life. (p. 39)

Group work Write a student guide to Germany in which you give new arrivals from abroad advice on what to expect and how to behave in Germany. Each student deals with one topic:
- food
- customs
- everyday life
- language (linguistic peculiarities)
- ...

The escape: A short story (2009)

Home

1

a) What does home mean to you? Note down as many associations as you can in one minute.

b) Then compare your associations with those of your partner. What do you have in common? What is different?

c) Find a definition of what home means to you and present it to the class.

Leaving Home

A lot of Pakistani people immigrated to England in the 1960s to escape from the political and economic problems that followed India's independence from Britain in 1947.

2

a) Look at the photos and describe them. The words in the box might help you.

suitcase | cotton textile mill | bus conductor | to face discrimination

b) Based on the photos, outline the life an immigrant presumably led after arriving in England in the 1960s.

Young Jamaican boy looks after his family's luggage, 1954

Immigrant from Pakistan 1950 at work in a spinning mill in West Yorkshire

Immigrant children playing in London, 1950s

A bus driver

Enoch Powell

Not all English people welcomed immigrants from the former colonies. British MP Enoch Powell gave a speech in which he strongly criticised mass immigration, especially immigration from the former colonies. His speech, held on 20 April 1968, is known as the "Rivers of Blood" speech, an allusion to Virgil's Aeneid (VI, l. 86f.), or "Birmingham speech", where the meeting of the Conservative Party took place.

Enoch Powell, 1912-1998

Pre-listening

3 → **S20:** How to listen/watch effectively

a) Read extracts from the speech.
  – Sum up each extract with one sentence.
  – Explain
    • the meaning of the Roman saying: "Those whom the gods wish to destroy, they first make mad."
    • what "sort of immigrants" Powell warns against.
    • what measures Powell suggests.
    • what sort of people Powell welcomes.
  – Analyse the language Powell uses to show his point of view.

		Annotations	Summary
5 10 15	It almost passes belief that at this moment 20 or 30 additional immigrant children are arriving from overseas in Wolverhampton alone every week – and that means 15 or 20 additional families a decade or two hence. Those whom the gods wish to destroy, they first make mad. We must be mad, literally mad, as a nation to be permitting the annual inflow of some 50,000 dependents, who are for the most part the material of the future growth of the immigrant descended population. It is like watching a nation busily engaged in heaping up its own funeral pyre. So insane are we that we actually permit unmarried persons to immigrate for the purpose of founding a family with spouses and fiancées whom they have never seen. [...]	**Wolverhampton** = E. Powell was MP for a Wolverhampton constituency **hence** = from now on **Those whom ... mad** = Roman saying attributed to Publius Syrus; **annual inflow** = the arrival [of people] every year **dependent** = a person who depends on the state for a home, food or money to **be engaged in doing sth** = to be busy doing sth; to **heap up sth** = etw. aufhäufen **funeral pyre** = Scheiterhaufen; **spouse** = a husband or a wife **fiancée** [fɪˈɑ̃ː(n)seɪ] = the woman a man is engaged to	
20 25 30	In these circumstances nothing will suffice but that the total inflow for settlement should be reduced at once to negligible proportions, and that the necessary legislative and administrative measures be taken without delay. I stress the words "for settlement." This has nothing to do with the entry of Commonwealth citizens, any more than of aliens, into this country, for the purposes of study or of improving their qualifications, like (for instance) the Commonwealth doctors who, to the advantage of their own countries, have enabled our hospital service to be expanded faster than would otherwise have been possible. They are not, and never have been, immigrants. [...]	**suffice** [səˈfaɪs] = to be enough for sth **negligible** [ˈneɡlɪdʒəbl] = insignificant **alien** = a person who is not a citizen of the country they live in **for instance** = for example	

35	As I look ahead, I am filled with foreboding. Like the Roman, I seem to see "the river Tiber foaming with much blood". [...] All I know is that to see, and not to speak, would be the great betrayal.	**foreboding** = a feeling that sth unpleasant or dangerous is going to happen **to see "The river Tiber foaming with much blood"** = In his prophesy to his son Aeneas, the mythological forefather of the Romans, Anchises, lays out the future to his son: before the Roman Empire will be finally established a lot of wars need to be fought on Italian soil. Whereas Anchises implies that a lot of suffering (wars) is needed until world power is finally reached, Powell misuses the quote to predict that mass immigration might lead to either a high crime rate or civil unrest.	

While listening

b) Watch the YouTube video. Then answer the questions below. **Webcode** WES-73652-04

1. What did E. Powell do before he gave the speech?	
2. How did people on the street react to the speech?	
3. How did Paul Uppal's parents feel about the speech?	
4. How much has become reality of what Powell predicted according to Paul Uppal?	
5. How does Bill Etheridge assess Powell's speech?	
6. What have immigrants contributed to according to Ian Austin?	

Post-listening

c) Speculate in class how Enoch Powell's speech might have influenced the immigrants' way of living at that time.

_____

_____

_____

_____

_____

_____

_____

_____

The escape

by Quaisra Shaharaz

In the packed prayer hall of Darul Uloom mosque[1] in Longsight[2], the Imam concluded the Eid[3] prayers with a passionate plea for world peace and terrorist activities in Pakistan to stop.
5 Seventy-three-year-old Samir, perched[4] on a plastic chair because of his bad leg, kept his hands raised, quietly mouthing his own personal prayer. "Please Allah Pak[5], bless her soul! And let me escape!" Rows of seated men had arisen from their prayer mats
10 and reached out to energetically hug others and offer the festive greeting, "*Eid Mubarak*[6]!" Samir took his time. There was no-one in particular he was seeking to greet or hug at this mosque. Most of the men around him were strangers and of the
15 younger generation, several sported[7] beards – a marked shift[8] between the two generations. His face remained clean shaven. Nowadays he prayed at the Cheadle mosque, joining the congregation of Arabs and other nationalities for the Taraveeh
20 prayers[9] during *Ramadhan*[10]. Nostalgia tugging[11] at him, on a whim[12], Samir had asked his son to drop him off in Longsight to offer his Eid prayers at his old community mosque. Painfully rising to his feet Samir began the hugging ritual, smiling
25 cordially[13]. Unlike the others leaving the hall, he loitered[14]; in no hurry to get out. At the door he dutifully dropped a five pound note in the collection fund box. Whilst looking for his shoes he bumped into his old friend, Manzoor – they
30 greeted, smiled broadly and warmly hugged. Outside, in the chilly autumn day, his friend, who lived a street away from the mosque, invited him to his house for the Eid hospitality of Vermicelles, *sewayian*[15] and *chana chaat*[16]. The smile slid off[17]
35 Samir's face; he was reluctant to visit his friend's house – afraid of the old memories, shying away from the normality, the marital bliss[18] of his friend's home. In particular he was loath to[19] witness the little intimacies between husband and wife. The
40 look. The laugh. The teasing banter. Instead he waved goodbye to his friend and stood waiting for his son. "I'm being picked up," he informed a young man kindly offering him a lift home, before sauntering[20] on his bad leg down the street. "I have
45 all the time in the world!" He wryly[21] muttered[22] to himself, savouring[23] the walk down streets he had cycled and scooted along[24] for over three decades. A lot had changed, the area now thriving with[25] different migrant communities; the Pakistanis and
50 the Bengalis living side by side with the Irish and the Somalis. Many Asian stores and shops had sprung up. The Bengali Sari and travel agent shops jostled[26] happily alongside the Pakistani ones and

the Chinese takeaway. Mosques catering to the
55 needs of Muslim community had sprung up, from the small Duncan Road mosque in a semi-detached corner house to the purpose-built Darul Uloom centre on Stamford Road. The Bengali mosque for the Bengali community on one corner of Buller
60 Road was only a few feet away from the Pakistani and Arab Makki Masjid on the other corner. Not surprisingly on Fridays, for the *Juma* prayers, the street was gridlocked[27], with an occasional police car monitoring the situation. He noted that the
65 Roman Catholic Church and its primary school on Montgomery Road had disappeared, joining the quaint[28] little National Westminster Bank branch that had been in the middle of Beresford Road with a communal vegetable plot at the back. That had
70 been pulled down twenty odd years ago. St Agnes church was still there, however, at the junction of West Point and Hamilton Road and it still enjoyed healthy Sunday morning congregations.
Samir stopped outside a shop on Beresford Road
75 that had been called Joy Town twenty one years earlier. It had been his children's favourite toyshop, especially on Eid day, when they ran to it with their *Eidhi* money, eager to buy cars, skipping ropes and doll's china crockery sets. In its place
80 there now stood a grocery superstore with stalls of vegetables and fruits hogging[29] the pavement area. On Fridays and Saturdays families, like Samir's, who had moved out of the area still returned to do their shopping, visiting their favourite halal meat[30]
85 and grocery stores; carting boxes of fresh mangoes, bags of basmati rice and chapatti flour back to their cars. The hustle and bustle of these shops always bought out a smile in him. His son, Maqbool, a well-to-do sportswear manager, dutifully returned to
90 pick him up half an hour later. By that time, Samir was shivering with the autumn chill in his *shalwar kameez*[31] and *shervani*[32] and gladly got into the warm car. He had wanted to go to Sanam Sweet Centre to buy a few boxes of Asian sweets to distribute
95 to friends but he hesitated, suddenly overcome by trepidation[33]. "Do you want to go somewhere else, Father?" his son asked, as if reading his mind. Samir shook his head; loath to inconvenience[34] his son further, feeling guilty for already taking up enough
100 of his time. "No. Let's go home," he murmured, eyes closed. He had a large five bedroom detached house[35] but with his wife and family gone all the joy of living had fled. He kept himself in the master bedroom, hating to enter the other rooms in the
105 house, especially the one with his wife's clothes. Only when the grandchildren visited did he unlock

some of the doors. He spent his time in his new favourite spot, the chair at the dining table next to the window and radiator. He sat there leafing
110 through *The Times*, the *Daily Jang* and *The Nation*, watching the traffic go past on the busy road. His son dropped him off at the door with the words, "Will collect you in an hour's time." Samir nodded and watched him drive away before letting himself
115 into the house. Another hour to kill. He shrugged. It was better here on his own, with the TV and the newspaper keeping him company, than politely waiting around at someone else's house for dinner. He felt hungry; but the dining table in front of him
120 lay dismally[36] bare[37]. On Eid days it was normally stacked with bowls of delicious food: boiled eggs, *sewayain*, *chana chats* and a hot tray of *Shami kebabs*. And these were just the breakfast starters, heralding[38] a busy festive day of eating. Last year
125 his entire family had been there. If he closed his eyes he could see his children helping themselves to the food, with him happily beginning the *Eidhi* money giving ritual. Five pounds notes for the little ones, ten for the older teenagers, and crispy twenty
130 pound notes for his daughters and daughters-in-law. In the steamy warm kitchen with the noisy fan purring[39] away at the window, the smell from a pot of pilau rice[40] and trays of roast chicken and kebabs in the oven would set everyone's mouths
135 watering. Dinner was a prompt affair[41]; always at one o'clock, served by the women of his household, moving elegantly around the room; their rustling *ghrarars* and *lenghas*[42] sweeping the floor and the long *dupattas*[43] hanging at their sides. The boys
140 would be in their *shalwar kameez* and *sherwanis*. By two, the whole family would be sitting around the table chatting, relaxed and happy, some still spooning away trifle[44] and *gajar halwa*[45].

The thought of all that food set Samir's stomach
145 groaning[46]. He could not wait that long. In the kitchen he tipped some cornflakes into a bowl; it was not *chana chat* or *sewayian* but would keep him going. He twice checked his pocket for the money, mentally counting the number of notes he
150 should have. This was the bit of Eid day that he particularly enjoyed, glimpsing[47] the excited faces of his grandchildren taking the *Eidhi* from his hand. In the old days a one pound coin delighted his children. After dinner they excitedly ran off to Joy
155 Town to buy gifts of their choice. When Maqbool arrived, Samir was well into his second hard-boiled egg, smiling sheepishly[48] at his son, who mentally chided[49] himself for leaving his father to eat alone at home. Samir's whole family was gathered in
160 his eldest daughter's house and he was the last to arrive. In the living room, his second daughter-in-law, Mehnaz, stood up out of respect to vacate[50]

her seat for him. "Stay seated my dear," he offered, perching himself instead on a chair near the door.
165 The women were busy in the kitchen, sorting out the crockery and the sauces. All had happily adopted the British custom of bringing a dish since their mother had died. His eldest daughter was carrying a tray of roast meat through the hallway
170 to the dining room. Catching her eye, Samir smiled politely.

His youngest grandson, Rahel, jumped into his lap, startling him[51] and bringing a smile to his face. Samir lifted him up to offer a tight hug. Then
175 holding out a five-pound note he beckoned[52] to his older grandson, a six-year-old, who was stood scowling[53] a few feet away. The child shyly sidled to his grandfather's side, plucked the note from his hand and ran off. "Would you like something to eat
180 before dinner?" His daughter came to enquire, the blender[54] with the mint sauce in her hand. Samir shook his head. Nodding, she disappeared into the kitchen leaving Samir to smile, watch, listen and respond where appropriate. That is until the seat
185 became too uncomfortable for his bad leg, forcing him to take the one vacated by his eldest grandson near the window. He bleakly stared out through the net curtains, watching passers-by, who probably had no idea that in this Muslim home they were
190 celebrating *Eid ul Fitr*. Eyes filling up, Samir kept his face averted towards the window; there was nothing to celebrate on his first Eid without his beloved wife. Sorrow suffocated[55]; desperation tearing at him. If he could only turn the clock back.
195 How he longed to have this Eid dinner at his own home and with her hosting it; instead of sitting awkwardly here as an interloper[56]. An hour later, he dutifully spooned food into his mouth; making no comments apart from the polite "everything is very
200 nice" to the women of his family. He did not pick on the chillis or criticise the curry sauces as he had always done with his wife's cooking. His sons, of a different generation and attitude, were happily munching away[57] at their roast meats, whilst he
205 stealthily[58] hid a raw bit of chicken leg under a napkin on his plate. By the time the *gajar halwa* and tea were served, Samir's mind was made up. He waited; heartbeat accelerating. When there was a lull[59] in the lively conversation he ventured[60] to
210 inform his family, licking his dry lips carefully. "I want to tell you something …" They turned to stare. His daughter, Roxanna, hushed her little girl sitting on her lap with the words, "Abu-ji is speaking, shush!" "I want to go back home – to Pakistan."
215 Samir announced, "To visit my family … stay there for a few months. It'll be good for me … it's the right time … with your mother gone … I need a change of scene and I have plenty of time now!" he

Annotations
[36] **dismally** = miserably
[37] **bare** = empty
[38] **to herald** = to signal
[39] **purring** = to make a low continuous sound
[40] **pilau rice** = a hot spicy dish of rice, vegetables and meat or fish
[41] **prompt affair** = here: punctual event
[42] **gharars and lenghas** = traditional outfit worn by Muslim women
[43] **dupatta** = veil
[44] **trifle** = *Süßspeise*
[45] **gajar halwa** = a sweet Indian or Pakistani dish made of carrots
[46] **to groan** = to moan
[47] **to glimpse** = to catch sight of
[48] **sheepishly** = feeling embarrassed
[49] **to chide** = to criticize sb
[50] **to vacate** = to leave a seat so that sb else can use it
[51] **to startle sb** = surprise sb by shocking them slightly
[52] **to beckon** = to signal sb with your hand
[53] **to scowl** = to look at sb angrily
[54] **blender** = *Mixgerät*
[55] **to suffocate** = here: took Samir's breath
[56] **interloper** = a person who is in a place where they do not belong
[57] **to munch away** = to eat noisily
[58] **stealthily** = quietly and secretly
[59] **lull** = a quiet period in the conversation
[60] **to venture** = to say sth carefully because it might upset people

Annotations

61 **abyss** = a deep wide space that seems to have no bottom

62 **prudently** = sensibly and carefully done when making decisions

63 **covertly** = secretly

64 **to intercept** = to stop sth that is going from one place to another

65 **to gush with sth** = to express sth so emotionally and often that it does not seem sincere

66 **to batter** = here: *durch den Kopf gehen*

67 **astutely** = very cleverly done

68 **tell-tale sign** = *Anzeichen*

69 **Anarkali Bazaar** = one of the oldest bazaars in South Asia, famous for its food stalls and embroidery

70 **Mall Road** = a major road in Lahore with many historical buildings dating back to the British Raj

71 **outskirts** = the parts of a town furthest away from the city centre

72 **tangle wood bushes** = *dichtes Gebüsch*

73 **adamantly** = *unnachgiebig, hartnäckig*

74 **ancestral home** = family home

75 **hatham prayer** = special Muslim prayer for the soul of a deceased person

76 **to traipse back** = here: to travel reluctantly

77 **to be insistent on doing sth** = *auf etwas bestehen*

78 **to crush** = to make sb sad and depressed

79 **quarry** = *Steinbruch*

80 **kiln** = oven for baking bricks

81 **to take one's fill** = *genug von etwas haben*

82 **to etch a picture** = here: to make a picture so that you can see it very clearly in your mind

explained, smiling. "It would be lovely to visit some
220 places of my old life. Also good to spend some time
with my sister and brother and their families."
Complete silence greeted his words. "A few months!
Are you sure about this, father? We'll miss you!"
His eldest daughter had found her tongue. "You'll
225 all be fine without me. Anyway you can phone me
every day … you've all got busy lives and families,
so it won't be that bad to have me disappear for a
few months. I'll hardly be missed … This trip will be
good for me … I need to go …" He stopped himself
230 from saying, "I need to escape," voice petering
away, giving them a glimpse of the abyss[61] inside
him. Discomforted and not knowing what was the
right thing to say, they prudently[62] ended the
discussion. Their father had always made his own
235 decisions – very rarely paying any attention to
other people's opinions. Their mother had battled
for years to influence him, and died having never
quite succeeded. "Where will you stay? Lahore?"
His youngest daughter, Rosie, boldly asked. "Yes! In
240 our family home of course, with my brother –
where else?" he replied sharply, annoyed at his
daughter's question and semi-hostile tone. Rosie
did not bother answering. Instead she covertly[63]
exchanged a pointed look with her sister, which
245 their father neatly intercepted[64]. Samir's face
tightened. "You need to understand Rosie that just
as this is your family – I have the same back home
… They care about me and I want me to spend time
with them." His tone harsher than he intended. The
250 word "back home" had just slipped out of him
again. It was a curious use. For a few seconds he
was lost in thought. Why did he say that? Was
Manchester not his "home"? After all he had spent
over forty years of his life in this city? The other
255 place was just his birthplace, his country of origin
and reminder of his youth. Surely these facts should
make Manchester his home? He shrugged these
thoughts aside, willing his mood to lighten; he now
had a goal: to occupy his mind with tasks, and he
260 loved tasks above all. The big task facing him now
was what presents to take for his family and his
two college friends in Lahore. He promised himself
that this time the three friends would treat
themselves to a walk through the tall, elegant
265 Victorian corridors of the Government College of
Lahore where he had studied. Three days later,
Samir had flown out from Manchester airport,
taking his "other family" in Lahore by surprise.
They gushed with[65] greetings, hurriedly assembling
270 their shocked faces even though inside they were
all amok. "What was he doing here, all of sudden?
How long was he going to stay? Which other
relatives was he visiting and for how long?" These
questions battered[66] simultaneously in all their
275 heads. Samir's face fell, quickly averting his eyes,
astutely[67] picking up the tell-tale signs[68] from their
faces and body language. Two days later, after
visiting the local Anarkali Bazaar[69], taking a
leisurely walk down the famous Mall Road[70], and
280 spending time with his sister's family in her villa in
the Defence area, he headed for the village where
his parents were buried. There he was amicably
greeted by his host, a second cousin, who hosted all
relatives visiting his parents' graves. After some
285 refreshments, Samir headed for the cemetery on
the outskirts[71] of the village. Well maintained, tall
tangle wood bushes[72] grew around it, keeping the
wolves out. Eyes blurred, Samir gazed down at his
parents' graves. His father had adamantly[73] made it
290 clear that he did not want to be buried in the
overcrowded city cemeteries. "I want fresh air,
shade of a tree and plenty of space around – and
make sure you leave space for your mother. Don't
just throw us in any hole!" As obedient sons, they
295 honoured their father's wish and duly visited the
village of their father's ancestral home[74] and bought
a plot of land. Thereafter his sister and brother
made annual journeys to the village, to offer a feast
and *hatham* prayers[75] for their parents souls. Samir
300 perched himself on the low wall circling the plot
with his parents' graves. The tranquillity around
him had him thinking about his own burial place.
Of course it would be Manchester's Southern
Cemetery. He could not imagine his children
305 traipsing back[76] to Pakistan to visit his grave in a
land that was foreign to them. He now understood
why his father was insistent on[77] keeping a place
for his wife. Remembering his Sabiya, he bowed his
head. The loneliness crushed[78]. He ached to have
310 her back. Two years ago they were both here,
sitting at the same spot. He watched a herd of milk
buffaloes being shepherded back to the village.
Feeling a tiny bite, he looked down at a line of ants
running down the brickwork. Laden with small
315 scraps of leaves, the ants were zigzagging around
his feet. He moved his foot away and glanced over
his shoulders at the brick making quarry[79]. and
kiln[80], spotting a group of peasant men pushing
trolleys stacked with bricks. Two women were
320 carrying small baskets loaded with baked bricks on
their heads. Feeling sorry for them and the hard
work that the women had to do in order to feed
their families, Samir was reminded of the second
mission that had brought him to this village – his
325 wife's charitable work. He had to visit the widow.
He turned to look back at the graves, taking his
fill[81], etching the picture[82] in his head. Was this
going to be his final farewell? Standing over his
mother's grave, soft sobs shook his large body. It
330 was a strange world. To be buried continents away

from one's own parents. Why was he crying? For his parents who had died decades ago or for his beloved Sabiya? "Life is a cycle!" He mused. He was in his seventies but still demurred from[83] being
335 called "old." God only knew where the rest of his ancestors were buried – most probably in India, before the partition. People were born and slid through the cycle of life and then disappeared, with some leaving no trace.
340 "Samir, stop thinking like this – it's morbid[84]!" He raised his hands to say a final fervent prayer over his parents' mounds[85]. His host family had gone to a lot of trouble in their offer of hospitality. The women had begun scurrying around[86] the
345 courtyard the moment he arrived. A hen had been snatched from the chicken coop[87] in the far end of the courtyard and quickly dispatched[88] to the cooking pot. The rice for the lamb biryani[89] had been soaked[90]. The pink custard powder was
350 energetically whisked[91] in a bowl. Not content with the home cooking for their special "velati"[92] guest from "London," the host had enlisted the help of the village cook. A fabulous chef, it was widely said that people always licked their fingers after eating
355 his tasty chicken shorba[93]. The women had happily obliged. Mina, the daughter-in-law was seven months pregnant, expecting her first child, and hated squatting[94] on the floor whilst cooking on a pedestal stove[95]. As well as that, she had to maintain
360 her modesty; it was quite challenging, keeping herself well draped in front of the male guest. Her pregnancy was causing her a lot of embarrassment. She was "huge," everyone kept telling her. With a last lingering glance at his parents' graves, Samir
365 followed the path to the village central square with its old majestic looking Minar tree where his driver was waiting. His brother had kindly loaned both their driver and the car for his use whilst he used his motorcycle. Ahead of him he saw a young man
370 pulling a suitcase and dragging something else. Bemused, Samir stared wide-eyed, temporarily transported to another time and place. He still kept his bedroll[96] canvas[97] bag in his garage in England, never having had the heart to throw it away. It was
375 a memento[98], a part of his life. Too many memories were caught up with it. The frayed brown leather suitcase, stuffed with all his important documents, including his British nationality, was still kept under his bed. There are special moments etched
380 on peoples' minds; for Samir it was the one of him dragging a big bedroll and a large suitcase from Victoria coach station through the streets of London: deeply mortifying[99] to this day. Why his arm and fingers did not fall off still amazed him.
385 Tired, hungry and harassed[100], he and his friend stumbled thankfully into a Victorian house with a Bed and Breakfast sign; two Pakistani migrants from up north wanting to try their fortunes down south in London. It was actually his friend's
390 breezy[101] confidence, smart use of English, cocky[102] winsome smile and flirtatious winks that had successfully got them a room late at night, winning over the elegant old lady with her purple rinse[103]. The purple hair colour of many older women in
395 those early days fascinated him. Why did they like such a strange colour? Samir shuddered, tasting the raw fear he had felt then as they desperately sought[104] a place for the night. "What if we don't find a room, where will we go and what will we
400 do?" He had silently agonised[105], panicking at the darkness falling around them. It was his friend's optimism and high spirits that had saved him from making a fool of himself. There was a moment he was ready to squat on the pavement and shed bitter
405 tears, bewailing[106] his stupidity in leaving a warm room and a cosy bed in Blackburn[107]. Sharing a double bed with his friend capped[108] the humiliation of that day further. His friend had joked at their sleeping quarters and went soundly
410 to sleep. Samir had sidled to the edge of the bed, shivering in the thin, coarse blanket making his face itch, afraid to pull it over himself and of waking his friend. In the end, he had got up and pulled out his own five inch[109] thick Pakistani quilt
415 from the bed roll. His love affair with the English capital was both doomed and short-lived – it was not for him – too anonymous. He knew no-one and felt shy and uncomfortable wherever he went – stumbling and stammering over the carefully
420 chosen English words and phrases he had mastered to buy bus tickets, packets of Benson and Hedges[110] or order something to eat. Intimidated by the huge buildings and mad evening traffic, he smiled when he saw brown faces, mainly of Sikhs[111] and
425 Indians. He did not come across many Pakistanis. After taking some souvenir photographs with an expensive camera he had brought from Pakistan, posing in his smart suit in front of one of the Trafalgar Square lions and outside the queen's
430 Buckingham Palace gates with the guards, Samir had happily fled. He wished his friend well with his love of London. Years later, when he came across him he laughed aloud. His friend had become a true Londoner, down to the cockney accent[112]. For
435 Samir, London was simply too much, making his life a misery and stripping away his self-esteem. Lacking his friend's confidence, easy going manner and ability to make new friends, Samir missed the cosy comfort of a small town like Blackburn. After
440 two weeks he had escaped, happily dragging his bed roll and his brown leather suitcase with him. He went to another friend, who welcomed him

Annotations

[83] **to demur from doing sth =** *sich sträuben, etwas zu tun*
[84] **morbid** = horrible
[85] **mound** = a large pile of earth
[86] **to scurry around** = to run with quick short steps
[87] **coop** = a cage for chickens
[88] **to be dispatched** = to be killed
[89] **biryani** = a South Asian dish made from rice with meat, fish or vegetables
[90] **to soak** = to put sth in water
[91] **to whisk** = to mix
[92] **velati** = English
[93] **shorba** = a Pakistani curry
[94] **to squat** = to sit on your heels
[95] **pedestal stove** = *Standofen*
[96] **bedroll** = a thick piece of material that can be rolled up and used for sleeping
[97] **canvas** = *Segeltuch*
[98] **memento** = *Souvenir*
[99] **mortifying** = humiliating
[100] **harassed** = troubled
[101] **breezy** = cheerful
[102] **cocky** = too confident in yourself in a way that annoys other people
[103] **rinse** = here: hair colour
[104] **sought** (to seek) = to look for
[105] **to agonise** = to worry for a long time
[106] **to bewail** = to express great sadness about sth
[107] **Blackburn** = a town in the northwest of England, known for its textile industry
[108] **to cap** = to top
[109] **inch** = *2,54 cm*
[110] **Benson and Hedges** = cigarette brand
[111] **Sikh** = one of the world's major religions on the Indian subcontinent
[112] **cockney accent** = accent spoken in the East End of London

Annotations
113 **to hog** = to use
114 **hub** = the most important part of a place
115 **to stay put** = to stay somewhere
116 **Keema lobia** = black eyed peas with ground meat
117 **painstakingly** = thoroughly
118 **Darwen** = a small town near Blackburn
119 **to scoff** = to make fun of
120 **to scurry** = to hurry
121 **demeaning** = humiliating
122 **Abba** = Indian address for "father"
123 **grotty** = unpleasant
124 **to term** = to use a particular name for sth
125 **pay packet** = an envelope containing your wages
126 **crown** = an old British coin worth 25 pence
127 **frugal** = using only as much money or food as is neccessary
128 **to feel duty bound** = to feel that you have to do sth because it is your duty
129 **menial** = not skilled
130 **Enoch Powell** = see pre-reading activity
131 **Idi Amin** = (1925 –2003) He was a Ugandan military officer who was the President of Uganda from 1971 to 1979. He is also known as the "Butcher of Uganda", one of the cruellest despots in African history.
132 **to be dismal** = to be sad and miserably
133 **khoti** = apartment
134 **terraced house** = *Reihenhaus*
135 **detached house** = *frei stehendes Haus*
136 **to sever** = to cut sth off
137 **to gush** = here: to express suddenly and strongly
138 **Bismillah!** = Muslim exclamation "In the name of God"
139 **bethak** = sitting room
140 **crocheted** = *gehäkelt*
141 **beaded** = decorated with pearls

with open arms, letting him join two other tenants in his two-bedroom terraced house. Apart from the kitchen all three rooms were used.

Even the front room had a single bed hogging[113] the area near the window and the open coal fire. That was the owner's room. The kitchen, with its big coal fire warming the room, was the hub[114] of their communal life, where they took turns cooking meals, smoking and chatting, lounging on hard wooden chairs around a small kitchen wooden table. Three of them had young families in Pakistan. Samir stayed put[115], intent on earning money to support his family back home by doing overtime and long shifts. *Keema lobia*[116] became his favourite dish. He became a good cook, very proud of his culinary skills. His first chapatti painstakingly[117] rolled with a long empty sterilised milk bottle was a good try. His three fellow home mates praised him heartily, rewarding him with the teasing words, "Your cooking is better than our wives' back home!" His landlord found him a job in the cotton textile mill, after he was pressured to turn down a job in a special nursing home in Darwen[118]. "You will be working with mentally ill people, are you mad? You'll become mad yourself!" His fellow tenants had cruelly scoffed[119], frightening him into scurrying[120] into the reception room and leaving a hurried note to say no to the job before he had even started.

In the Darwen textile mill, the huge dark machines intimidated him; but he quickly mastered the skill of working with and around them. It was dull and demeaning[121] work. With his good education behind him, he often heard himself dryly echoing "If Abba[122] sees me doing this, he'll have a fit!" His father had forked out a lot of money for the fees for a top college and expected him to do a "clean" respectable office job, not working in some "grotty"[123] mill as his youngest son once termed[124] it years later. The pay packet[125], however, had kept him smiling. The thrill of counting the bank notes through the little top corner, and feeling the angles of the six and three penny bits through the brown paper, and the occasional half-crowns[126] – small sums but mighty big pleasures they provided then. In those frugal[127] days, they felt duty bound[128] to keep each other in check; the talk then was always about "going back home". They were not here to waste money on luxuries or on themselves. Exceptions were only made for gifts for their children. Samir had not only his wife and one daughter to support, but also his father to appease, who had never forgiven him for leaving home and doing menial[129] jobs in mills in "Velat." The only thing that could win over his father would be the building of a new house, to illustrate his economic well-being and to support his younger brother's family. Three years later, having had enough of textile mills and with his family having joined him, he escaped to the big city of Manchester and started his own manufacturing business. It was a time when knitwear manufacturing was a booming industry in the Northwest and Ardwick had become a manufacturing area. Many Pakistani migrants entered this trade. Samir too purchased an old factory for his knitwear business. It was also a time of social and communal uncertainty. Enoch Powell[130] had done his bit; frightening the host community with his racist speech citing "the rivers of blood" and leaving the migrants in fear of being thrown out of the country.

When the Ugandan refugees started to arrive in the early nineteen seventies, after their expulsion by Idi Amin[131], his friends were very dismal[132] about their own fate in the UK, fearing that they too would be thrown out. For some, the mission or the next urgent goal was to build houses back home to return to if things really got bad in England.

Unlike his friends, Samir had faith in the British justice system and its fairness. He never for one moment believed that something similar could happen in Britain. Unlike some of his friends his savings went not into a *khoti*[133] or a villa in Lahore, but in gradually working his way up to a better standard of living for his family, progressing from a terraced house[134] to a detached house[135] in a good area. He concentrated on his children, their education and careers.

And the decades simply slipped away, melting away his youth and gradually severing[136] the links with his homeland. His retirement was forced on him; he did not welcome it. Samir smiled at the young man with the suitcase and turned into the village lane to pay a special call. In the widow's home there was panic as the youngest of the three girls whispered to the others that a man from *Velat* was standing outside their door. When their mother spotted the foreign visitor she nearly fainted, but recovered soon enough. Bursting into sobs she stared at the husband of their benefactor, muttering behind the fold of her long shawl, and gushing[137] the welcome greeting: "*Bismillah! Bismillah!*"[138] She owed a lot to this man's wife. Her three teenage daughters had rushed ahead into their *bethak*[139], to make the room presentable. The crocheted[140]-edged table cloth was quickly straightened and dusted, the mirrored beaded[141] cushions on the leather settee hurriedly plumped up and the pair of knitting needles and women's magazine snatched and shoved under the table. Red-faced and brimming with pleasure, the widow led their very "special" guest into their humble living room, with the walls lined with their best china propped on wooden sills. It was a quaint[142] sight for him, reminding him of the old days when his father would take him to tour some village for a "taste of the other life and warm hospitality of the rural people." Samir did not know what to say; both touched and embarrassed by their humility and behaviour.

"Please don't bring any refreshments, Cola or Miranda bottles or such – I have a bad stomach," he glibly[143] lied, saving them the bother and cost of purchasing the bottles from the local village shop. "I just wanted to see how you all are – and how your daughters are doing – I know my wife always visited you – as she did with the other homes she sponsored …" He stopped, eyes filling up, his Sabiya in front of him. The widow again burst into loud sobs. "We are so sorry about your wife's death, she was such a wonderful soul and so good to us! We miss her so much, and she phoned us every month – calling us to the butcher's house to chat with us … always checking that we had enough money for my daughter's expenses and enough grain!" "Yes – she was a good soul! And we all miss her!" Samir lowered his head to hide his tear swollen eyes. The widow touched by his grief, stared in wonder, mouth open, showing her row of uneven top teeth and two missing lower molars[144]. She quickly closed her mouth in embarrassment when he looked up. Samir looked at the girls shyly staring at him, and could not stop the outburst. His sobbing caused the girls' eyes to fill up. They were used to crying from an early age. Their mother had become a crying machine and often they ended up aping[145] her. Today they found the sight of this older man from England, crying over his wife, very poignant[146]. He was thinking, "My wife has made a difference to these wretched girls' lives!" Sobering[147], he wiped his cheeks clean with a tissue proffered[148] shyly by the eldest daughter. As if reading his mind, the widow reminded him, "Your wife got my oldest daughter married, she helped us with the dowry[149] … here is that daughter … she's visiting us at the moment." Then her gaze switched to her other daughters. "Who will now finance these girls' weddings?" Poverty had forced her into straight talking, to unabashedly[150] appeal to the good nature of well off people like him. Samir had thought ahead. His pension, even if he did not touch the rest of his savings, would be enough to support this household – an ideal way of honouring his wife and her dying wish. Her last words to all her children and to him had been, "Do not forget all the families that I've been supporting in my life – earn their heartfelt prayers by helping them. Don't forget to keep my register[151] of widows safe. Don't let anyone die of poverty or ill health! Display your

humanity and offer generously your *zakat*[152]."

His eyes on the four heads modestly draped with dupattas[153], Samir meditated on one possible way for these girls to get out of this poverty trap and offered. "Sister please educate your daughters … send them to any colleges that you like. I'll pay all their fees and other costs." The girls' eyes widened and lit up in wonder. The *Velati* man would do that for them! Go to the town college. The girls' minds were swimming. Their poignant looks and smiling faces cut him to his soul. His own children, including his two daughters, had been educated to the highest degree level and had access to great opportunities. Did these poor girls not have a right to the same? He was suddenly struck and dismayed[154] by the inequality of life. How some had everything whilst others simply worried about the next meal!

The youngest girl moved away from the doorway as Samir's village host, who had followed him to the widow's house, entered the room. Catching Samir's eyes, the host signalled to him that dinner was waiting. Samir hastened[155] to add before rising from the settee. "Don't worry about anything, Sister. I'll take care of your financial situation and make sure that you get your remittances[156] on time, including for the wheat[157]. You have our phone numbers, Please phone for any extra financial help needed. I'll take care of the furniture for your daughter's dowries just as my Sabiya did for your eldest daughter … I have to go now and may Allah Pak look after you all!" He felt in his jacket pocket and shyly placed a three-thousand rupee[158] note in the youngest girl's hand, lowering his gaze in embarrassment in the face of their gratitude. He politely followed his host out of the small courtyard before turning to look back at the girls shyly peeping out of their door. "This is their humble world!" he mused, "And I live in a large house all by myself." The thought terrified him. He politely smiled to the other villagers that he passed in the lane. There was no-one he recognised and no welcoming look of sudden recognition. And why should there be? He chided[159] himself. He was over seventy years old – and so far he had not seen a soul of that age group in the village. That night he returned to Lahore to his brother's family. Fear of hospitality had made him flee the village, afraid that if he stayed the night his hosts would incur the cost[160] of breakfast and afternoon dinner the following day. He was familiar with their generosity and excellent hospitality. Already they had spent a lot on his behalf[161]. Until the entire dining table was covered with plates of cakes, pastries, boiled eggs and parathas[162] they would not be happy. In his brother's home there was no element of guilt

Annotations
[142] **quaint** = strangely old-fashioned
[143] **glibly** = *vorschnell*
[144] **molar** = *Backenzahn*
[145] **to ape** = to imitate
[146] **poignant** = moving
[147] **to sober** = here: to pull oneself together
[148] **to proffer** = to offer
[149] **dowry** = money that a wife or her family must pay to her husband when they get married
[150] **unabashedly** = *hemmungslos*
[151] **register** = list of names
[152] **zakat** = a contribution or alms given by Muslims to people in need
[153] **dupatta** = a long piece of material worn around the head and neck by women in India
[154] **to be dismayed** = to be sad and worried
[155] **to hasten** = to hurry
[156] **remittance** = payment
[157] **wheat** = *Weizen*
[158] **rupee** = 3.000 rupees ~ 23 Euro
[159] **to chide** = to criticise
[160] **to incur costs** = to have to pay costs
[161] **on his behalf** = *seinetwegen*
[162] **paratha** = a type of South Asian bread made without yeast

Annotations

163 **kulcha** = a type of flat bread

164 **lassi** = yoghurt-based drink

165 **Mughal** = The Mughal Empire (1526-1857) was one of the largest empires in South Asia

166 **Data Gunj Darbar** = a well-known Islamic shrine in Lahore, the most sacred place in Lahore

167 **to pay homage to** = to show respect for sb by doing or saying sth

168 **daig** = cauldron of rice

169 **pilau rice** = a rice dish made of rice, spices, vegetables, meat and dried fruits

170 **to lounge** = to lie around

171 **to rustle up** = to make sth quickly without planning it

172 **to slip in** = to mention sth casually

173 **to accord sb** = to give sb

174 **laundry** = dirty washing

175 **chasten** = *schelten*

176 **chitchat** = conversation about unimportant things

177 **to ruminate** = to think deeply about sth

178 **musing** = a period of thinking carefully about sth

– no waiting upon ceremony. They knew what he liked, and so for breakfast his brother would fetch some warm *kulchas*[163] from the local bakery and the tea would be supplied by his sister-in-law. Drinking a cool glass of *lassi*[164], Samir instructed the driver to take him back to Lahore, the city of his birth, the old Mughal[165] capital of India. He wanted to call on the way at the famous Data Gunj Darbar[166], a favourite shrine of his mother. In his childhood days she eagerly took him to pay homage to[167] the saint buried in the tomb, visited by thousands every day from all over the world. Outside in the Darbar courtyard, the *daig*[168] men were fast at work, serving food from their big pots to the needy and to those keen to take the *tabark*, food offerings, home for their family. When the man distributing bags of pilau rice[169] touched him on his arm, Samir was lost for words and nodded, taking the bag of rice with him inside the building. In the large hall amidst the crowd of male and female devotees, peering through the open windows at the tomb draped with a green and gold embroidered sheet, Samir offered special prayers for his wife's soul, tears gushing out of his eyes. Then a prayer for himself. He repeated the word "escape" again. As he sheepishly entered his ancestral home, the mouths of his brother's family fell open. They had not expected him back that night. In fact, they thought he was touring another city and here he was, large as life. Both parties energetically avoided eye contact. His brother's family quickly recovered. They had been lounging[170] around on sofas. It was eight o'clock and the popular drama was about to be telecast. The wife and daughter began panicking. Was their guest fed or did they have to scurry to the kitchen to rustle up[171] a meal for him? Reading their minds perfectly, Samir wryly held the bag of rice in front of him. "I got my meal from the Darbar, I'm sure it's delicious. Don't worry about me, just carry on watching." With those words he left them to their drama, before excusing himself. "I'll go up to my room and have a shower."

"Yes, please do!" His sister-in-law quickly offered with a toothy grin and orangey *sak*-stained lips, sitting down to enjoy the drama with her daughter. He came down precisely after nine pm, having given them time to finish watching their serial. In that time, he had showered, eaten the rice from the bag with his fingers and started to gather his belongings. They were expecting him and hurried to greet him, his niece standing up. "Are you sure you will not want a meal?" His brother asked, not happy at Samir not eating.

"The *darbar daig* rice was wonderful. Good to eat *tabark* sometimes. It reminds us gently what life is all about – our stomachs. Getting food into our bellies is what we work for, don't we?" His brother cynically nodded, a director of a firm and now retired. He still had two daughters whose marriage and dowries he had to arrange. It was not just the matter of food for him. He envied his brother for having all his children wed and settled. No worries, saving that of having lost a wife. Aloud he instructed. "Bano, go and make tea for your uncle!" A smile fixed on her face, the eldest daughter left for the kitchen, whilst everyone else watched the news. "Tomorrow morning I will check flight times." Samir slipped in[172] the information whilst sipping his tea. Heads turned, TV forgotten, surprise written on their faces. "What brother! Already? You've only been here for just a week!" The sister-in-law rushed to speak. "I think a week is enough – time to go home!" He replied, a gentle smile peeping across his features as he remembered his daughter Rosie. Dumbfounded, they stared back at him, but did not challenge or question him further as to why. "He must be missing his children," his brother echoed in his head. Once more all heads turned to the programme. As the eldest daughter got up to take the cups back to the kitchen, she smiled at her uncle asking if he wanted some more tea. He smiled back; it was the first full smile she had accorded him[173] since he had arrived. Then she surprised him and her parents further with her kind offer. "Uncle, please give me your laundry[174]. I will see to it before you leave." "You stupid girl! Your uncle is not going yet!" Her father chided, red-faced. "He was only saying it. We are not going to let him go yet." His wife quickly echoed the same. "No brother, you are not going yet." "Don't worry, Bano! I'll get my clothes washed at home." Samir said, surprising himself.

Twice he had used the term "home." Was not this his home, the place where he was born? Chastened[175] and the smile deleted, the eldest daughter took the tray of crockery back to the kitchen. In the lounge her uncle from England had already decided. He stayed up for some more polite talk and then went up to his air conditioned room. Picking up the remaining items littering the dressing table he threw them into his suitcase. His love affair with the city of his birth was over. On the plane he found himself sitting next to a man called Ibrahim, of his age group and size; both overweight and uncomfortable with the economy seats and the narrow leg space in front of them. After exchanging polite chitchat[176] they soon got into serious talking and were onto the question as to why they were visiting their country of birth and youth. "The homeland?" Samir ruminated[177] over the term and shared his musing[178] aloud with his fellow passenger, who had similar home circumstances, including being a widower.

780 "The one that you have just visited, or the one that you are returning to? The place where you have spent most of your adult life? Which homeland are you trying to escape from?" Samir elaborated, making the man's sun beaten forehead groove[179]

785 into three deep pleats[180]. "Escape?" Ibrahim was disconcerted[181] by the term. Samir nonchalantly[182] went onto explain. "I am escaping back to the UK – and to a new home." "New home?" "Want to join me?"

790 The man looked blankly at him, wondering whether this was a joke. Samir chuckling[183] went on to explain.

He returned home not having met the two college friends or walked down the tall nineteenth

795 century corridors of the Government College of Lahore. Strangely, it really did not matter to him. Two weeks after his arrival, Samir had moved to an elderly people's home, leaving his five bed roomed detached house to his four children but

800 keeping his savings and shares[184] to see to[185] the needs of the family he had promised to support. He made a new will, instructing his Solicitor[186] that when he died one of his children would carry on supporting the widow and her daughters. He got

805 his eldest daughter to phone the widow, to reassure her that he had not forgotten his promise. Social and cultural parameters[187] had to be maintained[188]. He was a man and would keep his distance from the widow and not compromise her honour[189], her

810 *izzat*[190]. They needed his financial help which his wife used to provide; now he would take over her role. When he spoke to his brother on arrival in Manchester, he was asked when he would return to his homeland. After a pause Samir asked,

815 "Homeland? Which homeland? I'm home ..." An awkward silence followed. Then he had added laughing, "You can visit me next time." A week later, the friend he had met on the plane arrived with his daughter, carrying his suitcase. Ibrahim took

820 the room three doors away from Samir's, his gales of laughter[191] echoing down the corridor. Pure joy raced through Samir lifting his spirit as he rushed to show his friend around the home, enthusiastically explaining and reassuring, introducing him to the other house guests he had befriended, Penny and Derrick. "It's the right decision my friend. You won't regret it. Wave goodbye to loneliness and heartache ... We are the new English *babus*[192], living in old people's homes, the ones we used to ridicule

835 once upon a time! Meals on wheels[193] for us now – we have worked so hard – time to enjoy ourselves now, hey!"

WHILE READING

Samir's life in Manchester

4

a) Describe how Samir spends his retirement at home. (p. 52 f.)

b) Find out about the newspapers Samir reads and explain why they are listed here.

c) Analyse the descriptions of the Eid festival held at Samir's house the previous year and the current one at his eldest daughter's house and compare them. (p. 53)

5

a) While you read the short story collect information about Samir's family and draw a family tree.

b) Examine to what extent Samir's children have assimilated into English society.

c) Analyse the father-children relationship.

Eid

A family celebrating Eid

6

a) Collect all the information about the customs of Eid as mentioned in the short story. (Look up customs you don't understand on the internet.)
b) Explain the meaning of Eid to a partner.
c) Analyse the importance of Eid to Samir and his family.

Samir's visit to Lahore

7

a) Compare how his families in England and Pakistan react to his visit.
b) Analyse Samir's relationship to his parents.
c) Describe Sabiya's project and explain its importance to Samir.
d) State why Samir wants to go back to England.

POST-READING

The meaning of home

8

Analyse Samir's understanding of home in the course of the story by analysing the extracts.

Language support

I think Samir is/can be described as … This can be seen in line … where … Evidence can be found in line …

quote	analysis
"I want to go back home – to Pakistan." Samir announced, "To visit my family … stay there for a few months. It'll be good for me … it's the right time … with your mother gone … I need a change of scene and I have plenty of time now!" he explained, smiling. "It would be lovely to visit some places of my old life. Also good to spend some time with my sister and brother and their families." (p. 53)	
"Tomorrow morning I will check flight times." Samir slipped in the information whilst sipping his tea. Heads turned, TV forgotten, surprise written on their faces. "What brother! Already? You've only been here for just a week!" The sister-in-law rushed to speak. "I think a week is enough – time to go home!" He replied, a gentle smile peeping across his features as he remembered his daughter Rosie. (p. 58)	

"Don't worry, Bano! I'll get my clothes washed at home." Samir said, surprising himself. Twice he had used the term "home." Was not this his home, the place where he was born? Chastened and the smile deleted, the eldest daughter took the tray of crockery back to the kitchen. In the lounge her uncle from England had already decided. He stayed up for some more polite talk and then went up to his air conditioned room. Picking up the remaining items littering the dressing table he threw them into his suitcase. His love affair with the city of his birth was over. (p. 58)	
On the plane he found himself sitting next to a man called Ibrahim, of his age group and size; both overweight and uncomfortable with the economy seats and the narrow leg space in front of them. After exchanging polite chitchat they soon got into serious talking and were onto the question as to why they were visiting their country of birth and youth. "The homeland?" Samir ruminated over the term and shared his musing aloud with his fellow passenger, who had similar home circumstances, including being a widower. "The one that you have just visited, or the one that you are returning to? The place where you have spent most of your adult life? Which homeland are you trying to escape from?" Samir elaborated, making the man's sun beaten forehead groove into three deep pleats. "Escape?" Ibrahim was disconcerted by the term. Samir nonchalantly went onto explain. "I am escaping back to the UK – and to a new home." "New home?" "Want to join me?" […] He returned home not having met the two college friends or walked down the tall nineteenth century corridors of the Government College of Lahore. Strangely, it really did not matter to him. (p. 58 f.)	
When he spoke to his brother on arrival in Manchester, he was asked when he would return to his homeland. After a pause Samir asked, "Homeland? Which homeland? I'm home…." An awkward silence followed. Then he had added laughing, "You can visit me next time." A week later, the friend he had met on the plane arrived with his daughter, carrying his suitcase. Ibrahim took the room three doors away from Samir's, his gales of laughter echoing down the corridor. Pure joy raced through Samir lifting his spirit as he rushed to show his friend around the home, enthusiastically explaining and reassuring, introducing him to the other house guests he had befriended, Penny and Derrick. (p. 59)	

The atmosphere

9

a) Contrast the atmosphere at the beginning with that at the end.

Read the passages from p. 52, l. 1–53, l. 124. → **Workshop:** Analysing atmosphere

Beginning and end of passages	
In the packed prayer hall … And these were just the breakfast starters, heralding a busy festive day of eating. (pp. 52–53) The thought of all that food … "I want to tell you something." (p. 53)	On the plane he found himself sitting … – "We have worked so hard – time to enjoy ourselves now, hey!" (pp. 58–59)

- Then note down which atmosphere they convey.
- Describe what language is used to create the different atmospheres.

Language support

The atmosphere can be described as … This is suggested (on page …) in line … where it says … This is implied when … This can be concluded from …	calm | convivial | cosy | happy | homely | relaxed emotional | heavy | hostile | oppressive | stifling tense | lively | gloomy
to create an atmosphere of … a(n) … atmosphere pervades the passage	The use of (words, adjectives, emotive language, word fields) such as … suggests … By employing words such as … the author implies …

b) Explain what has changed for Samir in the course of the story.

The values
10

a) Explain the following quotation: "Social and cultural parameters had to be maintained." (p. 59)
b) Analyse the values Samir and his wife have pursued throughout their lives.
c) Describe how Enoch Powell's speech has influenced Samir and his friends' lives. Compare your results with your ideas from the pre-reading part.

A conversation
11

a) List Samir's activities during his visit to Pakistan and analyse how he feels about them.
b) Imagine Samir and his daughter Rosie talk about his visit to Pakistan. Write their conversation with a partner and act it out. Decide when it takes place. (Before the trip? In a phone call during his trip? Or in the retirement home?)

Samir's activities	How does Samir feel about them?
his stays with his brother (p. 54., p. 58) …	they "gushed" => Samir feels that they are rather shocked about his surprise visit. …

Samir's life in England
12

a) Collect all the information about Samir's life and his development, starting with his arrival in England up to his retirement.
b) Compare the social positions Samir has had in Pakistan and in England.
c) You are a journalist running a feature on immigrants and their life in England.

    CHOOSE

- Interview Samir. Consider personal aspects of his life as an immigrant as well as historical and social ones.
- Write a feature on Samir's life as an immigrant. For your newspaper article come up with a catchy headline.
  - Before writing: Write notes about the "who", "what", "when", "where", "why" and "how".
  - While writing: Begin your article with an introduction to your topic.
  - Use your notes. Divide your article into paragraphs. Choose adjectives and adverbs that create a lively impression of your topic. Use quotes that Samir might have said.
  - After writing: Check the spelling and grammar. Are your paragraphs easy to understand? Does your headline catch the reader's attention? Does your last paragraph round up the article?
    → **S8:** How to improve your text

The title
13

a) Explain the title of the story.
b) Comment: Do you think the title fits? What other titles can you suggest?

Loose change: A short story (2005)

The National Portrait Gallery

The National Portrait Gallery is a famous art gallery in London. It opened in 1856 and hosts about 195,000 portraits of the most historically important and famous British citizens.

a) **Pair work** Choose the picture you like best: First describe it and then explain why you like it.

Germaine Greer
by Paula Rego
pastel on paper laid on aluminium, 1995

Darcey Bussell
by Allen Jones
oil on canvas, 1994

Alan Bennett
by Tom Wood
oil on canvas laid on panel, 1993

b) **Group work** Do some research about the people portrayed in the pictures above.
Find out when they live(d) and what they are famous for.
c) Present your findings to your group members.
d) Discuss what these people have in common and speculate on why the author Andrea Levy mentions them in her short story. Why might Laylor, a young woman you will meet in the story, prefer a photo of football legend David Beckham over them?

The beginning

a) Read the beginning of the short story:

"I am not in the habit of making friends of strangers. I'm a Londoner. Not even little grey-haired old ladies passing comment on the weather can shame a response from me. I'm a Londoner - aloof sweats from my pores. But I was in a bit of a predicament; my period was two days early and I was caught unprepared."

Characterize the narrator on the basis of this extract. Choose an adjective from the box below and explain your choice. Think of two more adjectives. → **Workshop:** Analysing characters

unfriendly | stiff | indifferent | distant | unsympathetic | cold | reserved | unsociable | self-confident | lonely

b) Speculate about why the author introduces her narrator/character in such a way.

Loose change
by Andrea Levy

Annotations

1 **aloof** = distant
2 **predicament** = unpleasant situation
3 **National Portrait Gallery** = a famous art gallery in London
4 **bleak** = cold and unpleasant
5 **numb** = when your fingers are numb you can hardly feel anything in them
6 **iron filings** (pl.) = *Eisenspäne*
7 **to tumble** = to fall
8 **jaw line** = *Kieferpartie*
9 **whack** = blow
10 **to bulge** = to stick out
11 **coppers** = brown coins that are not valuable; loose change
12 **puddle** = a small amount of water
13 **gaze** = a long and steady look
14 **as keen as a cat with string** = as excited as a cat that is playing with string
15 **cubicle** = *Kabine*
16 **to leave dangling** = to leave sb in an uncertain state
17 **to flutter** = to move lightly and quickly
18 **doodle** = a line, a circle that you draw when you are bored
19 **mournful** = very sad
20 **glum** = sad, quite unhappy
21 **to curl your lip** = to move your lip upwards and sideways to show that you think sb/sth is stupid
22 **to jangle** = *klirren, klimpern*
23 **to tip back** = to put back

I am not in the habit of making friends of strangers, I'm a Londoner. Not even little grey-haired old ladies passing comment on the weather can shame a response from me. I'm a Londoner – aloof[1] sweats
5 from my pores. But I was in a bit of a predicament[2]; my period was two days early and I was caught unprepared.
I'd just gone into the National Portrait Gallery[3] to get out of the cold. It had begun to feel, as I'd
10 walked through the bleak[4] streets, like acid was being thrown at my exposed skin. My fingers were numb[5], searching in my purse for change for the tampon machine; I barely felt the pull of the zip. But I didn't have any coins. I was forced to ask in a
15 loud voice in this small lavatory, "Has anyone got three twenty-pence-pieces?"
Everyone seemed to leave the place at once – all of them Londoners I was sure of it. Only she was left – fixing her hair in the mirror.
20 "Do you have change?"
She turned round slowly as I held out a ten-pound note. She had the most spectacular eyebrows. I could see the lines of black hair, like magnetised iron filings[6], tumbling[7] across her eyes and almost
25 joining above her nose. I must have been staring to recall them so clearly. She had wide black eyes and a round face with such a solid jaw line[8] that she looked to have taken a gentle whack[9] from Tom and Jerry's cartoon frying pan. She dug into the pocket
30 of her jacket and pulled out a bulging[10] handful of money. It was coppers[11] mostly. Some of it tinkled on to the floor. But she had change; too much – I didn't want a bag full of the stuff myself.
"Have you a five-pound note as well?" I asked.
35 She dropped the coins on to the basin area, spreading them out into the soapy puddles[12] of water that were lying there. Then she said: "You look?" She had an accent but I couldn't tell then where it was from; I thought maybe Spain.
40 "Is this all you've got?" I asked. She nodded. "Well, look, let me just take this now …"
I picked three damp coins out of the pile, "Then I'll get some change in the shop and pay them back to you." Her gaze[13] was as keen as a cat with string[14].
45 "Do you understand? Only I don't want all those coins."

"Yes," she said softly.
I was grateful. I took the money. But when I emerged from the cubicle[15] the girl and her handful
50 of change were gone.
I found her again staring at the portrait of Darcy Bussell. Her head was inclining from one side to the other as if the painting were a dress she might soon try on for size. I approached her about the
55 money but she just said, "This is good picture."
Was it my explanation left dangling[16] or the fact that she liked the dreadful painting that caused my mouth to gape?
"Really, you like it?" I said.
60 "She doesn't look real. It looks like …" Her eyelids fluttered[17] sleepily as she searched to the right word, "a dream".
That particular picture always reminded me of the doodles[18] girls drew in their rough books at school.
65 "You don't like?" she asked. I shrugged. "You show me one you like," she said.
As I mentioned before, I'm not in the habit of making friends of strangers, but there was something about this girl. Her eyes were encircled
70 with dark shadows so that even when she smiled – introducing herself cheerfully as Laylor – they remained as mournful[19] as a glum[20] kid at a party. I took this fraternisation as defeat but I had to introduce her to a better portrait.
75 Alan Bennett with his mysterious little brown bag didn't impress her at all. She preferred the photograph of Beckham. Germaine Geer made her top lip curl[21] and as for A. S. Byatt, she laughed out loud. "This is child make this?"
80 We were almost making a scene. Laylor couldn't keep her voice down and people were beginning to watch us I wanted to be released from my obligation.
"Look, let me buy us both a cup of tea," I said. "Then
85 I can give you back your money."
She brought out her handful of change again as we sat down at a table – eagerly passing it across to me to take some for the tea.
"No, I'll get this," I said.
90 Her money jangled[22] like a win on a slot machine as she tipped it back[23] into her pocket. When I got back with the tea, I pushed over the twenty-pences

I owed her. She began playing with them on the tabletop – pushing one around the other two in a
95 figure of eight. Suddenly she leant towards me as if there were a conspiracy[24] between us and said, "I like art." With that announcement[25] a light briefly came into those dull[26] eyes to reveal that she was no more than eighteen. A student perhaps.
100 "Where are you from?" I asked.
"Uzbekistan[27]," she said.
Was that the Balkans? I wasn't sure. "Where is that?"
She licked her finger, then with great concentration
105 drew an outline on the tabletop. "This is Uzbekistan," she said. She licked her finger again to carefully plop a wet dot on the map saying, "And I come from here – Tashkent[23]."
"And where is all this?" I said, indicating the area
110 around the little map with its slowly evaporating borders and town. She screwed up her face[29] as if to say nowhere.
"Are you on holiday?" I asked.
She nodded.
115 "How long are you here for?"
Leaning her elbows on the table she took a sip of her tea. "Ehh, it's bitter!" she shouted.
"Put some sugar in it," I said, pushing the sugar sachets[30] toward her.
120 She was reluctant, "Is for free?" she asked.
"Yes, take one."
The sugar spilled as she clumsily opened the packet. I laughed it off but she, with the focus of a prayer, put her cup up to the edge of the table and swept
125 the sugar into it with the side of her hand. The rest of the detritus[31] that was on the tabletop fell into the tea as well. Some crumbs, a tiny scrap of paper and a curly black hair floated on the surface of her drink. I felt sick as she put the cup back to
130 her mouth.
"Pour that one away, I'll get you another one."
Just as I said that a young boy arrived at our table and stood, legs astride, before her. He pushed down the hood on his padded[32] coat. His head was curious
135 – flat as a cardboard cut-out – with hair stuck to his sweaty forehead in black curlicues[33]. And his face was as doggedly[34] determined as two fists raised. They began talking in whatever language it was they spoke. Laylor's tone pleading – the
140 boy's aggrieved[35]. Laylor took the money from her pocket and held it up to him. She slapped his hand away when he tried to wrest[36] all the coins from her palm. Then, as abruptly as he had appeared, he left. Laylor called something after him. Everyone turned
145 to stare at her, except the boy, who just carried on.
"Who was that?"
With the teacup resting on her lip, she said, "My brother. He want to know where we sleep tonight."
"Oh yes, where's that?" I was rummaging[37] through

150 the contents of my bag for a tissue, so it was casually[38] asked.
"It's a square we have slept before."
"Which hotel is it?" I thought of the Russell Hotel[39], that was on a square with uniformed attendants[40],
155 bed turning-down-facilities, old-world-style.
She was picking the curly black hair off her tongue when she said, "No hotel, just the square."
It was then that I began to notice things I had not seen before: dirt under each of her chipped
160 fingernails, the collar of her blouse crumpled and unironed, a tiny cut on her cheek, a fringe that looked to have been cut with blunt nail-clippers. I found a tissue and used it to wipe my sweating palms.
165 "How do you mean just in the square?"
"We sleep out in the square," she said. It was so simple she spread her hand to suggest the lie of her bed.
"Outside?" She nodded. "Tonight?"
170 "Yes." The memory of the bitter cold still tingled[41] at my fingertips as I said, "Why?" It took her no more than two breaths to tell me the story. She and her brother had had to leave their country, Uzbekistan, when their parents, who were journalists, were
175 arrested. It was arranged very quickly – friends of their parents acquired[42] passports for them and put them on to a plane. They had been in England for three days but they knew no one here. This country was just a safe place. Now all the money they had
180 could be lifted in the palm of a hand to a stranger in a toilet. So they were sleeping rough – in the shelter of the square, covered in blankets, on top of some cardboard.
At the next table a woman was complaining loudly
185 that there was too much froth in her coffee. Her companion was relating the miserable tale of her daughter's attempt to get into publishing. What did they think about the strange girl sitting opposite me?
190 Nothing. Only I knew what a menacing place Laylor's world had become. She'd lost a tooth. I noticed the ugly gap when she smiled at me saying, "I love London."
She had sought me out – sifted me from the crowd.
195 This young woman was desperate for help. She'd even cunningly[43] made me obliged to her[44].
"I have picture of Tower Bridge at home on wall although I have not seen yet."
But why me? I had my son to think of. Why pick
200 on a single mother with a young son? We haven't got the time. Those two women at the next table, with their matching handbags and shoes, they did nothing but lunch. Why hadn't she approached them instead?
205 "From little girl, I always want to see it …" she went on.

Annotations

[24] **conspiracy** = a secret plan by a group of people to do sth harmful
[25] **announcement** = a spoken statement that informs people about sth
[26] **dull** = not bright or shiny
[27] **Uzbekistan** = a country in Central Asia, country of the former Soviet Union
[28] **Tashkent** = the capital of Uzbekistan
[29] to **screw up your face** = to contract your muscles of your face
[30] **sachet** = a closed plastic or paper package
[31] **detritus** = natural waste material
[32] **padded** = *gefüttert*
[33] **curlicue** = here: black curls
[34] **doggedly** = in a way that shows that you do not give up easily
[35] **aggrieved** = feeling that you have been treated unfairly
[36] to **wrest** = to take sth from sb they do not want to give suddenly or violently
[37] to **rummage** = to move things around when you search for sth, e.g. in your bag
[38] **casually** = not showing much care or attention
[39] **Russell Hotel** = a historic five-star hotel
[40] **attendant** = servant
[41] to **tingle** = to feel as if a lot of small sharp needles are pushing into e.g. your finger
[42] to **acquire** = to obtain sth by buying it or by being given it
[43] **cunningly** = in a clever way especially by tricking sb
[44] to **feel obliged to sb** = *sich jmd. gegenüber verpflichtet fühlen*

Annotations

45 **Croydon** = town in south London. In the 1990s, the church formed the Croydon Refugee Day Centre (CRDC).

46 to **tramp through** = walking with noisy steps

47 **mildewed** = *verschimmelt*

48 **bone china** = *feines Porzellan*

49 to **smear** = to make sth dirty/greasy

50 to **leer** = to smile at sb with an evil interest in them

51 to **slump** = to sit or fall down heavily

52 to **yank** = to pull sb hard, quickly and suddenly

53 **tender-hearted** = having a kind and gentle nature

54 **benevolence** = kindness, generosity, helpfulness

55 **Good Samaritan** = reference to the parable told by Luke in the Christian gospel about helping others who are in danger

56 to **scrounge sth from sb** = *bei jdm etwas schnorren*

57 to **quiver** = to shake slightly

58 **poached** = cooked in a small amount of liquid; *gedünstet*

59 to **frown** = to make a serious expression by bringing your eyebrows together

60 **Velcro** = *Klettverschlüsse*

I didn't know anything about people in her situation. Didn't they have to go somewhere? Croydon[45], was it? Couldn't she have gone to the police? Or some charity?

My life was hard enough without this stranger tramping through[46] it. She smelt of mildewed[47] washing. Imagine her dragging that awful stink into my kitchen. Cupping her filthy hands round my bone china[48]. Smearing[49] my white linen. Her big face with its pantomime eyebrows leering[50] over my son. Slumping[51] on to my sofa and kicking off her muddy boots as she yanked[52] me down into my particular hell. How would I ever get rid of her?

"You know where is Tower Bridge?"

Perhaps there was something tender-hearted[53] in my face. When my grandma first came to England from the Caribbean she lived through days as lonely and cold as an open grave. The story she told all her grandchildren was about the stranger who woke her while she was sleeping in a doorway and offered her a warm bed for the night. It was this act of benevolence[54] that kept my grandmother alive. She was convinced of it. Her Good Samaritan[55].

"Is something wrong?" the girl asked.

Now my grandmother talks with passion about scrounging[56] refugees; those asylum seekers who can't even speak the language, storming the country and making it difficult for her and everyone else.

"Last week …" she began, her voice quivering[57], "I was in home." This was embarrassing. I couldn't turn the other way, the girl was staring straight at me. "This day, Friday," she went on, "I cooked fish for my mother and brother." The whites of her eyes were becoming soft and pink; she was going to cry. "This day Friday I am here in London," she said, "And I worry I will not see my mother again."

Only a savage would turn away when it was merely kindness that was needed. I resolved to help her. I had three warm bedrooms, one of them empty. I would make her dinner. Fried chicken or maybe poached[58] fish in wine. I would run her a bath filled with bubbles. Wrap her in thick towels heated on a rail. I would then hunt out some warm clothes and after I had put my son to bed I would make her cocoa. We would sit and talk. I would let her tell me all that she had been through. Wipe her tears and assure her that she was now safe. I would phone a colleague from school and ask him for advice.

Then in the morning I would take Laylor to wherever she needed to go. And before we said goodbye I would press my phone number into her hand.

All Laylor's grandchildren would know my name.

Her nose was running with snot. She pulled down that sleeve of her jacket to drag it across her face and said, "I must find my brother."

I didn't have any more tissues. "I'll get you something to wipe your nose," I said.

I got up from the table. She watched me, frowning[59]; the tiny hairs of her eyebrows locking together like Velcro[60]. I walked to the counter where the serviettes were lying in a neat pile. I picked up four. Then standing straight I walked on. Not back to Laylor but up the stairs to the exit. I pushed through the revolving doors and threw myself out in the cold.

WHILE READING

3 Read the short story. Then answer the following questions.

a) Why does the narrator go into the National Portrait Gallery?

b) Why do all the customers leave the lavatory according to the narrator?

c) How does the narrator feel when the young woman sweeps the sugar into her cup of tea and why?

d) Where does the narrator first think that the sister and brother are spending the night? Explain what makes her think so.

e) What reason does the young woman give for why she and her brother had to leave the country?

f) How does the narrator imagine she might be viewed by the girl's grandchildren and why?

The grandmother's story

4

a) Read the excerpt and describe what the narrator's grandmother experienced.

When my grandma first came to England from the Caribbean she lived through days as lonely and cold as an open grave. The story she told all her grandchildren was about the stranger who woke her while she was sleeping in a doorway and offered her a warm bed for the night. It was this act of benevolence that kept my grandmother alive. She was convinced of it. Her Good Samaritan. (p. 66)

b) Look up the parable of the "Good Samaritan" in the *Gospel of Luke*. Share the details of the story in class.

c) **Pair work** Find out about immigrants from the Caribbean on the following website:
Webcode WES-73652-05

Exchange your findings with a partner. Talk about
- who belongs to the Windrush generation.
- why they are called the Windrush generation.
- what made them come to England.
- what problems they faced in England.

d) Explain what the grandmother thinks of refugees and asylum seekers.

"SS Empire Windrush" arrives in England with workers from the Caribbean

The structure

5

A short story is often divided into five parts. Identify the different parts of a short story in "Loose change" and explain their function.

> resolution or denouement | rising action | exposition | climax | falling action

	Parts of a story	Lines	Function
1			
2			
3			
4			
5			

POST-READING

The characters

6

a) Collect all the information about the three characters in the grid below.

	The narrator	The girl and the boy
home country		
living conditions		
parents		

b) Compare the young woman's story with that of the narrator. What is similar in their family's story? Where do they differ?

7

Analyse how the narrator's attitude towards the woman develops in the course of the story by examining the language used in the passages below. In the end you are going to use your findings to write your analysis.

→ **S9:** How to structure a text   → **S8:** How to improve your text

a) **Group work** Each group member looks at some extracts A–C quoted below and analyses the narrator's attitude towards the young woman. Afterwards share your findings.
   – Read your extracts. Choose some suitable expressions from the box below to describe the narrator's feelings.
   – Then prove your ideas in the text.

Language support

sympathetic towards sb	angry at sb	reproachful	feel pity for sb	helpful	annoyed with sb
be condescending to sb	horrified by	embarrassed	embarrassing	disgusted with sb
solicitous	motherly	to care for sb	reckless

I think the narrator is/can be described as …
This can be seen in line … where … | Evidence can be found in line …

unlike | whereas | compared to | in comparison with | in contrast to

A

quote	analysis
She turned round slowly as I held out a ten-pound note. She had the most spectacular eyebrows. I could see the lines of black hair, like magnetised iron filings, tumbling across her eyes and almost joining above her nose. I must have been staring to recall them so clearly. She had wide black eyes and a round face with such a solid jawline that she looked to have taken a gentle whack from Tom and Jerry's cartoon frying pan. She dug into the pocket of her jacket and pulled out a bulging handful of money. It was coppers mostly. Some of it tinkled on to the floor. But she had change: too much – I didn't want a bag full of the stuff myself. (p. 64)	
As I mentioned before, I'm not in the habit of making friends of strangers, but there was something about this girl. Her eyes were encircled with dark shadows so that even when she smiled – introducing herself cheerfully as Laylor – they remained as mournful as a glum kid at a party. I took this fraternisation as defeat but I had to introduce her to a better portrait. (p. 64)	
The sugar spilled as she clumsily opened the packet. I laughed it off but she, with the focus of a prayer, put her cup up to the edge of the table and swept the sugar into it with the side of her hand. The rest of the detritus that was on the tabletop fell into the tea as well. Some crumbs, a tiny scrap of paper and a curly black hair floated on the surface of her drink. I felt sick as she put the cup back to her mouth. "Pour that one away, I'll get you another one." (p. 65)	

B

quote	analysis
"Which hotel is it?" I thought of the Russell Hotel, that was on a square with uniformed attendants, bed turning-down facilities, old-world style. She was picking the curly black hair off her tongue when she said, "No hotel, just the square." It was then I began to notice things I had not seen before: dirt under each of her chipped fingernails, the collar of her blouse crumpled and unironed, a tiny cut on her cheek, a fringe that looked to have been cut with blunt nail-clippers. I found a tissue and used it to wipe my sweating palms. "How do you mean just in the square?" "We sleep out in the square," she said. It was so simple she spread her hands to suggest the lie of her bed. (p. 65)	
She had sought me out – sifted me from the crowd. This young woman was desperate for help. She'd even cunningly made me obliged to her. (p. 65)	
But why me? I had my son to think of. Why pick on a single mother with a young son? We haven't got the time. Those two women at the next table, with their matching handbags and shoes, they did nothing but lunch. Why hadn't she approached them instead? [...] I didn't know anything about people in her situation. Didn't they have to go somewhere? Croydon, was it? Couldn't she have gone to the police? Or some charity? My life was hard enough without this stranger tramping through it. She smelt of mildewed washing. Imagine her dragging that awful stink into my kitchen. Cupping her filthy hands round my bone china. Smearing my white linen. Her big face with its pantomime eyebrows leering over my son. Slumping on to my sofa and kicking off her muddy boots as she yanked me down into her particular hell. How would I ever get rid of her? (pp. 65 f)	

C

quote	analysis
"Last week …" she began, her voice quivering, "I was in home." This was embarrassing. I couldn't turn the other way, the girl was staring straight at me. "This day, Friday," she went on, "I cooked fish for my mother and brother." The whites of her eyes were becoming soft and pink; she was going to cry. "This day Friday I am here in London," she said. "And I worry I will not see my mother again." Only a savage would turn away when it was merely kindness that was needed. I resolved to help her. I had three warm bedrooms, one of them empty. I would make her dinner. Fried chicken or maybe poached fish in wine. I would run her a bath filled with bubbles. Wrap her in thick towels heated on a rail. I would then hunt out some warm clothes and after I had put my son to bed I would make her cocoa. We would sit and talk. I would let her tell me all that she had been through. Wipe her tears and assure her that she was now safe. (p. 66)	

b) Now that you have shared your findings, write your analysis. There is language support in the box below.

Introduction	The short story "Loose change" written by Andrea Levy in 2005 is about …
Body	At the beginning the narrator's attitude can be described as … This can be seen in line … when she/the author … By using emotive language … Furthermore, … In addition, … However, … Although … Whereas at the beginning …
Conclusion	In conclusion, one can say that the narrator's attitude towards the young woman (Laylor) …

8 → **S2:** Checklist: Creative writing

Back home the narrator reflects upon her meeting with the young woman, assessing her decision to leave the woman back in the café. Write her inner monologue. Consider the situation the young woman is in as well as the narrator's family background.

9 Group work

There are many references in the short story. Analyse their function and explain how they contribute to the message of the story. The table below will help you.

Info

Intertextuality

When writers borrow ideas or quotations from other texts, they often do so in order to give their work different layers of meaning. This can happen openly (e. g. by using allusions such as the reference to the portraits) or covertly (e. g. by means of modifying the title). This way, a short story can be read and interpreted from different perspectives.

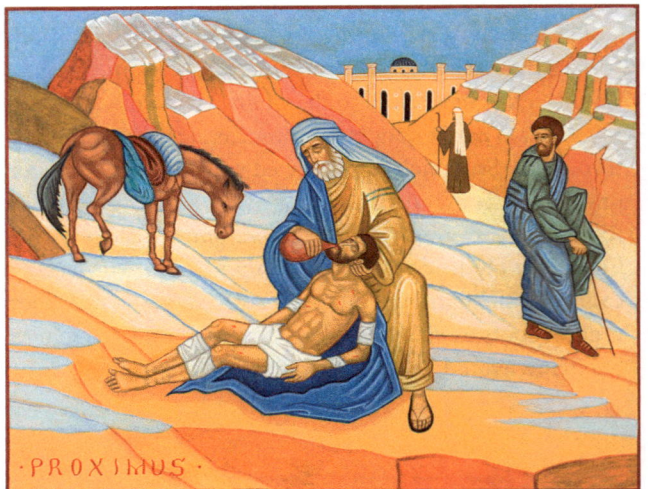

The Good Samaritan

- The portraits in the National Portrait Gallery
- The two women sitting at the table
- The Good Samaritan
- The narrator's grandmother

Portraits	Who do the portraits show? Where do the people portrayed come from? What is the purpose of the portraits in the National Portrait Gallery in general? How do portraits contribute to the collective memory of a nation?
The two women	What do the two women talk about? Why does the author include their talking in her short story? How do they contribute to the young woman's misery?
The Good Samaritan	What is the story about? What is the message of the parable? How can it be related to the short story? Where do you find parallels between the parable and the short story?
The narrator's grandmother	Where does she come from? How did she start her life in England? What is her attitude towards refugees and asylum seekers? Why? How does the grandmother's story influence the outcome of the story?

The rain missed my face and fell straight to my shoes: A short story (2005)

PRE-READING

1

Read the title of the story. Speculate what it could be about and what topics or themes it might be dealing with.

The rain missed my face and fell straight to my shoes
by Saeed Taji Farouky

I'm looking for change in my pocket, flicking¹ through the coins all one- and two pence pieces. I'm trying to make up at least two pounds with all the spare coins because Faris said he can't let me into the theatre any more for free. Otherwise his boss is going to get suspicious and Faris would maybe loose his job so I have to give him some change. I turn over everything I have, which is only eighty-seven pence anyway. He starts counting the coins and I can see it isn't going to be enough. People are behind me in the queue, getting impatient. Faris looks behind him in the booth, then to me, "It's not even a pound, Samir." I have to lean down to speak quietly through the gap in the glass, "I know. I don't have enough. It's OK for now, isn't it?" "Just go inside, there are other people waiting. I don't have time to argue now." Faris is scowling², trying not to look me in the eyes. But there's a familiarity we have that means he understands me by now, he knows that I always do this. Faris piles the coins next to the ticket machine and yells for the next person in line. I used to feel guilty when I tried to get into Faris's theatre³ for free, but not any more, not since I started letting him on to the tube⁴ for nothing – not even one or two pounds. I walk with my ticket into the foyer and look for someone else I recognise. I know it'll all either be Youssef or Hamza. Youssef is Egyptian so he gets along well with me. Hamza is I think from Somalia – we don't have much in common; not much. He can't speak English very well, or Arabic, so we can only have very simple conversations about his family. I can tell that Hamza doesn't like me coming in to the cinema, and he's worried about his job as well, but he doesn't know that everyone lets their friends in for free – even the boss and the English people working here. That's why I prefer it when Youssef is at the gate because he knows that there's nothing to worry about. This time it's Youssef and he smiles and puts out his arms for a hug when he sees me.

His hairy arms tickle my neck when he leans in to hug me. He has a thin beard that pricks my face. The other customers in the queue turn to look at us, two men hugging, but Youssef doesn't care. He's a very private man, but somehow he never seems afraid if people notice him. He's never afraid to let people stare at him and wonder who he is. I'm the opposite: I always get anxious when people look at me; I try to make out their reactions to everything I do. I worry they're looking for something that isn't really in me, but if they look hard enough, they might see it anyway. I'm smiling when Youssef hugs me because I haven't seen him in more than two weeks. I'm usually at the cinema every day, sometimes a few times a day. "Samir! You son of a bitch!" "Don't swear so loud, people will hear you." Youssef is hugging me with one hand and tearing tickets with the other. People have to step around us to get through the gate. "Where were you, I haven't seen you in weeks. Hamza says you haven't been, either." "No, I was visiting my Mum, she was sick in hospital. I had to go stay with her in hospital." "Your Mum was sick? I didn't know. I'm sorry." He takes back his arm from around me and steps to the side to tear someone else's ticket. I can see everyone else is getting impatient because he's ignoring them and not telling anyone their screen number⁵. Some people are trying to listen to our conversation. Youssef smiles to his customers as he's talking to me: "I hope she's OK now, huh?" "No, she died." Some more people get their tickets torn and walk past us through the gates. We both stand beside each other for a few moments in silence. Customers pass by. Youssef doesn't look at me but puts one hand on my shoulder and is trying to say something sensible while he's tearing the tickets. I finally have to move out of the way to let the other customers through, and his hand falls from my shoulder. I give him a few seconds to think of something to say, but I don't want to make him uncomfortable, with the

Annotations
¹ to **flick** = to move sth up and down with sudden quick movements
² to **scowl** = to look at sth/sb angrily
³ **theatre** = cinema
⁴ **the tube** = the underground *(U-Bahn)*
⁵ **screen number** = *Kinosaalnummer*

71

Annotations
6 to **sneak/snuck past**
= to go somewhere
secretly without
permission
7 to **billow** = to rise
and fall
8 **they** = i.e. the
narrator's family
members
9 **shallow** = superficial

customers all standing around us, I don't want to
embarrass him. "I'll see you after the film, Youssef
85 …" "No, I'll see you in there," he says to me. "I'm
coming in now." Youssef looks over his shoulder to
the far end of the foyer. The toilet door swings
open, and I see Hamza clumsily pushing his way
out carrying a mop in one hand and bucket in the
90 other. Youssef tries to wave him over, but Hamza
doesn't see him. He's just finished the day's third
cleaning, mopping up all the shit and piss and
disgusting things people leave behind in cheap
toilets when they don't care about them. I used to
95 do that job as well, anyone who works in the
cinema has to do all the jobs – except Hamza who
doesn't sell or tear tickets because of his English.
When he sees Youssef waving, he carefully puts the
mop and bucket into the service closet and walks
100 over. His dark black skin shines blue under the
halogen lights of the foyer, thin arms pressed
tightly to his sides and hands forced into his
pockets. Youssef asks Hamza to tear the tickets in
his place, and Hamza says OK because Youssef has
105 a personality that makes people want to do what
he says. He doesn't push, but he always manages to
convince you that his ideas are clever or sensible.
While I was working there, he always got me to
count the money at the end of the night, which was
110 the worst job, and no one wanted to do it because it
was so boring and you were always the last to
leave. He also managed to convince me, every
Friday night, to take a few pounds from the till and
go drinking with him. I never wanted to steal and I
115 didn't want to drink before I worked there but
Youssef makes me want to do all of that. He takes
my arm and walks me through the swinging doors
and into one of the theatres, looking for spaces at
the back right, under the balcony. That's where you
120 always find the people who got in for free or people
who just snuck6 in or people who paid for one
ticket in the morning and stayed in the cinema all
day moving from film to film, sometimes sleeping
behind the seats if no one saw them. Youssef and I
125 take the empty seats behind two boys I recognise,
two boys that I always see here. They sit next to
each other and pass a mobile phone between them,
sometimes both talking on it, sometimes just
writing messages. Next to us, there's one Arab or
130 Iranian man who is a bit older than me and has a
beard and looks like a religious man, but I always
see him drinking cans of beer in his seat. He's
sitting next to the air conditioner vent. I see one
black guy who once brought a prostitute in, or
135 maybe not a prostitute but a girl who didn't mind
doing things in a cinema and that's what they did.
I also see a fat white man who usually sits a few
rows ahead and at the end of the film always asks

Youssef and me and anyone else I'm with "What
140 did you boys think of *that*?" Especially when it's a
film about war: "What did you think about *that*?"
With his arms waving and the loose skin billowing7.
There are some other people around but I don't
recognise them. Everyone else, the real customers,
145 are sitting further up so they can see the screen.
Back here no one cares if we talk because they8're
not here to see the film anyway, so Youssef and I
talk and he asks me what happened to my mother
and I tell him. I tell him that she was in Cairo when
150 she got sick and they wanted her to go to hospital
there, but no one could pay for it. So they thought
she could get treated in London for free, but of
course they had to pay for the plane ticket and still
no one had the money. My family tried to put
155 everything they had together but it still wasn't
enough, and at the same time my cousin was
having a baby so they needed that money. That's
when I stole the whole day's till from the cinema,
and with that I bought the plane ticket. The next
160 day I lost my job. All this Youssef knew. But since
my Mum made it to London, that was seventeen
days ago, I hadn't seen him or been to the cinema
at all. I was staying with my Mum in hospital. At
midnight I would go to work in the underground
165 stations until 8 a.m., then I could go back to the
hospital.

"After seventeen days she died. It was very slow.
And I have to spend all my money again to send
her body back to Cairo. I can't even go with her. I
170 have to look for another job." I'm trying to raise my
voice above the sounds of the screaming coming
from the film. It's a film about a woman who finds
out her daughter is being followed by a killer, that's
what I understand so far, and the woman now is
175 trying to find out who the killer is and what he
wants with her daughter. Youssef says in Arabic
the things that we always say when someone
else dies, that is "She will live on inside you," and
"God have mercy on you," and "God give you
180 good health." These things we never really have
to think about because they are phrases already
written by generations and hundreds of years of
people's parents dying. Generations of killing
children and starving and being murdered in the
185 name of God. We can recite these phrases and
then forget about the death and move on. I know
Youssef won't forget, but it always sounds shallow9
when someone uses these phrases. And the person
grieving knows those words all sound empty and
190 insincere but there's nothing anyone can do about
it. We keep using them. The killer turns out to be
someone the mother knows and now she's chasing
him across the city. There's a policeman with her,
and the policeman's father was shot before when

195 he was also a policeman. "Samir, I know someone who can do it properly here, who can do a Muslim funeral here." "No, she's supposed to be buried in Cairo. Everyone there is waiting for me to send her but I don't have the money. I need money." It 200 reminds me of when I would break something in my grandmother's house. The place was filled with antiques and whenever we went to visit, when I was younger, I would always break something. She would tell me it was all right as long as I paid for 205 it, and I would say "Later," but I never did pay for anything. "I don't have anything I can give you." Youssef is talking to me but looking straight ahead, his eyes on the screen. "I wasn't expecting anything from you." I turn my head to face him. "That's not 210 what I meant. I just wanted to tell you." Now the woman and the policeman find the killer just before he reaches the daughter. The daughter doesn't know he's after her. The policeman gets shot and dies before the killer falls from the roof or from a 215 balcony. The lights come up and everyone slides from out of their chairs and throws empty boxes and cups on the floor and the fat white man sees us and his eyes get wide. "Well, what did you boys think of that?" He crosses his arms over his belly 220 and looks at both of us with relish[10], waiting for a reply, but I'm not going to say anything. Youssef finally offers this: "I think the girl was stupid, she should have known he was coming to kill her!" The fat man nods his head, "I was thinking that as well," 225 and smiles broadly to himself as he limps[11] out of the cinema with the other customers.

When I stole the money from the cinema, everyone else said they wouldn't tell the boss it was me. They knew it was me because I'd been talking 230 about it for a few days, but all of us working there stayed together and usually let the rest of the staff get away with whatever they were doing. No one wants to cause problems for themselves, and the best way to avoid that is to do your job. Don't say 235 anything if you aren't asked. We're all illegal so no point in bringing trouble on all of us. They said they wouldn't tell the boss who it was but everyone knew and someone must have said something in the end because the boss told me straight, the next 240 morning, that I didn't have a job there any more. But that didn't bother me, because I had already taken the money the night before and hidden it in my flat. Now I think it would have been better if I had just taken the money for myself. Just kept it. 245 My mother died anyway, better for her to have died in Cairo with the family and then be buried there straight away. I say that to Youssef but he tries to make me feel better and says, "There was no way to know, was there? You couldn't have known. You did 250 what you could." Now I have to go through losing

her and losing all the money at the same time. As Youssef and I walk out of the cinema, Hamza follows to tell us something. He's trying to give us a message, but he's difficult to understand because 255 of his English. Youssef and I eventually figure out that the message has to do with the boss; he says I can't come to the cinema any more since I lost my job. If he seems me here again he'll call the police and have me arrested. Youssef laughs because he 260 laughs when he's nervous. My face is straight, I don't have the energy to react. When Hamza says the word "police", I imagine the policeman from the film. I imagine him chasing me in a taxi and getting shot before I fall off a roof. Now I'll have to 265 find somewhere else to waste hours of every day. Somewhere else dark to hide in when I can't bear to go back to the flat and I can't afford a proper meal. I'll have to find somewhere else to buy my hashish from.

270 The next night I meet Youssef outside the cinema when he's done working, and he brings Aqil with him, a friend from Iraq. Aqil was in the army there but they thought because he had a doctorate degree in physics he shouldn't be in the army. 275 So the government said he could work on their physics programme, but he escaped to come to England instead. Aqil is short and very wide, now he wears thick glasses and has his hair combed over the top. When he was younger he was very 280 handsome – he showed me a picture of himself when he was a weight-lifter. He also used to be on the National Weight-Lifting Team, then he came to London and started working in a video shop. He watches the news all day on the shop's television 285 even though he's supposed to play the new films. We walk to a café not far from the cinema, on one of the smaller streets behind Charing Cross Road. There's a Turkish guy who runs the place, they sell fish and chips and pies. Aqil sits facing me and 290 looks into his cup of coffee for a few minutes before starting with, "Samir, can you believe Blair[12]? He is such a fool! I'm serious, he is a fool if he thinks he can control Iraq like this: Be democratic ..." he lays down his coffee and holds his two hands up 295 as though he's aiming a rifle at my chest "... or I'll kill you. This is his foreign policy." I look down at his fingers pointed to my chest. That's how our conversations always begin, then we go on from there insulting European and American leaders. 300 At some point in every conversation Aqil will say, "And don't forget, it's really our fault. We let them push us around like this ..." and no one's satisfied by the end of it. I once saw Aqil crying when they were showing on TV pictures of people in Iraq, 305 men on the streets of Baghdad, stealing things from the National Museum[13] and smashing everything to

Annotations
[10] **with relish** = with pleasure
[11] to **limp** = to walk slowly or with difficulty as if one leg is injured
[12] **Blair** = Tony Blair (*1953), former leader of the Labour Party (1994-2007) and UK Prime Minister from 1997 to 2007
[13] **The National Museum** = The museum's official name is The Iraq Museum, inspired by the name of the British Museum in London. It was founded by a British archaeologist after the Great War in 1922 and hosted exhibits from the Mesopotamian, Babylonian and Persian civilization. It was looted in the course of the 2003 invasion of Iraq. Despite international efforts, only some of the stolen artefacts were returned.

73

Annotations

[14] **antique** = an old and valuable piece or object

[15] **King Farouk** = He was King of Egypt and the Sudan from 1936-1952 and was overthrown in a military coup d'état *(Staatsstreich)*. He died in exile in 1965.

[16] **revolution** = The 1952 coup d'état aimed at abolishing the constitutional monarchy in Egypt, establishing a republic and ending the British occupation of the country that had started in 1882.

[17] **to suck** = to take sth by force

[18] **to come by** = to make a short visit to see sb

[19] **Holland Park** = An affluent area in Kensington, London, with Victorian houses and several embassies. It has a park of the same name.

pieces. The city and the windows and someone's car and banks and people's houses, all being taken to bits. "Those statues," he said, pointing to images

310 of stolen antiques[14] on the screen, "were made when Europeans were still running around in the mud! Living in caves!" I drink my third coffee and Aqil asks about my mother. He must have heard from someone else that she was sick. I don't say

315 anything, but Youssef shakes his head and waves a finger at Aqil. We talk about marriage instead. I've been thinking about it for months now, but I haven't met anyone I love. We decide maybe I don't have to wait to find someone I love. Then on the TV

320 there are pictures of piles of dead bodies but I can't tell if they're American or Iraqi. We've been sitting in the café for two and a half hours by now, waiting for our night shifts to start. I can see girls walking past outside – girls dressed up to go out with their

325 friends, girls in suits on their way back from work (maybe they have to work late or they're sleeping with the boss), girls already drunk, girls who look scared to walk in the streets alone, girls who look really ill and they're trying to find someone to pay

330 them for sex. While looking out of the door, looking at the girls passing, I ask Aqil if he knows where I can get some money. I carefully ask, "What about you, do you have any money I can borrow?" He has his fingers locked together, resting on the table,

335 and he opens his hands to answer with enthusiasm, "If I knew where to get money, I would get it!" and Youssef and I laugh with him. It's pathetic and we know it's true but we laugh with him. Everyone is always looking for ways to make money. I once

340 went round to people in the streets with a stolen stereo and tried to persuade someone to buy it, but no one would even talk to me. I didn't steal it but the man who stole it asked me to sell it for him and said I could keep some of the money. I hated to

345 think of myself as a criminal. I thought if I stayed far away from the guy who stole it, if I didn't get close to him, I would be fine. I mean, I would still be clean. But it didn't work and I couldn't sell the stereo and I still felt like a thief. That made me

350 sick. Aqil would often say about himself, "I left my country to escape from criminals and I came here, and I became a criminal!" That's how I felt with the stereo. But Aqil reads a lot and watches the news all day so he always thinks too much about what he's

355 going through. Youssef and I try not to think about it; we go to the cinema and watch films instead.

Aqil comes in to see me one night when I'm working in the kitchen of Café Tangier. I got the job from someone Youssef knows who used to be in the

360 military in Egypt. His father was something like a captain under King Farouk[15] and he had to leave the country with the king during the revolution[16].

Youssef's friend got me a job serving tables at the Tangier and that was good money. Sometimes I

365 could overcharge tourists, or foreigners who had just arrived in London, by one or two pounds and they wouldn't notice because they couldn't read the menue. But I can't serve in the restaurant any more after the police came and found me and

370 some Hungarian girls working without papers. So I moved to the kitchen. I can still work in the kitchen and probably no one will find me there. That's what I mean by feeling like a criminal. I'm not doing anything illegal, I'm only trying to

375 make a living. Washing up in a kitchen, my family wouldn't believe it. That would be a disgrace. That's why I don't tell them what I'm doing. I tell them instead that I'm doing fine and I'm happy and making money. I can't tell them I came to London

380 to become a criminal. When I look at myself, I don't see a criminal. I don't see a good man. All I want is to live simply. I don't want to get rich, suck[17] the money out of this country. No one would believe that, they don't imagine that at all. I want to tell

385 them, "I'm only trying to earn a living. You have to work too – I'm just working". That's what it's like in the kitchen.

Aqil comes by[18] to tell me there's a car coming in from France. His cousin is coming to London for

390 the weekend to meet him and pick up a few days of work building around Holland Park[19]. There are a lot of rich Arabs in Holland Park who pay to have work done. Some of them prefer to have other Arabs working for them. Some people say

395 it's because they want to give back to the poorer ones in London, to show their appreciation, but I think it's because they want to be reminded of what things were like for them at home, when they had servants and maids. "We can go with them to

400 Paris. It's my cousin who moved to Syria, he speaks French." "What would they do there?" "We could find something else there. My brother can help us find work." "What kind of work?" "I don't know. He says it's better than here." But I don't speak French.

405 I don't know Paris at all. By now I'm used to where things are in London: where the money is, where there are jobs going and which ones are safe. That takes a lot of time to learn. I stand over the sink, with Aqil next to me hovering like he's waiting for

410 an answer right now. He's sitting on the counter and his legs don't touch the floor. I stop washing and hold my hands down to let some of the soap drip from my fingers. My shirt was white, now it's grey, spattered with water from the sink. I'm

415 thinking about Paris and what it must look like at night compared to London, whether it also has a Soho with mini-cabs and empty beer cans and girls who look sick and counting the money in the till

until midnight. And mothers coming over because
420 they have no money and dying in the city.

I hear Aqil's voice mumbling, but I don't hear the
words clearly. I look over and see his lips moving
with the same sound but I don't hear his voice. I
hear the words to an old song, one where the diva
425 sings, "The world is a cigarette and a drink, when
people abandon you ..." and her voice moans with
the floating sound of the strings. Most people
would say that means the cigarette and the drink
are all you have left. But I always thought she
430 was saying that everywhere you can see chances.
Everywhere you see little insignificant things that
can comfort you. Maybe it's a drink or a cigarette
or a girl but when everything is lost, you find
suddenly there are little pieces everywhere that
435 give you hope, more hope than when things were
going well. You can see hope in everything. This is
what I'm hearing until Aqil jumps down from the
counter and brushes his hands on his trousers. He
starts to look apologetic[20] as he turns to walk out
440 of the kitchen. He pauses before the door to say,
"Youssef is coming with me," and that's the sound
of the orchestra rising in a crescendo. I know I'll
be alone if I decide not to go with them. I couldn't
stand being alone. I turn to face Aqil and he can see
445 on my face what I'm thinking: that I'm afraid to go
to Paris. This is like everything else that controls
me. I leave the restaurant early. There aren't many
customers anyway so I'll finish washing in the
morning. I stand in the doorway and I see the rain
450 hitting the pavement in some spots where it's lit
orange by the street lamps. I remember then that
I still have a hole in my left shoe, where the sole[21]
is split, and if I walk out like this the water's going
to soak[22] through my sock and get my foot wet.
455 I'm feeling sick now, sick in my stomach like I'm
hungry or I have a hangover but I can't get rid of
the sensation. Even when I eat something, I'm just
sick thinking of what Aqil mentioned. The idea of
going to Paris. I buy four cans of cheap beer from
460 the newsagent's and I open the first one just as
I'm stepping on to the tube to get me out of Stoke

Newington[23] and all the way down to south London
where I can hide behind the warehouses and
factories. My foot is already soaking wet. I wish
465 I could have done something like the man who
escaped from Egypt with King Farouk. I could be
running from something dangerous – that would
be honourable. But I'm just running around looking
for spare jobs and trying to avoid the police. If I
470 was in exile with the king, no one would look at
me like I was a criminal. I could say, "I did it for my
country," or, "I did it for my king," and it would be
glorious. English people would understand that's
something you have to do, so save your king, and
475 that would be a good reason to be on the run or
to be afraid all the time. That would be a good
reason to hide my money and buy four cans of beer
every once in a while and drink them on my own.
Or a good reason to bring your mother over and
480 watch her die, because that's how people in exile
have to live. My family could be angry at me but
they couldn't be ashamed of me because everyone
would know I did it for my country first, and I was
willing to die for my country. But I didn't die and I
485 escaped to London. That's my fantasy.

I'm still feeling sick on the tube, and people are
watching me now drinking my beer and still
wearing my dirty clothes from work. In front of
me is a girl sleeping with her head resting on the
490 glass. I can still see the oil from other people's hair
smeared on the glass but the girl doesn't seem to
notice. She's very young, the girl, and starting to
look pretty. I scratch my back through my shirt.
Then I have to reach under my shirt to scratch the
495 skin properly, with my nails. The girl opens her
eyes while I'm still looking at her, but I forget to
smile. She quickly shuts her eyes again, pretending
to sleep. I don't know what else to say to her,
except, "I had to escape from the revolution. They
500 were going to kill me if I didn't escape, because I
wanted to save my king. Because I love my king."
I only say that because I'm a little drunk by now.
Otherwise it's just my own fantasy.

Annotations
20 **apologetic** =
sorry (for causing
a problem)
21 **sole** = the bottom
part of the shoe
22 **to soak** = to make
sth completely
wet
23 **Stoke Newington**
= a multicultural
area in the
borough of
Hackney in north-
east London with
large Asian and
Afro-Caribbean
communities.
One of the men
who attacked the
London public
transport system
on 27 July 2005
was a resident of
this area.

WHILE READING

The narrator

a) Collect all the information about the narrator while you read the short story.

_____

_____

_____

His personal information	
His outer appearance	
His cultural background	
His relationship to other people	
His beliefs and values (towards his mother, family and girls)	
What other people think of him	

b) Explain why, for the narrator, living in exile would be better than living like an illegal immigrant. (p. 75)

c) Based on your findings from a) and b) write the narrator's character analysis. Choose suitable adjectives to describe the character. → **Workshop:** Analysing characters

Language support

The short story "The rain missed my face and fell straight to my shoes" written by Saeed Taji Farouky in 2005 is about ...

For a start, the narrator can be described as ... This can be seen in line ... when ...

Furthermore, the author presents/pictures/portrays him as ...

The relationship between ... can be characterized as ...

The description contains a lot of/a large number of/many details of ...

These details refer to/allude to/apply to ...

This trait becomes apparent when he ... Another feature is ...

What is also striking about him is ... In addition to this ...

Moreover, ...

One might draw the conclusion that ... One can infer that/conclude that ...

Thus it is only too obvious that ...

Summing up one might say that ... Taking everything into consideration ... To sum up ...

Aqil

3

a) Explain what Aqil means when he says about himself: "I left my country to escape from criminals and I came here, and I became a criminal!" (p. 74)

b) "I once saw Aqil crying when they were showing on TV pictures of people in Iraq, men on the streets of Baghdad, stealing things from the National Museum and smashing everything to pieces." (p. 73)

- Read the online article and outline the most important aspects (in English). **Webcode** WES-73652-06
- Write Aqil's inner monologue in which he reflects upon the importance of the exhibits in the museum. Use the information from the online article.

The Iraq War (2003)

4

a) Find out about the Iraq War and the attitude of European and American leaders towards it.
- reasons for starting the war
- countries involved
- the leaders' attitudes towards the war
- the outcome of the war

b) Explain Aqil's attitude towards European and American leaders. (p. 73 f.)

Air raid on Bagdad, 2003

Life as an illegal immigrant

5

a) Describe the jobs the illegal immigrants have to do in order to make ends meet.

b) Contrast the characters' lives at home to their lives abroad (in England).
Consider (legal/illegal) jobs, social positions, and family ties.

> **Language support**
>
> whereas | unlike | compared to | by comparison | in comparison with | in contrast to

POST-READING

6

a) List all the topics/themes the short story deals with. Then compare them to your speculations from task 1 in the pre-reading section.
Milling around: Choose one of the topics you find relevant and prepare a two-minute talk on it: Explain its importance for the story, provide evidence from the text and say how it contributes to the message or idea of the story.

> **Language support**
>
> My topic is ... | I'm talking about ... | The importance of the topic becomes clear when ... | This can be seen on page ... in line ... when ... | Apart from that ... | The idea of the short story is to show how ... | Finally, ...

b) Discuss in class what the message of the short story is.

The setting

7

a) Explain how the cinema as a confined indoor setting contributes to the overall message the short story conveys.

b) Analyse the function of the horror film. (p. 73 f.)

AN IMMIGRANT IN BRITAIN: AQIL

8 **Hot seat**

You are going to interview Aqil to find out what life is like for an immigrant in Britain.
2-3 students take Aqil's role. Make sure you put yourself in Aqil's shoes and act
from his point of view. To get prepared do task a) below. Another group acts as interviewers,
who try to find out as many details about Aqil as possible. Do task b) (cf. p. 78).
A third group is the observers, who evaluate the questions and the answers and give
the others feedback on their performance. You need to be well-informed about Aqil.

a) Collect all the information about Aqil in a mind map. Give line references.

Short story   **The postcolonial experience:** The rain missed my face ...

2

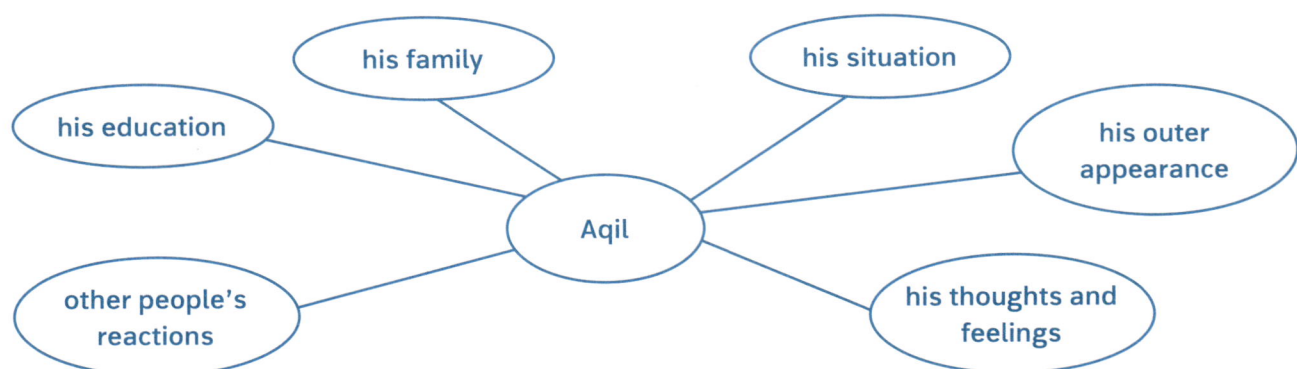

b) Then prepare questions about ...
- his name, age, and nationality
- his outward appearance
- his development
- his everyday life as an immigrant in Britain
- his problems
- his hopes and fears
- ...

c) Hot seat: Choose one person to be Aqil and have him sit in the middle while you ask him questions. In the course of the interview, Aqil can be replaced by another student.

d) Evaluate the performance. Give feedback on ...
- how well the students considered the details mentioned in the short story,
- how accurate the performances were,
- how well the students could be understood in terms of grammatical correctness, choice of words, and voice.

e) Optional: You are a journalist writing for a magazine and have come across Aqil. Write an article about him featuring his life before and after his escape, his hopes and fears as well as his present situation.

The title

9

The title of this short story is rather unusual: "The rain missed my face and fell straight to my shoes".

a) Think: Explain the title. Look at some words more closely. Think about ...
- why the author chooses a rainy situation for the title.
- why the rain misses the narrator's face.
- why the rain falls to his shoes.
- what the rain symbolizes.

b) Pair: Exchange your ideas with a partner.

c) Share: Discuss in class to what extent this title fits the content of the story.

d) Think of other titles that would fit the short story.

The characters in the future

10

a) Pick an immigrant from this short story. Revise the information about this character.

b) Portray his life twenty years later. Consider ...
- what job he might have
- how he has developed financially
- where and how he lives
- what his family situation might be like
- how he leads his everyday life
- what his dreams are
- what he would have changed if he could turn back time
- ...

She shall not be moved: A short story (2005)

PRE-READING

1

Research information about the author Shereen Pandit on the internet.

2 **Think–Pair–Share:**

a) Think: Look at the photos and speculate about the short story's contents. Consider the information you have found about the author. Take notes.

b) Pair: Exchange your ideas with a partner.

c) Share: Present your ideas to the class.

She shall not be moved
by Shereen Pandit

I swear, if it hadn't been so late, I'd have done something about it. Or if the previous two number 201 buses hadn't vanished into thin air. Or if it hadn't been so cold. Or if I didn't have Mariam
5 with me, her almost turning blue with the cold. Yes, I would definitely have done something about it, there and then. I would have given him a piece of my mind. And them.

But the thing is, it was late, and the buses *hadn't*
10 come for more than an hour. And this being London, it was pretty darned[1] cold and there was Mariam, shivering next to me. So I was highly pleased, I tell you, when that bus finally pulled up[2]. I paid. That's
another thing, it was the last change I had on me
15 and I couldn't afford to get chucked off[3], could I?

Anyhow, this bus finally comes, I put Mariam up alongside me, while I pay. Then I try to move her along into the bus ahead of me. Only, we can't move. The aisle is blocked by this huge woman,
20 with a pram in the middle of the aisle[4]. She seems to be Somali, from her clothes – long dark dress, hair covered with a veil[5], like what nuns used to wear, arms covered to the wrists, nothing but face and hands showing. The driver shouts at me to
25 move down the bus, only I can't because of the pram. I'm about to say to him, well get this woman

Annotations
[1] **darned** = (informal) extremely
[2] to **pull up** = (of a bus) to stop
[3] to **be chucked off** = to be forced to leave a place
[4] **aisle** = *Gang*
[5] **veil** = *Schleier*

Annotations

6 **rinse** = haircolour
7 **prune** = a dried plum that is often eaten cooked; *Dörrpflaume*
8 **Pauline in EastEnders** = a fictional character from the popular soap opera called *EastEnders*, which deals with working-class life in London. *EastEnders* has been broadcast since 1985.
9 **mac** = short for mackintosh, a coat made of water-proofed material
10 **to tackle** = to speak to sb about a problem
11 **havoc** = a situation in which there is a lot of chaos or confusion
12 **nonchalant** = behaving in a calm and relaxed way
13 **gleam** = an expression of a feeling that shows in sb's eyes
14 **to jam** = to press one's lips
15 **to scramble** = to move quickly using your hands
16 **to jerk** = to move suddenly
17 **skinny to boot** = *sehr dünn*
18 **so-and-so** = used to refer to a person whose name you don't know
19 **haughty** = arrogant
20 **to accommodate** = here: *jmdm entgegenkommen*
21 **strapping** = tall and strong
22 **to yell at sb** = to shout loudly at sb, especially when you are angry
23 **wrapper** = a piece of cloth worn around your body
24 **scornful** = contemptuous, *verächtlich*

to move out of the way – it's one of those modern buses with a special place for prams – when I see what the problem is.

30 There are these two women, sitting in those fold up seats in the pram space. White, fifty-ish, wrinkles full of powder and grey roots under the blonde rinse[6], mouths like dried up prunes[7], both of them. One of them's wearing a buttoned up cardie like
35 Pauline in EastEnders[8]. The other one's wearing a colourless crumpled and none too clean mac[9] of some kind. The big-breasted, big-bottomed type. Both looked strong enough in the arm to lift a good few down the pubs every night.
40 They're sitting right under that notice which says: "Please allow wheelchair users and those with prams priority in using this space". Which means, these two are supposed to get up so the Somali woman can put her pram in the space left when
45 their seats fold up. Only, they're staring hard out of the window, pretending they haven't heard a word of what's going on, and if they did, it's nothing to do with them.

As I said, they didn't look like the kind to tackle[10]
50 unless you wanted a real scene. I wouldn't have put it past the likes of them to use some pretty rough language, regardless of whether there were kids around. Me, I don't like exposing Mariam to unpleasantness. So I turn to the driver, who's still
55 yelling down the aisle from behind his glassed in box. I reckon it's his job to tell the women to move. I mean why should I do his dirty work?

There're two empty seats right opposite the women. They can just move over the aisle. I look
60 hard at them, trying to will them to look around. They finally can't resist looking round to see the havoc[11] they've caused. They're still trying to be nonchalant[12], but you can see this gleam[13] of satisfaction in their eyes, their mouths growing
65 even thinner as they jam[14] their lips grimly together, as if to say: "That'll show you who's boss!".

I take the chance to point the empty seats out to them. Politely. I'm doing as my mum said when I was young, always show them we're better. So,
70 even though I've got a small kid with me, I'm not scrambling[15] to grab the seat. Usually I let Mariam sit down because buses jerking[16] around can be dangerous for kids, especially kids like Mariam, small for her age and skinny to boot[17]. But do these
75 old so-and-so's[18] take the seat I'm pointing out to them? Not likely. They look at me, then look at the seats as if they're a pile of dogdirt I'm offering. Then they mutter something to each other, turn up their noses and stare out the window again, like it's
80 nothing to do with them.

The Somali woman, meantime, has squashed herself tight up against the side of the aisle, just

below the stairs. If anyone really wants to, th can squeeze past and go on upstairs. Her face
85 tight too. Lips set. Eyes blank. Head held high. S looks like a haughty[19] queen. She's done her best accommodate[20] other passengers by leaving the what inches she can, and now she just shuts off a looks into space.

90 Through all this, the driver's been yelling on a off. Finally, his door swings open – the glassed bit leading into the bus, I mean. Right, I think, he he comes, he's going to make the old witches mo He's not scared of them, big strapping[21] bloke,
95 doesn't have to be scared of anyone or anythin Besides, he's got right on his side. They can't ev complain amongst themselves, let alone to h employers that he's taking sides with the Som women just because they're both black

100 But oh no! He comes at this Somali woman yells at her[22] that either she folds up the pram she leaves the bus. He's all over her, leaning rig into her face and shouting. I reckon he's going hit her. I hate violence and I turn Mariam's fa
105 away. I don't like her seeing ugliness like this. T Somali woman doesn't give an inch. Except to tu aside disdainfully because this bloke's spit is flyi in her face. Pulling her wrapper[23] more close about her, she says scornfully[24] that she's not doi
110 either. And you can see why not. Her baby's asle in the pram and she's already got another small o hanging onto her. One hand on the pram, anoth on the toddler.

Her face is full of contempt for this driver, b
115 her voice isn't rude or loud or anything. Just fir She's paid, she's got these kids, she's staying p He shouts and storms. Eventually he gives up a goes back and starts the bus so it jerks and she a the kid and the pram nearly go flying, except f
120 the pram being stuck. Me, I'm totally shocked his attitude. I'm really building up a head of stea here. If it wasn't for all the stuff I said before, at th stage I really would have given him a go. But he gone back and there's nothing I can do about hir

125 I tell the Somali woman to sit down in the emp seat, thinking she can at least hold the small o on her lap and maybe I could steady the pra while Mariam sits next to her. She shakes h head wordlessly. It's like she's used up all h
130 words on the driver. I reckon maybe, in spite her looking so proud and firm, she's too timid give the women a go. Maybe she's worried, bei black and a foreigner, probably a refugee and a Maybe she also doesn't like a scene and is alrea
135 embarrassed enough by the women. Maybe if she said something to them directly, I would ha backed her. But how could I go and attack them o of the blue, make them move, if she's not sayi

anything to them?

The two women, deciding that they aren't having enough fun, start a loud conversation with each other about how they're not getting up, no way. Cardie reckons to Mac that "they" – meaning women with prams, or does she mean black women – just pretend "they" want to park the pram and then snatch the seats. "They" want everything their way. Definitely black people this time. And on and on they go. I'm fuming, amongst other things, because Mariam is being subjected to all this racist hogwash²⁵. But what's the point in having a go? It'll only lead to a row lasting the whole bus ride and I probably will get chucked off then for stirring. Even if I'm in the right. They can say what they like about anti-racist laws, but I've yet to see them stop people like these two slinging their poison around. I look at the other passengers in the second half of the bus, past the stairs. All white. No-one's saying anything, no-one's seeing anything, no-one's hearing anything. Not their business. Mariam starts to nudge²⁶ me and whispers to me to tell the driver to tell the old witches to move. She doesn't call them that, though. Calls them "those two ladies". Ladies my backside.

Mariam's language is polite, but this is a kid with attitude. Got it from me, I guess. I used to be known as a kid with attitude too. They can have our seats, she says loudly. I nod, but say nothing. Mariam decides to go on, so I feel like really nudging her hard, only I don't hold with hurting kids. They are the problem, she says even more loudly. I look at them again, still saying nothing. I'm still thinking that with the Somali woman saying nothing to them and the driver on their side, I'm going to end up outside in the cold with Mariam, minus the fare, if I take them on.

This is what I'm thinking, but not saying to Mariam. Kids, there are things they just don't understand. I mean, Mariam would definitely not get to her dance lesson on time and then she'd be right miffed²⁷. And then there's the busfare and the fees and the time and everything all wasted.

Mariam glares²⁸ at the women. She glares at me. I know what she's thinking. How many times have I told her to stand up against wrongdoing. How many times have I pushed her into standing up against bullies at school, whether they're bullying her or someone else. And her only such a small kid for her age.

We try to bring her up thinking about right and wrong. Like how many times have I told her that I'm only living in this miserable country because I'd got into trouble back home, fighting for our rights. There are political posters and slogans all over the house. One of them's got Pastor Neumuller's²⁹ speech: "First they came for the Jews …"³⁰ and all that. She knows, all right. She knows that I should be speaking up for this Somali woman.

And here I'm saying nothing, doing nothing. Every once in a while, when people get on and mutter about the aisle being blocked, the driver shouts at the Somali woman. She stands there like a rock. Cardie and Mac have restarted their loud conversation about "them" wanting to take everything over. I laugh in their faces and start agreeing loudly with Mariam, but I don't say anything to them. The bus is filling up. At a couple of stops some pretty yobbo³¹ looking types get on. You know, tattoos, earrings all over their faces, hair sticking up. The type that I can't afford to get tangled with³². I don't fancy a boot in my face. Or in Mariam's. While those two probably watch and cheer. The yobbos just squeeze past the Somali woman. It's a couple of blokes in collars and ties that swear at her before they force a path upstairs, nearly making her let go of the pram and fall. You can't always tell by appearances, can you.

Then the bus empties a bit. Another middle aged woman gets on, about the same age as the two troublemakers. But this one's sort of frailer looking. Now my mum, when we were kids, she'd only have given us what-for if we didn't get up and offer our seats to older people. I've still got the habit drilled into me. I don't like Mariam getting up, like I said, in case she falls, so usually I give up my seat. But this time, I sit tight. Mariam gives me a questioning look, then makes to get up for this new old lady, but I pull her down. Call me a reverse racist if you like, but if those white women won't get up for the Somali woman, then I'm not giving my seat or my kid's to one of their kind. No way. I didn't start this. Now they start a loud conversation about the "their" manners. Meaning me. I glare at them and say nothing. I can feel Mariam wriggling with impatience for me to mouth off³³ at them. But I reckon with the driver on their side, even against this poor woman with her pram and her kids, what chance have I got? He'd probably call the police for me, if I gave them lip. And guess whose side the police would be on! So I glare and sit tight. I stare straight ahead, like this old lady standing is nothing to do with me. I can feel my lips tighten with satisfaction at getting back at the other two. See how they feel when it's one of their kind getting a dose of it.

But I'm feeling right small inside. I feel like a real sod. Not only for not standing up for the Somali woman, but for not giving my seat to the old white woman. Plus Mariam starts hassling about getting up for the old woman. I almost blow my top at Mariam. I mean, can't she see what I'm doing?

Annotations
²⁵ **hogwash** = a stupid idea
²⁶ **to nudge** = to push so gently
²⁷ **miffed** = slightly angry or upset
²⁸ **to glare** = to look at sb in an angry way
²⁹ **Pastor Neumuller** = Martin Neumuller or Niemöller was a German theologian and pastor (1892-1984), he is well-known for his opposition to the Nazi regime.
³⁰ **"First they came …"** = see post-reading task, p. 85
³¹ **yobbo** = a rude and aggressive young man, a hooligan
³² to **tangle with** = to get involved in an argument or fight with sb
³³ to **mouth off** = to complain loudly about sth

Annotations

34 **barb** = a nasty remark to hurt sb's feelings

35 to **hurl abuse** = to shout abuse

36 to **rake sth up** = to mention sth unpleasant that happened in the past and that other people would like to forget

37 to **yak** = to talk continuously about things that are not very important

38 **bouncy** = lively, full of energy

Standing up to them? I pull her down again and glare at her, whispering "No!" fiercely at her as she struggles to stand up and give her seat to the old woman standing.

255 Then I feel like a right idiot, getting upset at Mariam. The kid's only doing what she's been taught. I make my excuses to Mariam, but she's not taking any notice of me. She doesn't exactly look like she wants to cry, like when she's mad at 260 me, though. Her face is just the same as usual, not swelling up and going red like it always does before she starts to cry, but her eyes have that sad, lost, grief-stricken look. I sit there feeling right helpless. I'm trying to remember where I know that look 265 from.

The bus is coming to a main shopping area, people are walking around with holly-printed plastic bags full of goodies. That makes me remember when Mariam had that look on her face. She had it when 270 she woke up in the night last Christmas and found her Dad stuffing her stocking. I feel sick at the thought of what she's thinking of me. The thing is, what can I do? You can teach kids to stand up against bullies, but sometimes they've got to learn 275 discretion is the better part of valour. I start to explain, but Mariam isn't taking any notice. She looks again at the old woman swaying about on the bus, trying to hold on to prevent herself falling. Then she gives me a look – like I've chucked away 280 her favourite teddy bear.

At last we get to Woodgreen and the troublemakers get off, slinging a last few barbs³⁴ over their shoulders. At that, the Somali woman finally snaps. She lets go of the pram and leans out the 285 doorway and shouts "racists!" after them. They're still hurling abuse³⁵ at her, as if they were the injured parties, as they disappear into the crowd, everybody staring. But thank god, it's Woodgreen and the sea of faces staring interestedly at us is as 290 much black as white.

The Somali woman starts to struggle to turn the pram so she can get off too. I offer to help her, muttering to her that she should report the driver. What's the good of that, she says bitterly. But 295 why do you think he's taking their part, I ask her, because I am truly confused. I mean he's a black man. The black woman is clearly in the right, so, as I said before, he can't get into trouble with the company if he tells the white women to get up or 300 get off.

The Somali woman gives me a long look: "Because he's a slave," she says. "He is a slave," she repeats loudly through the still open back door of the bus, at the driver collecting fares from passengers 305 boarding at the front. I realise from her attitude that they probably already played it all out, she and the women and the driver, before I got on the bus. "But me," she says, looking at me hard again, "I am not a slave. I would rather die than be one." Her 310 voice is like granite, hard and unmovable. Every word falls heavy as a stone between us, cuts into me like a diamond. I feel my face turn red as I take Mariam's hand. All through Mariam's class, that woman's words go round and round in my 315 head. I reckon it's me she's called a slave too, for not sticking up for her. And the thing is, I'm not even mad at her if that's what she's saying. I'm just upset at myself for not doing anything. And then there's Mariam. People reckon kids forget 320 things quickly. But I know Mariam. All afternoon I sit there watching her. I want to tell her she still shouldn't let people walk all over her, just because they're white, or stronger, or richer, or anything. I don't want her not to stick up for other people if 325 she sees wrong done to them. But I also want to tell her that you can't always do that – you've got to pick your moments. Then I ask myself what's the good of raking it all up³⁶ again? What's done is done. After her class, Mariam asks to go to the 330 bagel shop for a hot buttered bagel. This is our usual routine, our little treat. I suggest an extra special treat instead. I take Mariam for a pizza and let her have Coke as extra, extra special. She looks puzzled for a moment at all this, but then she's 335 yakking³⁷ away, back to her usual bouncy³⁸ self. I reckon there's nothing like a special treat to let kids forget bad memories. Soon she's blowing bubbles into her Coke through her straw. She's got a smear of pizza tomato on her cheek. So why can't I forget 340 the whole thing? Is it because I imagine a bit of Mariam's look of this afternoon still about her everytime she looks at me?

WHILE READING

The story

a) Read up to p. 80, l. 29. See if your ideas from the pre-reading task were correct.

b) How do you think the story will continue? Jot down some ideas. Then continue reading.

c) Compare your ideas with the short story. Were you right? Explain why or why not.

The narrator

4

a) **Pair work**: Choose some of the words from the box that describe your impression of the narrator best and explain your choice to your partner.

I think the narrator comes across as … To me, the narrator seems …

> annoyed | annoying | angry | sympathetic | embarrassed | embarrassing | cheerful | indifferent |
> insincere | hypocritical | pretentious | a little Miss Know-it-all | active | agitated | disappointed |
> disappointing | under stress | helpless

b) Explain what the narrator means when she says: "Call me a reverse racist …". (p. 81, l. 227)

c) Collect the narrator's excuses about why she does not help the Somali woman.

evidence	the narrator's excuses
p. 79, ll. 1/2	*"… if it hadn't been so late, I'd have done something about it."*

d) Comment on the excuses the narrator makes.

e) Contrast the narrator's beliefs and values with her behaviour. Use the chart below.

The narrator's beliefs and values	The narrator's behaviour
The narrator thinks that the two white women should leave their seats to the Somali woman. (p. 80, l. 40 ff.)	*The narrator doesn't intervene; expects the bus driver to do so. (p. 80, l. 54 ff.)*

f) Comment on your findings.

Mariam

5

a) Outline how the narrator brings up her child in terms of beliefs and values.

b) Analyse the function Mariam's role has for the short story.

c) The narrator says: "Mariam glares at the women. She glares at me. I know what she's thinking." (p. 81, l. 182). Put yourself into Mariam's shoes and write her inner monologue. → **S2:** Checklist: Creative writing

The Somali woman

6

a) Collect all the information about the Somali woman in a character map.

> *"long dark dress" (l. 21)*   *"huge woman with a pram" (l. 19 f.)*

b) Use your findings from a) to analyse the impression the Somali woman makes on the reader.

c) Explain what the Somali woman means when she says: "'Because he's a slave,' she says. 'He is a slave,' she repeats loudly through the still open back door of the bus." (p. 82, l. 302 f.)

d) **Pair work** In the evening the Somali woman talks to her friend about the incident on the bus. Write their dialogue. → **S2:** Checklist: Creative writing

The Passengers: The two women

7

a) Study the extracts below and describe the two women's behaviour.

> "There are these two women, sitting in those fold up seats in the pram space. White, fifty-ish, wrinkles full of powder and grey roots under the blonde rinse, mouths like dried up prunes, both of them. One of them's wearing a buttoned up cardie like Pauline in EastEnders. The other one's wearing a colourless crumpled and none too clean mac of some kind. The big-breasted, big-bottomed type. Both looked strong enough in the arm to lift a good few down the pubs every night."

> "They look at me, then look at the seats as if they're a pile of dogdirt I'm offering. Then they mutter something to each other, turn up their noses and stare out the window again, like it's nothing to do with them."

> "The two women, deciding that they aren't having enough fun, start a loud conversation with each other about how they're not getting up, no way. Cardie reckons to Mac that 'they' – meaning women with prams, or does she mean black women – just pretend 'they' want to park the pram and then snatch the seats. 'They' want everything their way. Definitely black people this time. And on and on they go."

b) Explain what the narrator means by "Cardie and Mac" (p. 81, l. 143, l. 202). What impression of the two women does she try to give?

The other passengers

8 **Group work (3)**

a) Using the extracts below, describe how other passengers react to the situation.

b) Analyse how their reaction is presented by the narrator.

c) Imagine you are one of the passengers. Write down their thoughts.

> (1) "I look at the other passengers in the second half of the bus, past the stairs. All white. No-one's saying anything, no-one's seeing anything, no-one's hearing anything. Not their business."

> (2) "The bus is filling up. At a couple of stops some pretty yobbo looking types get on. You know, tattoos, earrings all over their faces, hair sticking up. The type that I can't afford to get tangled with. I don't fancy a boot in my face. Or in Mariam's. While those two probably watch and cheer. The yobbos just squeeze past the Somali woman."

> (3) "It's a couple of blokes in collars and ties that swear at her before they force a path upstairs, nearly making her let go of the pram and fall. You can't always tell by appearances, can you."

POST-READING

The story

9

a) Go back to p. 70 and reread the info on intertextuality.

b) The narrator refers to a political speech made by Pastor Neumuller in 1946.

Info

Martin Niemöller (English: **Neumuller**) was a German-born theologian and pastor (1892-1984), who initially supported Adolf Hitler, but then turned against him. He was imprisoned from 1938 to 1945. He became famous for his speech that he gave in 1946 and that was then turned into various poetic forms "First they came …".

Read the following version. Analyse the poem, explain its message, and interpret its function for the short story. The following questions might help you to interpret this poem.

- What group of people are chosen and why?
- What stylistic devices are used and to what purpose?
- What does the speaker in the poem have in common with some of the characters in the short story?
- To what extent does the reference to this poem characterize or even criticise the narrator's behaviour in the short story?

First they came for the Communists
And I did not speak out
Because I was not a Communist

Then they came for the Socialists
5 And I did not speak out
Because I was not a Socialist

Then they came for the trade unionists
And I did not speak out
Because I was not a trade unionist

10 Then they came for the Jews
And I did not speak out
Because I was not a Jew

Then they came for me
And there was no one left
15 To speak out for me

The title

10

a) Speculate about why Shereen Pandit might have chosen this title for her short story.
Do you think the title fits the story? What would have happened if the Somali woman had moved?
Exchange your views with a partner.

b) Read an extract from Maya Angelou's poem "Our Grandmothers".

Info

Maya Angelou (1928–2014) was an influential African-American writer, professor and civil rights activist who is well-known for the recitation of her poem "On the pulse of morning" at the inauguration of Bill Clinton in 1993.

Having suffered from several catastrophes in her childhood, she was able to turn these terrible experiences into creative inspiration for her writing. She was awarded many prizes during her lifetime, such as the *Mother Teresa Award* (2006) and the *Presidential Medal of Freedom* (2011).

I shall not be moved is the title of her fifth poetry collection that was published in 1990 and that deals with themes such as the struggle of African Americans.

Our Grandmothers

She lay, skin down in the moist dirt,
the canebrake rustling
with the whispers of leaves, and
loud longing of hounds and
5 the ransack of hunters crackling the near
branches.

She muttered, lifting her head a nod toward
freedom,
I shall not, I shall not be moved.

10 She gathered her babies,
their tears slick as oil on black faces,
their young eyes canvassing mornings of madness.
Momma, is Master going to sell you
from us tomorrow?

15 Yes.
Unless you keep walking more
and talking less.
Yes.
Unless the keeper of our lives
20 releases me from all commandments.
Yes.
And your lives,
never mine to live,
will be executed upon the killing floor of
25 innocents.
Unless you match my heart and words,
saying with me,

I shall not be moved.

30 In Virginia tobacco fields,
leaning into the curve
of Steinway
pianos, along Arkansas roads,
in the red hills of Georgia,
into the palms of her chained hands, she
35 cried against calamity,
You have tried to destroy me
and though I perish daily,

I shall not be moved.

Her universe, often
40 summarized into one black body
falling finally from the tree to her feet,
made her cry each time into a new voice.
All my past hastens to defeat,
and strangers claim the glory of my love,
45 Iniquity has bound me to his bed.

yet, I must not be moved.

She heard the names,
swirling ribbons in the wind of history:
nigger, nigger bitch, heifer,
50 mammy, property, creature, ape, baboon,
whore, hot tail, thing, it.
She said, But my description cannot
fit your tongue, for
I have a certain way of being in this world,

55 and I shall not, I shall not be moved. (...)

c) Identify the historical background of the extract and describe the situation as portrayed in the poem. Use the right-hand column for your notes.

d) Analyse the extract and explain its message. Consider the role of the speaker, too.

e) Explain how the refrain of the poem "I shall not be moved" with its variations can be referred to the title of Shereen Pandit's short story.

The characters

11   CHOOSE

Group work (6)

Hot seat: Choose a character from the short story you would like to explore more deeply.
Divide the class into the number of characters you would like to explore. You also need a group of students to interview the character. Preparation: The character: In order to step into the role of this character, answer the questions below in your group.

- How old are you? How and where do you live?
- Who do you live with and in what surroundings?
- Where do you spend most of your time?
- Who do you like in particular, who do you like less or not at all, and why?

- Do you have any friends? If so, how do you spend your time with them?
- Do you love anybody? If so, what does this love mean to you?
- What is your financial situation like?
- What profession do you have? What is your profession like? Are you happy with it? Why, why not?
- What do you know about the incident on the bus? What do you think of it?
- What do you expect from life and from other people? How do you feel about life?
- How do you see yourself? Are you happy with yourself?
- What do others think of you?
- What are your dreams?
- What do you need?
- What makes you suffer?
- What do you like doing?
- What do you look like?
- How do you dress?
- What is your posture when you walk, stand or sit?
- What is physically characteristic of you?

As the interviewer, you ask questions, e.g. about this character's feelings, actions, and motives in the story. Presentation: One student takes the hot seat. The others ask him or her questions to find out about the character's feelings and motives.

OR

Group work (5)
Dramatic acting: Act out the scene from p. 88 ("… here he comes, he's going to make the old witches move. …") with a different ending.

MEDIATION

12

a) Before you read the text below, think about how you would explain the German term "Zivilcourage" to a non-German speaker. Exchange your explanations with a partner.

b) Read the text and start a mind map in which you include words and phrases that can be used when talking about moral courage. → **Workshop: Mediation** → **S19:** How to improve your mediation skills

What is "Zivilcourage"?

Moral courage or civil courage are terms referring to the German word "Zivilcourage". But what exactly is moral courage? What defines such behaviour?

5 Generally speaking, moral courage entails high social costs, such as negative consequences with hardly any rewards for the person showing such prosocial behaviour.

Other scientists define moral courage as brave 10 behaviour that someone shows when they become angry or indignant about a difficult situation in which they want to enforce their beliefs and values without considering their personal and negative consequences.

15 In what situations is moral courage needed? When human rights are violated, people are treated unfairly, foreigners or minorities are discriminated against, weaker people are verbally or physically attacked, sexually harassed or abused. These 20 situations usually have an imbalance of power in common, in which the person who wants to help faces one or more victims as well as one or more perpetrators.

Moral courage is an important virtue within society. 25 It is not innate behaviour but can be learned and trained through role plays, discussions and group exercises. In training courses participants learn how to recognize an emergency situation as such, how to behave fast and reasonably without endangering 30 one's own life and how to activate others to assist. They learn that small deeds matter such as calling the police or informing others. Studies have shown that these courses have a similar effect as those of first aid courses.

c) Your friend from your American partner school asks you to help him write an article on the issue of moral courage. You find the following website released by the German police department:

Webcode WES-73652-07

Write to your friend. First tell him about what moral courage is. Then continue by explaining the steps one should take and the advice the police give on their website. Read the online article.

◀ ◀ ▶   🔍   ▼ 🏠

Zivilcourage: Einschreiten – oder nicht?

Beherzt eingreifen, wenn andere Hilfe brauchen: In Notsituationen würden viele Menschen gern Zivilcourage zeigen. Experten erklären, wie man in brenzligen Situationen hilft – ohne sich selbst in Gefahr zu bringen.

Von Vivian Alterauge
Donnerstag, 11.12.2014   15:23 Uhr Hamburg

Tugce Albayrak zögerte nicht lange, als sie die Rufe zweier Teenagerinnen hörte. So berichten es Zeugen, die dabei waren am frühen Morgen des 15. November im McDonald's an der Autobahnauffahrt Offenbach-Kaiserlei. An jenem
5 Samstag, als Tugce Albayrak mit anderen Imbissgästen Sanel M. und dessen Freunde zurechtwies, die offenbar die beiden jungen Frauen belästigt hatten. Wenig später schlug Sanel M. die 22-Jährige so heftig, dass sie auf den Asphalt des Parkplatzes fiel. Sie erlag ihren Verletzungen.
10 Joey K., in einem Supermarkt in Hannover erschossen, starb vergangene Woche. Aktuellen Ermittlungen zufolge wollte der 21-Jährige helfen, als kurz vor Ladenschluss eine Kassiererin in einem Supermarkt von einem bewaffneten Mann bedroht wurde. Bei einem Handgemenge mit dem
15 Täter löste sich ein Schuss, Joey K. war tot. Vom Täter fehlt immer noch jede Spur.

Beide wollten helfen, beide hatten nur Sekunden, um zu entscheiden, was zu tun ist. Die Reaktionen auf die beiden Fälle haben gezeigt: Zivilcourage hat einen enorm hohen
20 Wert in der Gesellschaft. Zugleich wird deutlich: Mut bedeutet, Risiken einzugehen.

Wie soll jeder Einzelne abwägen, wenn sich die Frage stellt: einschreiten oder nicht?

Das Handeln ergebe sich aus einer Art Kosten-Nutzen-
25 Analyse, erklärt die Psychologin Monika Schanderl von der Uni Regensburg, die seit Jahren zum Thema Zivilcourage forscht. Im Kopf fänden blitzschnell eine Reihe von Abwägungen statt, etwa: Habe ich Schuldgefühle, wenn ich nicht eingreife? Entscheidend aber seien vier Schritte,
30 um aktiv zu werden.

• Zunächst müsse die Situation genau wahrgenommen werden, ohne jede Ablenkung wie Musik über Kopfhörer oder Zeitdruck.
• Dann die Frage: Ist das überhaupt eine Notsituation?
35 Streitet sich da nicht nur ein Pärchen?
• Man muss sich selbst verantwortlich fühlen: „Je mehr Personen anwesend sind, desto eher diffundiert die Verantwortung", sagt Schanderl. Sprich: Wenn niemand die Initiative ergreift, handelt keiner.

40 • Letztlich muss man sich fähig und kompetent fühlen, einzugreifen.

Doch wie greift man richtig ein? Es gehe nicht nur um das aktive Dazwischengehen, sagt Schanderl. Nur wer sich körperlich imstande fühlt, sollte bei Gewalttaten
45 aktiv eingreifen. Schließlich beherrsche nicht jeder Kampfsportarten. „Wenn der Täter direkt angegangen wird, macht ihn das oft noch aggressiver", sagt Schanderl. Wer dem Opfer helfe, überrascht stattdessen den Täter. „In der Zeit kann man mit dem Opfer fliehen."
50 Auch Andreas Mayer, Geschäftsführer der polizeilichen Kriminalprävention der Länder und es Bundes, sagt, von einem aktiven Eingreifen in eine Gewaltsituation sei eher abzuraten. Die bessere Alternative: Notruf wählen, den Kontakt halten, bis die Streife vor Ort ist.
55 Stets mit dem Fokus auf das Opfer, nicht den Täter. Wie man in solch einer Situation, wenn das Herz klopft und der Körper automatisch Adrenalin ausschüttet, richtig reagiert, kann man lernen. Seit zwanzig Jahren bietet die Polizei in München solche Schnellkurse an. Auch
60 Schanderl leitet solche Trainings, meist im Großraum Regensburg. Dort lernt man auch, wie man das Umfeld richtig mit einbindet. Konkrete Ansprachen sind zum Beispiel sehr wichtig: „Sie in dem roten Pullover rufen die Polizei", ein anderer kann vielleicht weitere Hilfe holen.
65 Es gibt staatliche und private Programme, gerade für Jugendliche, die für das Thema sensibilisieren. Beinahe jede Stadt habe ein Zivilcourage-Programm, sagt Mayer. Die Polizei habe etwa die „Aktion-tu-was" initiiert, zahlreiche Preise zeichnen zudem Mutige aus und sollen
70 zur Zivilcourage ermutigen. Mayer weiß allerdings auch: „Die Wegschau-Mentalität ist immer noch weit verbreitet." Das liege nicht unbedingt an Ignoranz. Sondern auch an der Tendenz, sich von der Gemeinschaft abzuwenden, das Umfeld kaum mehr wahrzunehmen. „Viele kennen
75 noch nicht einmal ihre Nachbarn im Mehrfamilienhaus." Dabei sei es schon couragiert, Fremde im Hausflur anzusprechen, um mögliche Einbrüche zu vermeiden.

Post-reading

THE SHORT STORIES

1 Group work (4)

Divide the class into five groups. Each group deals with one short story.

a) In your group, collect important aspects of your short story that you think are worth discussing or analysing. You will find some ideas below:

- Characters
- Living conditions
- Topics dealt with in the short story
- Reasons for immigrating
- Problems the characters face
- Setting (time and place)
- Decisive events or turning points

b) Each member works on a different topic. Use examples from the text to back up your results. Share the information with your group members. Then visualize the information in form of a documentation poster. Present the results to the class. It might look like this:

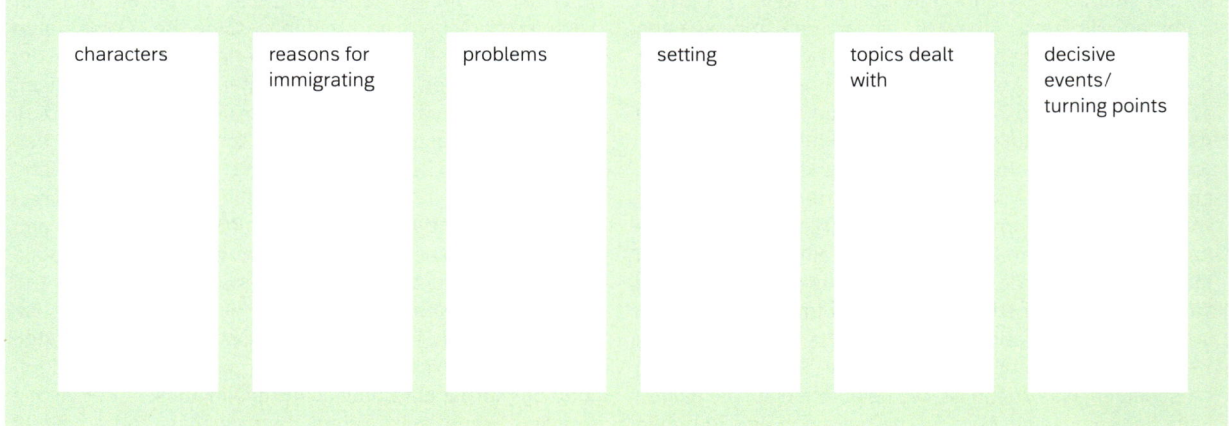

characters	reasons for immigrating	problems	setting	topics dealt with	decisive events/ turning points

c) A TV station runs a special programme about migrants and their lives. Interview one of the characters from your short story.
Find out about:

- their motives for coming
- how they were welcomed or accepted
- how and where they live
- how they like(d) it
- what they expect(ed) from life
- what difficulties they have or had to face and how they cope(d)
- ...

Optional: You may also choose the narrators from A. Levy or S. Pandit's short stories. In this case you need to adjust the aspects to the change in perspective.

Quotes

2

a) Look at the quotes on the next page from the short stories that you have read. Choose the one you like best. Explain the situation to which they belong and their relevance for the short story.

"I like to think of that moment in [her] parlor as the moment when the distance between Mala and me began to lessen." (Lahiri, p. 46)

"There are still times I am bewildered by each mile I have travelled, each meal I have eaten, each person I have known, each room in which I have slept. As ordinary as it all appears, there are times when it is beyond my imagination." (Lahiri, p. 46)

"'The homeland?' [He] ruminated over the term and shared his musing aloud with his fellow passenger, who had similar home circumstances, including being a widower. 'The one that you have just visited, or the one that you are returning to? The place where you have spent most of your adult life? Which homeland are you trying to escape from?'" (Shahraz, p. 58)

"We are the new English *babus*, living in old people's homes, the ones we used to ridicule once upon a time! Meals on wheels for us now – we have worked so hard – time to enjoy ourselves now, hey!" (Shahraz, p. 59)

"I am not in the habit of making friends of strangers." (Levy, p. 64)

"Only a savage would turn away when it was merely kindness that was needed. I resolved to help her." (Levy, p. 66)

"'Those statues', he said, pointing to images of stolen antiques on the screen, 'were made when Europeans were still running around in the mud! Living in caves!'" (Farouky, p. 74)

"I left my country to escape from criminals and I came here, and I became a criminal!" (Farouky, p. 75)

"I swear, if it hadn't been so late, I'd have done something about it." (Pandit, p. 79)
"'He is a slave,' she repeats loudly through the still open back door of the bus ..." (Pandit, p. 82)

b) Pair work Choose the short story you would recommend to your friend who wanted to learn something about the situation of immigrants. Explain your choice.

Important scenes

3   CHOOSE

Group work (4)

Each group deals with one short story. In your group you settle on a scene that you find the most important one from the short story. Choose one of the following activities:

a) Act out the scene. Then explain why you have chosen it and how it contributes to the overall message of the story.

b) Show a freeze-frame. Make the other students guess which scene you have chosen. Explain why you have chosen it and how it contributes to the overall message of the story.

c) Mime the scene. Make the other students guess which scene you have chosen. Explain why you have chosen it and how it contributes to the overall message of the story.

4

Find information about the current situation of a group of migrants mentioned in the short stories and prepare a short presentation on this topic.

What is postcolonialism?

1

In the pre-reading section you have already come across the term "postcolonialism". Read the following entries. Then make a mind map, in which you connect aspects of postcolonialism found in the pre-reading section and in the examples provided below.

- Post-colonial literature is writing which reflects, in a great variety of ways, the effects of colonialism. This might include the enforced mass migrations of the slave trade or the impact of colonialism upon indigenous societies.

- The study of the cultures of countries and regions, especially in Africa, Asia, and Latin America, whose histories are marked by colonialism, anti-colonial movements, and the transition to independence during the 20th century, and the study of their present-day influence on the societies and cultures of former colonizers.

- Postcolonialism often also involves the discussion of experiences such as slavery, migration, suppression and resistance, difference, race, gender, and place […]. The term is as much about conditions under imperialism and colonialism proper, as about conditions coming after the historical end of colonialism.

- In many works of literature, specifically those coming out of Africa, the Middle East, and the Indian subcontinent, we meet characters who are struggling with their identities in the wake of colonization, or the establishment of colonies in another nation. For example, the British had a colonial presence in India from the 1700s until India gained its independence in 1947. As you can imagine, the people of India, as well as the characters in Indian novels, must deal with the economic, political, and emotional effects that the British brought and left behind. This is true for literature that comes out of any colonized nation. In many cases, the literature stemming from these events is both emotional and political.

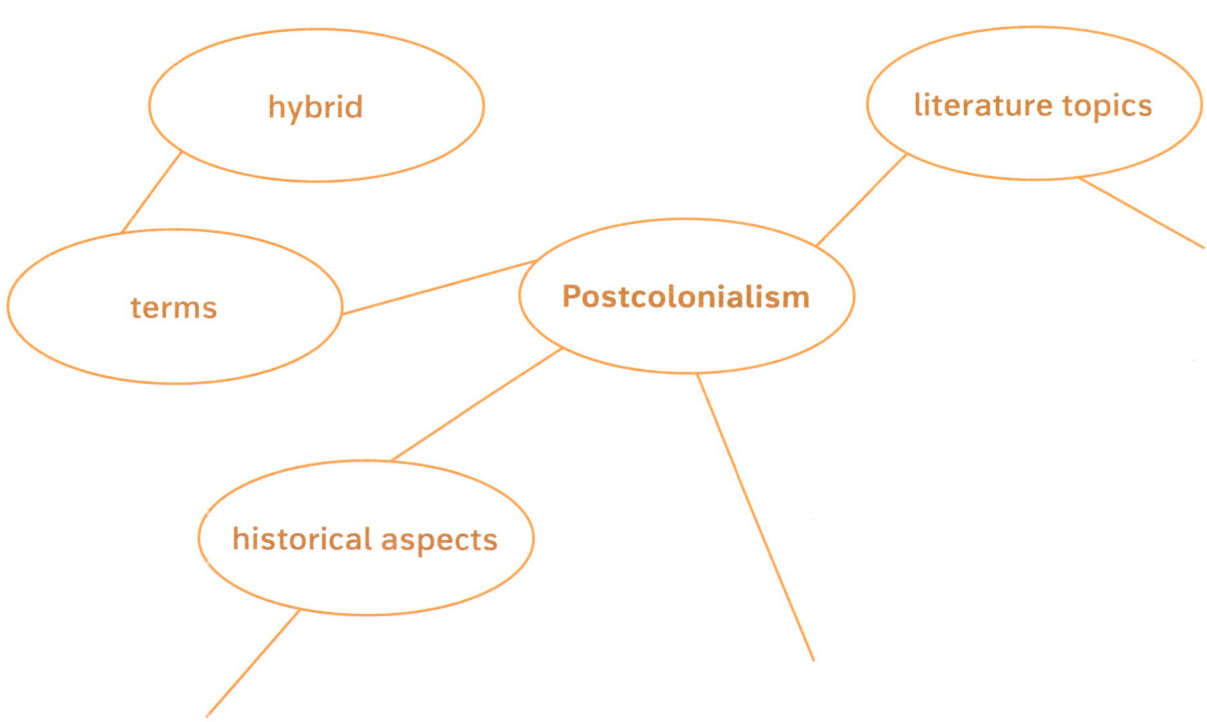

Understanding postcolonialism

2 → **S17:** Checklist: How to work with cartoons

a) Study the cartoon carefully, then describe it.
   The cartoon depicts … In the centre, you can see …

b) Analyse the characters and objects shown in the cartoon.

c) Explain the message of the cartoonist.

d) Explain why this cartoon can be classified as a postcolonial cartoon.

"JUST HOW LONG DO YOU ILLEGAL ALIENS PLAN ON STAYING IN OUR COUNTRY?"

Sarfraz Manzoor: British journalist of Pakistani origin

My family moved from Pakistan to the UK 40 years ago – how far we've come

In May 1974, Sarfraz Manzoor arrived from Pakistan with his mother and siblings to join his father in Luton, to build a new life. He reflects on the changes in his family – and in the world he grew up in – in the four decades since.

5   First published on Fri 9 May 2014 15.30 BST

How far we have come. Forty years ago this very week – 16 May 1974 – a plane that had set off from Lahore landed in London. Among the passengers was Rasool Bibi, a 41-year-old Pakistani woman, with her daughter, 12, and
10 sons, aged 11 and two. It was their first plane journey and the first time any of them had left Pakistan. I was the

Sarfraz Manzoor and his daughter Laila.
Photograph: Graham Turner

youngest of the children – I was almost three – and at the airport we waited nervously for our father to meet us and take us to our new home and our uncertain fate. In 1974, Harold Wilson was in Downing Street, Richard Nixon was vowing not to resign over Watergate and Abba had just won the Eurovision Song Contest with Waterloo.

My father, Mohammed Manzoor, had been in Britain for 11 years, visiting Pakistan only twice during that time. He had left my mother and his children in the hope of finding work in Britain that would enable him to send for us. When we joined him he was working on the production line at the Vauxhall car factory and that was how we came to live in Luton, in the Bury Park area.

I live in London now but often return to Luton. I recently visited Bury Park and stood on the rooftop of Nadeem Plaza, which offers one of the most striking views of the town.

Below me were streets lined with halal butchers and grocers, little changed from the days when I used to walk along them with my parents.

During the first few months, before we could afford secondhand beds, we slept on the floor or on two chairs turned to face each other. What might my parents have said had they predicted what would happen to them and us in the next four decades?

We didn't have a television set but the Saturday morning schedule for this weekend 40 years ago featured an animated series called Wait Till Your Father Gets Home in which "a conservative father butts heads with his family on various social attitudes of the day". That sounds like the story of my life. My father was an ambitious man – he had left his wife and children in Pakistan in the hope of a better life in Britain – but his ambition was tempered by reality. He could not imagine a world in which white people were friends and not just colleagues.

My family and home town did not equip me to talk to white people; my parents actively discouraged such interaction. My father and the other working class Pakistani men he fraternised with only knew work that was soul-destroying and low-paid. Work was endured not enjoyed; the same could also be said for marriage. I grew up in a world constrained by rigid certainties; life would follow a predetermined path and the route was largely determined by others.

Roads were closed because I was brown, because I was working class and because of my parents. It was against these limitations that I have spent the last 40 years resenting, raging, running and rebelling. My father came to Britain for economic reasons and I have struggled to process the unintended consequences of his decision.

As a little boy in the 70s, mine was an insular existence, enclosed within the Pakistani bubble of Bury Park and largely unaware that any other world existed. I was a teenager in the 80s, a decade of frustration as I realised I was different from my white friends who were allowed to have girlfriends and parties and free will. In the 90s, I left Luton and my family to study and live in Manchester only to be forced to return in the spring of 1995 for my father's death. I spent the next 10 years fearing an arranged marriage before finding the courage to reject it, and the fortune to find love.

This decade has been defined by marriage in 2010, and fatherhood the following year. When I first arrived in Britain my family consisted of my parents and their three children. In the years since there have been departures – the death of my father – and arrivals, and today the family includes my mother, her four children, their spouses and her seven grandchildren.

The family is bigger and broader: if someone had told my mother before she left Pakistan that two of her children would end up marrying white non-Pakistani partners, I doubt she would have believed it, or been able to conceive of it.

Progress can be painful and one theme of the last 40 years is of absolute certainties being challenged and unravelled on the journey from resentment to forgiveness and acceptance, some further down the road than others. I was the first person in my family to marry someone who was not a Pakistani Muslim and I am now the only fully non-white person in my own family. My daughter, Laila, is mixed race but her skin tone owes a larger debt to me than my wife. The other day I was taking her clothes off in preparation for bath-time. She looked down at her body and said "I'm brown!" It was said with surprise and delight, an entirely innocent observation. I recall having the same thought when I was a teenager but it was freighted with foreboding. The difference says everything about how far we have come.

My father is buried in Luton and my mother lives less than a 10-minute drive from the very first house she lived in. When I was young I didn't want to spend time with my parents or their friends. It is one of the more surprising aspects about the passing of time to learn that not only do I love the things I once resented – I need them too. I need them because as the previous generation slips into the arms of history, my generation finds itself the keeper of memories, the teller of stories. It will be my job to tell Laila about her Pakistani grandad and grandma and what life was like way back then.

My parents and that first generation were, of course, pioneers but what I have only recently come to realise is that we are all pioneers. My parents were the bridge between Pakistan and Britain, the old world and the new. I am the bridge between the almost vanished world of my parents and the unfolding life of my daughter. We are all pioneers; and when freedom is not feared we are all bridges.

I look at Laila and I see distant echoes of my father and of me but I also see how different her world will be. Her history includes the history of myself and my parents but it is not dominated by it. There are fewer rigid certainties to constrain her future, she can believe that no road is closed to her.

This story began with my mother arriving at Heathrow airport and it ends, or perhaps begins again, with my daughter's birth in an east London hospital. She could only exist now. She is the past, the present and the future – a joyous hope-filled reminder of how far we have come.

3

a) Read the article and summarize it in your own words.

_____

_____

_____

b) Explain: "We are all pioneers; and when freedom is not feared we are all bridges."

_____

_____

c) Analyse Sarfraz's attitude towards his childhood and youth by examining the language he uses.

_____

_____

d) Explain how this article reflects postcolonialism. Use the information from task 1.

_____

_____

_____

e) Discuss if Sarfraz Manzoor's story is a story of success.

Postcolonialism in the short stories

4 **Group work**

a) Each group deals with a different short story you have read in class. In your group analyse how the short story reflects aspects of postcolonialism.

b) Choose relevant quotations from your short story to prove your point.

c) Present your findings to the class.

Discussion

5

a) Explain Sarfraz Manzoor's statement: "My generation finds itself the keeper of memories, the teller of stories. It will be my job to tell Laila about her Pakistani grandad and grandma and what life was like way back then."

b) Discuss in class to what extent it is important to study postcolonial literature at school.

"No one leaves home unless home is the mouth of a shark"

1

Have you ever wondered how you would feel if you had to leave your country? Discuss with your partner.

2

a) Read the quotations about displacement, belonging and identity. Choose the one you like best and state why. Explain how displacement is presented in the quote.

- "What greater sorrow than being forced to leave behind my native earth?" – *Euripides, Electra*

- "How is it possible for people and places to change so entirely that they lose any connection with what they used to be? Can a man adapt to new things and new places without losing a part of himself?" – *Abdelrahman Munif*

- "mingling with the remains of the plane, equally fragmented, equally absurd, there floated the debris of the soul, broken memories, sloughed-off selves, severed mother tongues, violated privacies, untranslatable jokes, extinguished futures, lost loves, the forgotten meaning of hollow, booming words, land, belonging, home." – *Salman Rushdie, The Satanic Verses*

- "The fish,
  Even in the fisherman's net,
  Still carries
  The smell of the sea."
  – *Mourid Barghouti*

- "In Sri Lanka, when two strangers meet, they ask a series of questions that reveal family, ancestral village, and blood ties until they arrive at a common friend or relative. Then they say, 'Those are our people, so you are our people.' It's a small place. Everyone knows everyone. But in America, there are no such namings; it is possible to slip and slide here. It is possible to get lost in the nameless multitudes. There are no ropes binding one, holding one to the earth. Unbound by place or name, one is aware that it is possible to drift out into the atmosphere and beyond that, into the solitary darkness where there is no oxygen." – *Nayomi Munaweera, What Lies Between Us*

b) **Pair work** Pair up and devise a short scene in which your quotation is used.

3

a) Read the following extract from a poem written by British-Somali poet Warsan Shire.

Home
by Warsan Shire

no one leaves home unless
home is the mouth of a shark
you only run for the border
when you see the whole city running as well

5 [...]

Warsan Shire, *1988

no one leaves home unless home chases you
fire under feet
hot blood in your belly
it's not something you ever thought of doing
10 until the blade burnt threats into
your neck
and even then you carried the anthem under
your breath
only tearing up your passport in an airport toilet
15 sobbing as each mouthful of paper
made it clear that you wouldn't be going back.

you have to understand,
that no one puts their children in a boat
unless the water is safer than the land
20 no one burns their palms
under trains
beneath carriages
no one spends days and nights in the stomach of a truck
feeding on newspaper unless the miles travelled
25 means something more than journey.
no one crawls under fences
no one wants to be beaten
pitied

no one chooses refugee camps
30 or strip searches where your
body is left aching
or prison,
because prison is safer
than a city of fire
35 [...]

the
go home blacks
refugees
dirty immigrants
40 asylum seekers
sucking our country dry
niggers with their hands out
they smell strange
savage messed up their country and now they want
45 to mess ours up
how do the words
the dirty looks
roll off your backs
maybe because the blow is softer
50 than a limb torn off

[...]

no one leaves home until home is a sweaty voice in your ear
saying
leave,
55 run away from me now
i don't know what i've become
but i know that anywhere
is safer than here

b) Sum up in a few sentences what the poem is about.

c) Analyse how "home" is presented in the extract.

d) Optional: Write a short poem in which you express your idea of home.

4

a) Read the extract of an interview with Warsan Shire below and explain why the poet is committed to writing about people's war experiences.

"I'm from Somalia where there has been a war going on for my entire life. I grew up with a lot of horror in the backdrop – a lot of terrible things that have happened to people who are really close to me, and to my country, and to my parents; so it's in the home and it's even in you, it's on your skin and it's in your memories and your childhood. And my relatives and my friends and my mother's friends have experienced things that you can't
5 imagine, and they've put on this jacket of resiliency and a dark humour. But you don't know what they've been victims of, or what they've done to other people. Them being able to tell me, and then me writing it, it's cathartic, being able to share their stories, even if it is something really terrible, something really tragic. Sometimes I'm telling other people's stories to remove stigma and taboo, so that they don't have to feel ashamed; sometimes you use yourself as an example."

b) Discuss in class to what extent it is important to deal with stories about displacement.
Consider the following aspects: the immigrants' experiences in their new country, the situation in their home countries, and the authors' intentions in writing about displacement.

5 **Group work (4-5)**
Presentation of displacement, belonging and identity in the short stories
a) Divide the class into groups – one group for each short story dealt with in class. Each group prepares a five-minute talk about how displacement, belonging and identity are presented in the short stories.
b) Milling around: Find a partner who has dealt with a different short story and present your findings to each other.
c) Evaluate in a class what you find striking about the short stories: What do the short stories have in common when talking about displacement. How do they differ?

6 **Optional**
Write your own short story about displacement, identity and belonging.
a) First outline your ideas in the chart below.

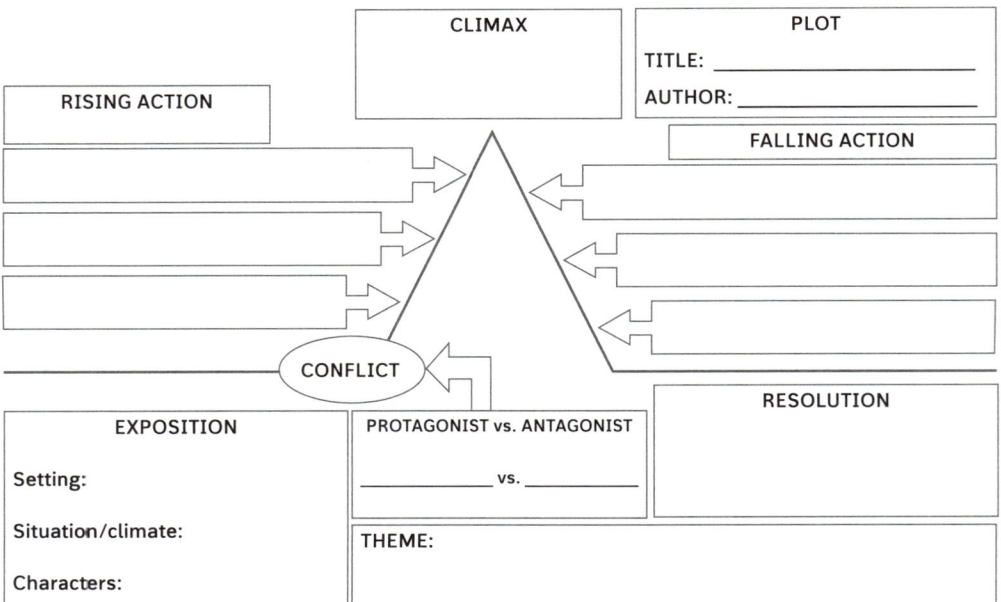

b) Write your own short story. → **S18:** How to improve your text

American core beliefs and cultures

When people from different cultural backgrounds live together, this can sometimes lead to conflicts or even cultural clashes. How do cultures clash in such a multicultural society as the United States of America? You will find out in this section.

 1

Read the info box below and outline some of the American core beliefs.

Info

American core beliefs

- **The Declaration of Independence (July 4, 1776)**, a document signed by the Thirteen Colonies seeking independence from British rule, states: *"We hold these truths to be self-evident, that all men are created equal, that they are endowed[1] by their creator with certain unalienable[2] rights, that among these are life, liberty and the pursuit of happiness."*
- **The Constitution**, drafted by George Washington among others and adopted in 1789, granted inherent rights, self-government and the separation of powers (meaning executive, legislative, and judicial governmental branches are kept separately). On December 15 in 1791, the "Bill of Rights" was written to enshrine the protection of people's basic individual liberties from governmental influence. These first ten amendments[3] include protection for freedom of speech, religion, the press; and the right to assemble. The Second Amendment states: *"A well-regulated Militia[4] being necessary to the security of a free State, the right of the people to keep and bear arms, shall not be infringed[5]…"*
- J. T. Adams (1878–1949) coined the term **"The American Dream"** in his book "The Epic of America" (1931) as follows: *"The dream of a land in which life should be better, richer, and fuller for every man with opportunities for each according to his abilities and achievement."*
- The **Pledge of Allegiance**[6] is a solemn oath[7] of loyalty to the United States declaimed as a part of flag-saluting ceremonies at public events or at the beginning of school days. The Pledge first appeared in 1892 but went through some modifications before reaching its current form in 1954, which reads: *"I pledge allegiance to the flag of the United States of America, and the republic for which it stands, one nation under God, indivisible[8], with liberty and justice for all."*
- Americans firmly believe in an open and dynamic society and its continuing progress, which is why America has always welcomed **immigrants,** provided that they can contribute. Due to America's diverse and multicultural population, one will encounter a variety of different people of varying ethnicities across the country.

Annotations
[1] **endowed** = equipped with particular features by birth
[2] **unalienable** = inalienable; not subject to being taken away from or given away
[3] **amendment** = a change of or an addition to the Constitution
[4] **Militia** = all able-bodied civilians eligible by law for military service
[5] **infringed** = actively break the terms of a law
[6] **allegiance** = someone's loyalty to and unconditional support of their country
[7] **oath** = vow/promise
[8] **indivisible** = unable to be divided or separated

FACTS AND FIGURES OF THE AMERICAN SOCIETY

2 **Group work** → **S18:** Checklist: How to analyse statistics

In the following task, your group will deal with different data and statistics about the American people.
- Analyse your preassigned material (M1 – M4) using the language support (cf. p. 103).
- Afterwards form new groups with members from M1 – M4. Discuss your solutions and draw conclusions.

(M1) Immigration waves and corresponding push and pull factors

time	group of immigrants	push factors driving people away from their country	pull factors drawing people towards a country
in the 17th century	European settlers		colonization
in the 17th century	Protestant groups, e.g. Puritans	religious persecution	colonization
up until 1808	Enslaved Africans	slavery (non-voluntary)	slavery (non-voluntary)
1815–1865	Irish migrants	famine	better living conditions
19th century	Germans	poverty	economic reward better living conditions
19th century	British	poverty	economic reward better living conditions
mid-19th century (until 1882)	Chinese		economic reward new jobs
1880–1920	European workers (largely Italian)		new jobs
1880–1920	Jewish people	religious persecution	
post WW2–1965	European immigrants		better living conditions
since 1965	Asian and Central American	crime, poverty	better future

(M2) Distribution of US population by race/ethnicity, 2010 and 2050

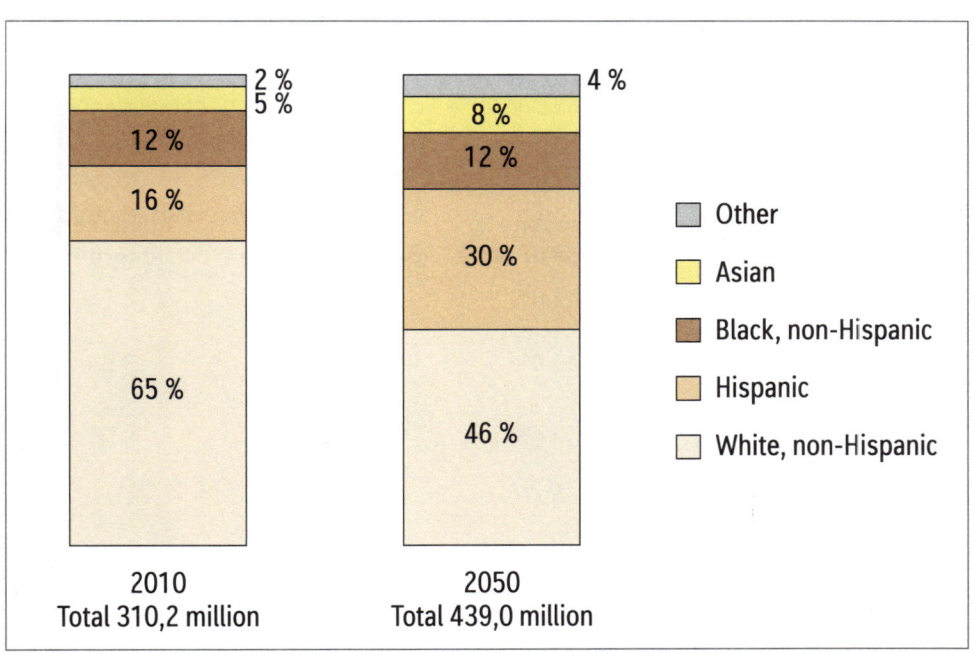

Source: US Census Bureau 2008, Projected Population by Single Year of Age, Sex, Race, and Hispanic Origin for the United States, July 1, 2000 to July 1, 2050.

(M3) Median household income by race/ethnicity of household head

Income varies widely across racial and ethnic groups in the United States

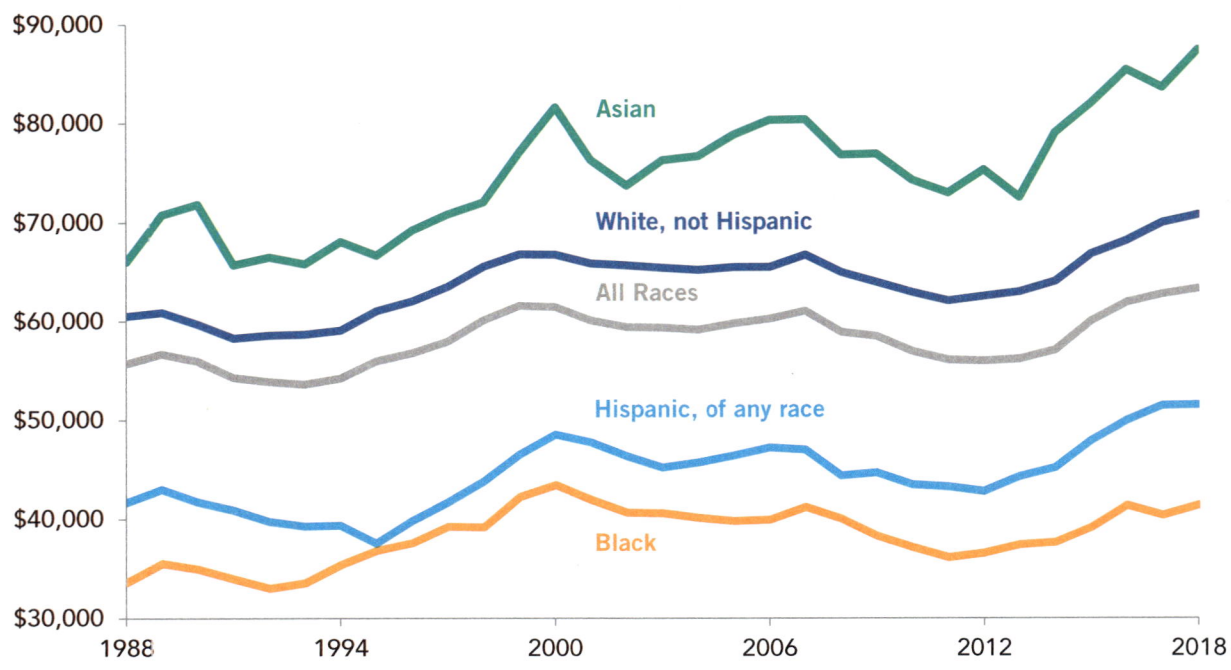

MEDIAN HOUSEHOLD INCOME BY RACE/ETHNICITY OF HOUSEHOLD HEAD (2018 DOLLARS)

SOURCE: United States Census Bureau, *Current Population Survey, 2019 Annual Social and Economic Supplement.*
© 2019 Peter G. Peterson Foundation

PGPF.ORG

(M4) Educational attainment of the population by race and Hispanic origin

	High school graduate or more	Some college or more	Associate's degree or more	Bachelor's degree or more	Advanced degree
White alone	88.8%	59.2%	42.8%	32.8%	12.1%
Non-Hispanic White alone	93.3%	63.8%	46.9%	36.2%	13.5%
Black alone	87.0%	52.9%	32.4%	22.5%	8.2%
Asian alone	89.1%	70.0%	60.4%	53.9%	21.4%
Hispanic (of any race)	66.7%	36.8%	22.7%	15.5%	4.7%

Source: US Census Bureau, 2015 Current Population Survey.

_____

_____

_____

Info

Analysing tables, graphs and charts

Step 1: **Introduction**
- state the title, type, subject, period of investigation and publication detail of the visual

Step 2: **Body**

A) Description
- describe notable, striking developments/changes/differences in the visuals; state whether absolute figures or percentages are used

B) Interpretation
- examine the changes/differences/developments by drawing conclusions or making predictions based on the figures; assess whether the figures are objective or biased

Step 3: **Conclusion**
- summarize what the results of your analysis tell you about the topic

Use ...

→ a clear structure (introduction, body, conclusion) with paragraphs and topic sentences.

→ specific vocabulary (cf. language support) and suitable linking words to logically connect your analysis.

→ the simple present tense.

Language support

- The (line) graph/bar/chart/table is about/shows/presents/provides information on/deals with ..., covering a period of ...
- The ... shows the distribution of ...
- The topic/subject/theme of the (line) graph/bar chart/table is ...
- It is taken from/The source of the data is .../... was published by ... on ...
- The chart compares/It shows the relationship between ... and ...
- The figures show/reveal how ... is divided/made up.
- The figures are subdivided into ... segments/sections which represent the ...
- All the figures are given as percentages/total numbers.
- The biggest/smallest section ...
- The highest/lowest figure/score is .../The figures reach a peak .../The overwhelming/vast majority ...
- to be at the top/bottom of the ranking
- to grow ... by ... %
- steep/strong/rapid growth
- ... is twice/three times as high as ...
- In comparison with/Compared to/In contrast to ...
- to go up/increase/rise/expand
- to go down/decrease/fall
- Almost no/Only a few ...
- Less than/More than/Nearly half of ...
- to remain constant/stable
- All in all/By and large, the statistics for ... reveal/show/present/indicate ...
- This development clearly shows/indicates that ...

FACTS AND FIGURES OF THE AMERICAN SOCIETY

3

There are many different metaphors for America and its integration of immigrants. Describe the following images and explain each metaphor using words from the word bank.

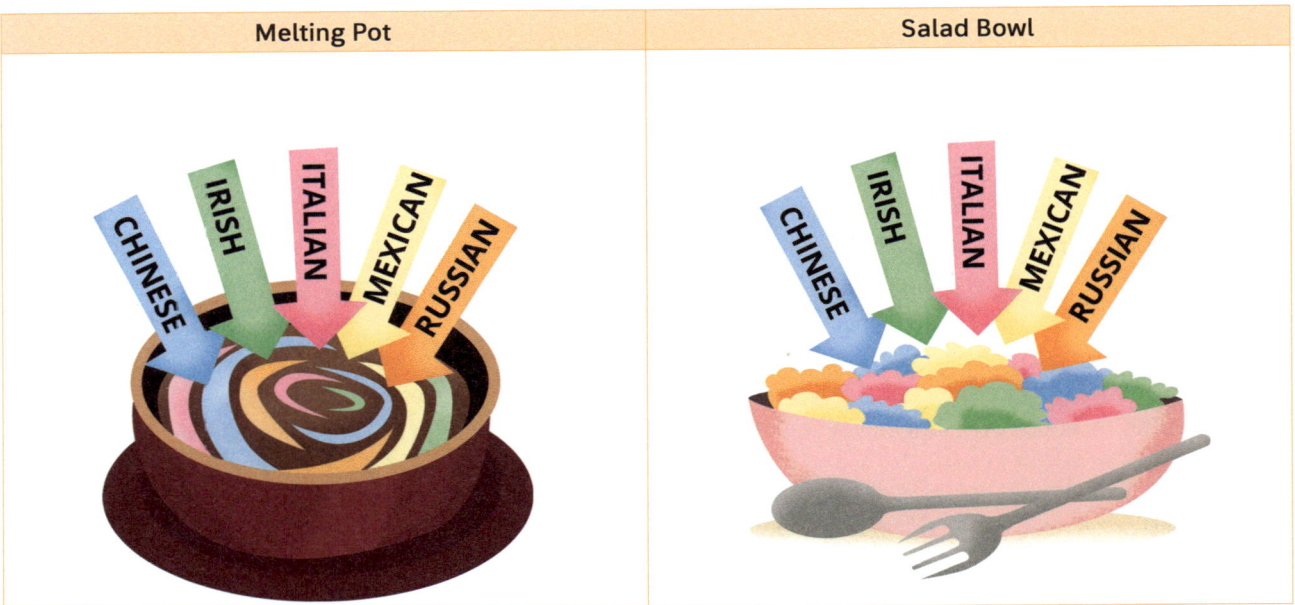

Melting Pot	Salad Bowl

abandon one's culture | acculturation/to acculturate | assimilation/to assimilate | cultural heritage/ backgrounds | cultural homogenization | distinct qualities | diversity | heterogeneous group | homogenous group | immigrants | integration | living together as a nation | living in harmony | mainstream | multiculturalism | one culture | perceptible differences | subcultures | traditional principles | to add something | to blend | to co-exist | to melt | to mix together | unity

Annotations

acculturation = the process of learning and conditioning oneself to the patterns or customs of a culture in order to live successfully in a different culture; the process of becoming adapted to a new or different culture

assimilation = the cultural absorption of a minority group into the main cultural body; the process of becoming an accepted part of a country or group

distinct = clearly different or belonging to a different type

heterogeneous = consisting of parts or members that are very different from each other

homogeneous = consisting of things or people that are all the same or all of the same type

homogenization = if something is homogenized, it is changed so that all its parts are similar or the same

4 CHOOSE

Recently the metaphors "American Quilt" and "American Pizza" have emerged for America and its integration of immigrants. Examine these metaphors and compare them to the "Melting Pot" and "Salad Bowl" metaphors.
OR
Sketch a visual representation of each metaphor, the "AQ" and the "AP".

AN IMMIGRANT TELLS HIS STORY

5 → **S20:** How to listen/watch effectively

You will hear Vietnamese Dieu Ha interviewing American Charles Jensen about US culture. Give short answers to the following questions (#1–10). You do not need to write complete sentences. Unless otherwise specified, one aspect is enough.

Webcode WES-73652-08

Annotations
Tet = Vietnamese New Year
Pho = Vietnamese street food, a soup

#	questions
1.	What does Dieu Ha want to learn/understand by interviewing Charles Jensen? (2 aspects)
2.	What is Charles Jensen's profession and where does he currently work? (2 aspects)
3.	Why is US culture difficult for Vietnamese students to grasp?
4.	How does Charles describe the "melting pot" metaphor?
5.	How does Charles describe the "salad bowl" metaphor and which example does he provide? (2 aspects)
6.	Which nationality is Charles' wife and where did they get married? (2 aspects)
7.	Why is Charles' wedding a great example of lived cultural diversity in the US?
8.	What is Charles' explanation for the prevailing racism in the US? (2 aspects)
9.	What is Charles' opinion about cultural diversity and racism in the US? (2 aspects)
10.	How does Charles depict the advantages of living in a culturally diverse American population?

6

Read the provided definition of a "culture clash". Discuss with clear reference to your previous findings whether or not the American cultural situation is likely to bring about cultural clashes. Give reasons!

Culture clash
A "culture clash" is a conflict between cultures, or a disagreement arising between two parties of different beliefs, values and practices. Criminal offences and delinquencies[1] often arise from culture clashes.
[1]**delinquency** = bad or criminal behaviour

a) Read the quote and the text by Nihal Adler on "Culture and Culture Clash". Outline what a culture clash is and illustrate it with some examples.

b) **Pair work** With a partner, discuss possible ways of handling cultural clashes in everyday life.

Info

Culture and Culture Clash: What is Culture?

Culture is when a group of people share the same customs, traditions, values, symbols, norms, rituals, styles of communication, dress, gestures, language and religion. These are then passed on to the children of that group, who in turn pass them on to their children and so on. It almost resembles a genetic coding.
The term "culture clash", or "culture conflict" was coined by anthropologists at the end of the 19th century [...].
What is a "culture clash"?
On a more general level, culture clash is a complex, multilayered phenomenon that can even occur within the same culture. Examine, for example, the subculture clashes in a society between the young and the old, the rich and the poor, youth of the same generation, men and women, or groups with dissimilar political or sexual orientations. On a more specific level, culture clash implies the meeting of two or more cultures and their difficulties in reconciling[1] their diverging characteristics within the framework in which they are obliged to coexist. [...] Fortunately, most cultural clashes are not severe. Unfortunately though, they can have a negative impact on the people involved in the conflicts if not dealt with carefully. Many words and phrases we use acknowledge cultural clashes like culture shock, interculturalism, multiculturalism, cultural differences, tolerance, diversity, sub-cultures, dominant culture, exclusion, inclusion, ostracism[2], misunderstandings, conflicts, discrimination, racism, different life experiences and perceptions, personal space, taboos, fringe culture, etc.
[1] **reconciling** = the process of making peace
[2] **ostracism** = the act of deliberately not including somebody in a group or activity

7   CHALLENGE   → **S7: Checklist:** Writing a blog post
In your local community, somebody has started a blog about living together in a multi-ethnic community. Make a contribution and write a post in which you share your thoughts about the challenges and chances of living together in a multi-ethnic society.

Gran Torino

PRE-VIEWING: DETROIT IN NUMBERS AND FIGURES

Detroit, the setting of Clint Eastwood's *Gran Torino,* has gone through a few changes – from car capital to a multicultural city with a high crime rate.

1

In order to get to know the setting of the film, read the short texts and look at the graphs and tables about Detroit. Note down information about
– Detroit's problems
– Detroit's racial composition
– its crime rate
– what you find most interesting about Detroit.

2 **CHALLENGE**

You have already got to know the different metaphors people use when talking about cultural diversity in the US (cf. p. 104). Using the information you have learned about Detroit, explain which metaphor best fits this city. Give reasons.

Ford Model T in Detroit, 1913, assembly line production

Detroit

Detroit, the most populous city in Michigan and the Metro Detroit area, serves as a vital port connecting the Great Lakes to the Saint Lawrence Seaway. Detroit is also known as the traditional automotive center of the world, and its name is synonymous with the US auto industry, as well as its musical legacies, which have earned it the nicknames Motor City and Motown[1]. As of 2016, Detroit's estimated population is just over 677,000, a steep decline from a peak of over 1.8 million in the 1950s. Detroit's
10 population in 2000 was 951,270, which dropped to only 713,777 by 2010. In 2016, the city's estimated population was 677,116. [...] In 1950, Detroit was the 4th largest city in the country, but its population has been in decline for the past 60 years. It has had the second largest population
15 decline in the country (second only to St. Louis). Because of this decline, Detroit now has a large number of abandoned buildings and homes and the area is dealing with urban decay[2].

Detroit's Decline

20 Detroit has been going through an economic decline for many years, in part due to urban decay as young, educated people move away from the city for better options. Other causes of Detroit's decline include segregation[3], politics, and of course, the collapse of the auto industry, which
25 the city relied on for many years. Between 1947 and 1963,

the city lost over 140,000 manufacturing jobs. In the next decade, Japanese car imports took up a greater share of the United States market, which took even more jobs from the region. Unfortunately, Detroit was dependent on a
30 single industry – automobiles – and the city's population dropped by over 40% from 1970 to 2006. Between 2000 and 2010, Detroit's population fell an astounding 25%, dropping the city from the 10th largest city in the country to the 18th. In 2010, Detroit's population was
35 713,000, a 60% decrease from its peak population of 1.8 million in 1950. Detroit is an extreme case of what has affected other major, old industrial cities in the country. As the industrial cities in the United States declined, only Detroit hit rock bottom[4] with $20 billion in unpaid bills in
40 2013 that led to the single largest municipal[5] bankruptcy in US history.

Detroit Diversity

Along with its population problem, Detroit also has a demographics problem with a wide age distribution.
45 31.1% of its population is under 18, 9.7% are 18-24, 29.5% are 25-44, 19.3% are 45-64 and 10.4% are 65 or older. The median age in Detroit is 31, and for every 100 females aged 18, there are 83 males. Detroit is also one of the poorest major cities in the United States, and poverty is
50 a real problem. The median household income dropped

from $29,526 in 2000 to $26,098 in 2009. A year later, it had fallen further to $25,787. In 2010, the mean income is below the US average by thousands. 1 in 3 residents in the city are in poverty. [...] In 1940, non-Hispanic
55 whites accounted for 90.4% of Detroit's population, but there has been a significant shift in its population to the suburbs since the 1950s. In 1910, only 6,000 black people lived in the city, which grew to 120,000 by 1930. Detroit is still one of the most racially segregated cities in the
60 country. While black people moved to Detroit from the 40s through the 70s to escape Jim Crow laws[6] elsewhere, they encountered exclusion from white areas, sometimes through economic discrimination or even violence. The traditional boundary between white and black regions
65 of the city is Eight Mile Road. Black people and African

Americans make up only 13% of the state's population as a whole but account for 82% of Detroit's population. [...].

Detroit Demographics
According to the most recent ACS, the racial composition of Detroit was:
Black or African American: 79.12%
White: 14.10%
Other race: 3.02%
Two or more races: 1.90%
Asian: 1.50%
Native American: 0.34%
Native Hawaiian or Pacific Islander: 0.02%

The map clearly shows the segregation of Detroit's metro area: Toward the top of the map, you can see the distinct line dividing black and white families ("8 Mile"). It has long been considered the racial dividing line. Black people are in green; Latinos in orange; Asians in red, white people in blue; all other races are in brown. Every dot represents a person. For a larger image use the provided webcode. **Webcode** WES-73652-09

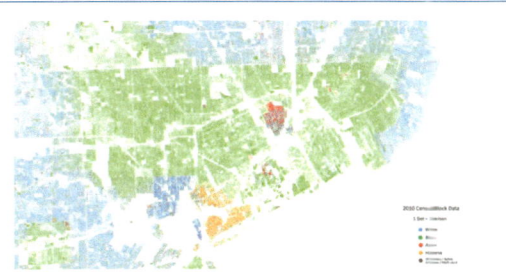

Another major problem in Detroit is its high crime rate, which is 3 times greater than the U.S. average. It was higher than in 99.2% of U.S. cities in 2017. The 2017 Detroit crime rate is about the same compared to 2016. The number of homicides stood at 267 – a decrease of 36 compared to 2016. In the last 5 years, Detroit has seen decreasing violent crime and decreasing property crime.

Annotations
[1] **Motown** = a style of music popular in the 1960s and 1970s, produced by an African American music company based in Detroit
[2] **urban decay** = urban decay refers to the deterioration of part of a town or city due to ageing, neglect, and lack of financial support for maintenance.
[3] **segregation** = the act or policy of separating people of different ethnic groups and treating them in a different ways
[4] **to hit rock bottom** = to reach the lowest or worst point of a decline
[5] **municipal** = connected with or belonging to a city that has its own local government
[6] **Jim Crow laws** = the former practice in the U.S. of using laws that allowed black people to be discriminated against and kept separate from white people, for example in schools

Language support

Talking about graphs
The graph/statistics shows/show ...
Looking at the bar chart, you can see that ...
The number of murders is higher/lower than ...
There are more/less ... than ... (cf. p. 103)

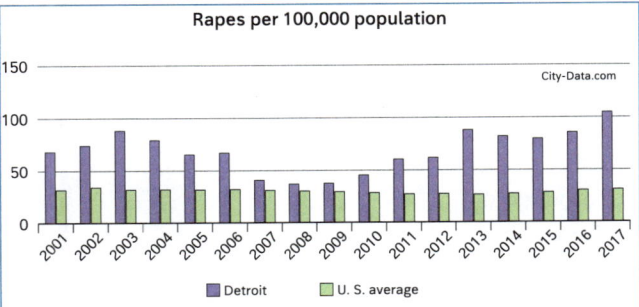

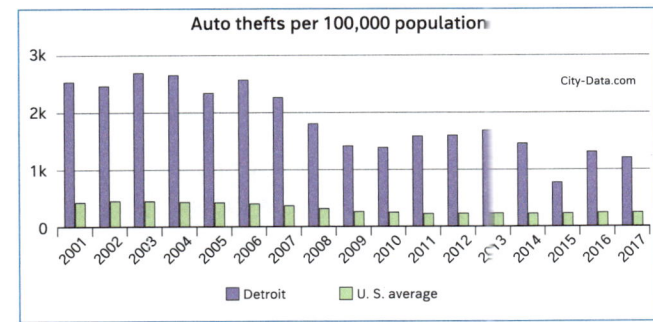

Source: City-Data.com

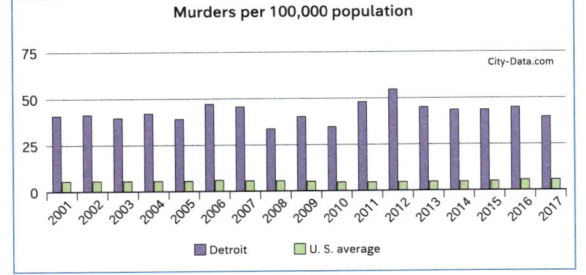

Webcode

WES-73652-10

PRE-VIEWING: GETTING CLOSER TO THE "GRAN TORINO"

Info

Muscle cars in America

In the 1960s and 1970s the so-called *muscle cars* or *supercars* played an important role in the American way of life – especially in the lives of young, white men, who loved high-performance cars. These cars were not that expensive and became a symbol of individuality, independence, endless mobility, liberty and manhood.

3 **Pair work**

*Gran Torino i*s not only the title of a movie, but also the name of a famous muscle car.

Take a look at the Gran Torino above. Speculate on the kind of people who would own such a car and what role it might play in the movie.

Language support

Description/layout of a poster

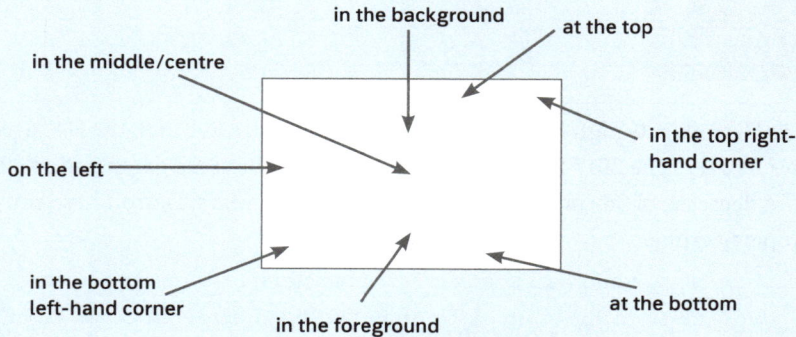

- In the film poster/In the picture I can see …/There is/are/seems to be …/One can see …
- The poster shows/illustrates/depicts …
- The field size is a close-up/medium shot/long shot …
- The layout emphasizes …/The layout is rather detailed/simple with …
- The focus of attention/What strikes the eye is the key/main image.
- The image of … is taking up the most space.
- There is a contrast between …/A contrast is clearly recognizable/visible.

Talking about content und genre

- When looking at the film poster, I think/feel/am reminded of …/
  Initially the image makes me think/gives the impression of …
- The choice of colours supports the idea of/suggests/contributes to …
- The film's mood and tone are reflected/illustrated by …/It can be assumed that … because …/
  … is a symbol of …/The choice of colours supports the idea of/suggests/contributes to …
- The movie poster appeals to audiences that enjoy movies containing dramatic tension/showing male views of the world/about protecting law and order, right and wrong/focusing on one protagonist, powerful and ready to take on the enemy …
- The film poster depicts/shows/portrays/represents/illustrates/conveys …
  which is why I believe/think …

Film posters, DVD covers, and trailers provide a selected visual preview attempting to catch and arouse the potential target groups' interest to advertise and promote the film.

4

Describe the film poster. Then, using it as a starting point, speculate on the content, genre (cf. examples below) and the potential audience of *Gran Torino*. Give reasons for your ideas and refer to your previous findings.

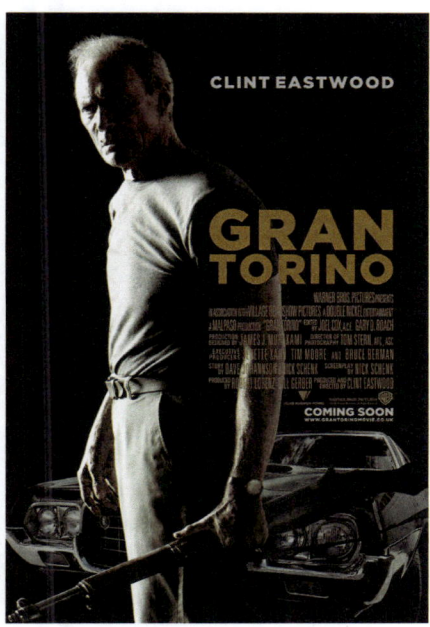

_____

_____

_____

_____

_____

_____

_____

_____

Info

Some examples of genres

action	crime	documentary	drama
• speed action • physical stunts and chases • rescues, battles, fights, escapes, destructive crises • often standard heroes and villains (good guy – bad guy)	• high speed with some mystery • action of a criminal mastermind versus the rise and fall of sinister criminals	• non-fiction • reporting on an issue of interest	• serious and plot-driven • rounded, real-life characters, settings, situations, and stories • characterized by an intense character development and interaction • vigorous human emotions
fantasy	**horror**	**romance**	**suspense/mystery**
• imaginative and fantasy themes • fairy-tale adventures or plots from Dark Ages • magic, supernatural elements	• large amount of violence in the plot • trying to awaken audience's worst fears and nightmares about the arrival of an evil force or event • often mythical creatures, such as ghosts, vampires, and zombies	• alternating tone from happy to tragic • love between two protagonists, e.g. love at first sight, forbidden love, love triangles and love requiring great sacrifices	• a person of authority, usually a detective, trying to solve a mysterious crime • clues, investigation, and logical reasoning • constant suspense created through visual cues or unusual plot twists

5   **Pair work**   → **S20:** How to listen/watch effectively

Now just listen to the trailer for *Gran Torino* twice – do not look at the images – and take notes on the following aspects. Exchange your findings, taking the film's content and genre into consideration.

Webcode WES-73652-11

- the number of speakers/their voices
- the speakers' feelings
- what is being said and done
- facts you understand
- background noise/music/other sounds
- the scenery/setting (time and place)

Language support

Talking about listening impressions

- I could hear/understand/pick up …/I could make out the words/phrases/names …
  I think I heard/I could hear the sound of …
- It sounded like/as if … because …/The voice appears to be …
  The person was screaming/whispering/mumbling …
- The voice of the speaker was/appeared to be loud/harsh/low/deep (…) due to/as/since …
- The music is loud/lively/soft/aggressive/melodious/fast/has a strong beat …
  There is instrumental/background music …/The background noise/music indicates that …
- The music creates/evokes an atmosphere/feeling of …/builds up/increases suspense.
- I imagine the setting might be …
- Perhaps there is/are …/Maybe someone is …
- I suppose something terrible/exciting/frightening/sad is happening because …
- I visualize/assume/suppose/imagine/believe that … because …

6   **Pair work**

a) Look at the following film stills and describe them (cf. Language support on p. 108).
b) Considering your previous findings with regard to the film poster, the trailer and the stills, revisit your ideas about the content and genre of *Gran Torino* and check if you need to change anything about your ideas.

PRE-VIEWING: REVISITING CINEMATOGRAPHY

In order to analyse and talk about *Gran Torino* properly you need some film specific terms and phrases. When dealing with films, camera operations and music or sound play vital roles in guiding and influencing the viewer as intended by the film maker. Before analysing specific key scenes of *Gran Torino*, have a look at the task:

7

Look at the table of the most common camera operations that are used in films. Match the functions on the right to the operations on the left.

I FIELD SIZE

Camera operations		Functions
A long shot	☐	**1** points out sth specific about sb/sth
B full shot	☐	**2** provides a complete picture of sb/sth
C medium shot	☐	**3** points out a particular detail about sb/sth
D close-up shot	☐	**4** presents the setting of the scene
E extreme close-up shot	☐	**5** provides a closer look at sb/sth

II CAMERA MOVEMENT

Camera operations		Functions
A static shot	☐	1 horizontal/vertical movement from a static position to shift focus towards or away from sb/sth
B zoom in/out	☐	2 creates the impression of following sb/sth
C panning/tilting shot	☐	3 no movement; creates a feeling of hesitation/calmness/slowness
D tracking shot	☐	4 puts focus on something or takes focus away

III CAMERA ANGLE AND POSITION

Camera operations		Functions
A overhead shot	☐	1 creates an overall impression of the scene
B high-angle shot/bird's eye	☐	2 creates a neutral impression
C eye-level shot	☐	3 makes sb/sth seem unimportant
D low-angle shot	☐	4 represents a character's perspective
E over-the-shoulder shot	☐	5 creates the impression of being involved in a conversation
F reverse-angle shot	☐	6 usually in connection with over-the-shoulder to show the other character's reaction/side
G point-of-view shot	☐	7 sets the scene that's to come
H establishing shot	☐	8 makes sb/sth look important

IV EDITING/MONTAGE

Camera operations		Functions
A fast cut	☐	1 opens/closes an action/scene slowly
B slow cut	☐	2 creates focus on sth specific or creates calm atmosphere
C fade in/fade out	☐	3 intensifies an action/moment
D cross-cut	☐	4 depicts action vividly
E slow motion	☐	5 focuses on contrast and thus creates suspense
F fast motion	☐	6 provides a comment on the action
G voice-over	☐	7 changes chronological order and therefore connects/disconnects action/moments
H flashback/flash forward	☐	8 focus on text and its meaning, gives additional information without adding voices or stressing the meaning of voices
I floating, superimposed text	☐	9 intensifies speed, creating the impression of change

Music/sound

1. **diegetic sounds:** sounds from 'the world inside the film', e.g. conversation, a window closing, footsteps
2. **non-diegetic sounds:** sounds from 'the world outside the film', e.g. film music, sounds creating suspense
3. **voice-over** (off-camera commentary): non-diegetic information by a narrator

Talking about cinematography

General phrases:

- The establishing shot of the film shows/portrays .../... is shown in a medium shot/(extreme) close-up
- ... brings the viewer closer to/creates a distance between ...
- The focus is on a ... in detail.
- The movement of ... is followed in a ... shot.
- The shots follow each other quickly/slowly.
- The viewer sees the character in .../There is a close-up of the character ...
- The scene is shot from X's point of view./... is seen from the perspective of ...
- The director uses a long shot of the setting/uses high-/low-/eye-level angel shots of ...
- The camera pans from left to right/tilts up/tilts down.

Effects of cinematography:

- ... describes characters indirectly/shows a character's emotions/draws attention to sth/describes the setting/evokes a certain atmosphere ...
- ... is presented in a low-angle shot/high-angle shot, which illustrates inferiority/vulnerability/superiority/power ...
- The point-of-view-shots make the audience experience the (emotional) perspective of ...
- The close-up is used to focus attention on .../reveals the character's feelings/makes the situation more intimate.
- ... is shown in a close-up so the viewer can see the reaction in his/her face when ...
- The over-the-shoulder shots include the viewers in the action.
- ... uses a fade-in/fade-out to ...
- The hand-held camera underlines .../gives the scene an unsteady quality/aims for authenticity.
- The light used in the scene is harsh/soft/bright/intense.
- The ... is used to focus on/draw attention to .../This ... emphasizes/stresses/indicates ...
- ... is used to build (up) suspense/tension/to create a certain effect/to convey a feeling of/to create a mood to set the scene.
- ... affects/touches the viewers.
- ... suggests/signifies that/provides a strong contrast to/serves as an insight into .../bridges two scenes

Music/sound:

- The music is upbeat/gloomy/aggressive/slow/fast-paced ...
- The rhythmic/background music contributes to the atmosphere of ...
- The effect of this scene is enhanced by the music/contributes to the mood/atmosphere of the scene.
- The music provides an extra feeling of tension/adds to the atmosphere.
- The scene is accompanied by soft/alarming/melancholic music.
- The lyrics suggest ...
- to build up suspense
- to show a certain mood/create a certain atmosphere
- to describe a character
- to foreshadow an event

8   Group work

Now you are going to watch the entire film.

- Form groups that focus on preassigned characters and take notes while watching the film.
- Continuously revise your findings in terms of character development and change.
- Be prepared to present your findings afterwards using a suitable form of visualization (e.g. graphic organizer, mind map, poster)
  - Walt Kowalski
  - Thao Vang Lor
  - Sue Lor
  - Father Janovich
  - Spider (Fong) and Smokie
  - Phong Lor (grandmother)

9   CHALLENGE   → **Workshop:** Analysing characters

Describe and analyse your character by giving a written characterization of him/her.

Language support

Talking about characters

General phrases:

- The main/principle character in the story is ...
- Another central character is ...
- ... is characterized/described/portrayed/depicted/ presented as .../proves to be ...
- As far as his/her character is concerned, it can be said that he/she is ...
- Concerning his/her character, it can be said that ... This character trait becomes apparent when ...
- ... seems to be ...
- The body language/The action reveals that ...
- His/Her statement "..." shows/proves/reveals that .../from this one can conclude that .../It is quite apparent that ...
- When saying that ... he/she reveals that he/she is/feels ...
- Proof of this can be found in/when ...
- This is an example of ...

- He/She has many positive personality traits/traits of character/characteristics.
- His/Her behaviour is marked by ....
- He/She shows ... behaviour.
- A positive/negative aspect of his/her behaviour is ...
- He/She reacts ...
- He/She gradually develops into .../In the course of the film he/she undergoes a development.
- ... remains unchanged.
- ... is/reacts/shows/seems to be/feels ...
- The motive/reason for his/her action ... is influenced by ...
- The relationship can be described as/characterized by ...

Useful linking words

giving examples	adding information	sequencing ideas	summarizing
for example for instance such as	and as well as too in addition also furthermore moreover/apart from in addition to/besides ...	the former, ..., the latter firstly, secondly, finally the first point is lastly the following last but not least	in short/in brief to summarize/to sum up in a nutshell/to put it in a nutshell to conclude/in conclusion/all in all/on the whole
giving reasons	**giving a result**	**contrasting ideas**	**comparing ideas**
due to/due to the fact that owing to/owing to the fact that because/because of since/as	therefore so/consequently this means that as a result/the result is that that is why hence thus	but/however/although/even though/despite/despite the fact that/in spite of/in spite of the fact that/nevertheless nonetheless/while/whereas	similarly equally likewise in the same way

relating information	reformulating	giving opinions	emphasizing facts
with regard to/with respect to referring to/regarding according to when it comes to	in other words to put it another way	in my/his/her opinion my opinion is I think/I believe in my view/from my point of view to my mind	in fact/obviously undoubtedly for this reason/again fortunately/unfortunately indeed

10 **CHOOSE**

Outline the plot of *Gran Torino* including the relationships between the characters by reconstructing the character map while watching the film. Draw arrows and label them. You may use different colours. Come up with different emoticons to indicate the different relationships (e.g. family = ♥, friends ☺, conflicts ☹, etc.).

OR Summarize the film *Gran Torino*. → **S1:** Checklist Summary

11 → **S16:** Checklist: Analysis of a film scene

Read the definitions of exposition and contrast on the next page. Afterwards watch the beginning of the film (00:00 – 11:25) and fill in the grid.

12

Discuss the function of using contrasts in the exposition – are there more differences or more similarities between Walt Kowalski and Thao Vang Lor's environment?

Exposition: The word exposition comes from Latin and its literal meaning is "a showing forth". It is used as a structural element for without it nothing would make sense. At the beginning of a film, a director is usually required to give a certain amount of essential information about the setting, plot, themes, atmosphere, main characters, and events like conflicts which are to come. He or she might also provide information about what has already happened. Thus, the exposition's function is to lead the viewers gently into the story.

Contrast: Contrast comes from the Latin word "contra stare", meaning to stand against. Contrasts are used to illustrate noticeable differences by bringing together dissimilar or opposing images, persons, places, or ideas to emphasize or clarify a theme, while heightening a certain feeling and creating a certain atmosphere.

	Walt Kowalski's environment	Thao Lor's environment
reason for the (family) get together		
location(s)		
family ties/family bonds		
religion – what is being said and done		
food		
people's general interactions		
atmosphere		
language(s)		
house		
some general information on and first impressions of the main characters Walt and Thao		
Walt and Thao's first encounter		
masculinity		
perception of the other		
values		

WHILE VIEWING: (UNWANTED) BIRTHDAY PRESENTS FOR WALT

Walt celebrates two birthdays on one day. Watch the *Birthday presents for Walt* scene (38:30-40:40).

13

Give short answers to the following tasks. You do not need to write complete sentences.

Task	Answer
1. State what Mitch and Karen give Walt as presents.	
2. Point out what these presents and Mitch and Karen's remarks suggest.	
3. Explain why Walt throws Mitch and Karen out of the house.	
4. Outline how Mitch and Karen feel about being thrown out.	

14 CHALLENGE → **S16:** Checklist: Analysis of a film scene

Analyse how cinematography is employed in the scene to visualise

a) Mitch and Karen putting Walt under pressure and

b) Walt's increasing irritation and anger. Use information from p. 111 ff.

15 → **S16:** Checklist: Analysis of a film scene

Re-watch Walt's second birthday party at the Lors' house (40:40-52:10) and complete the tasks a)- c).

Excerpts from the film script

SUE: Hey Walt. What are you up to?

WALT: [shows beer]

SUE: We have a barbecue. Do you wanna come over?

WALT: What do you think?

5 SUE: There is tons of food.

WALT: Yeah. Just keep your hands of my dog.

SUE: No worries. We only eat cats.

WALT: Really?

SUE: No, I'm kidding, you moron. Come on, you can be my

10 guest.

WALT: No, I'm fine right here. Son of a bitch.

SUE: Ok, so, what have you eaten today?

WALT: I had a piece of cake and a little beef turkey.

SUE: Come over and get something to eat. We got beer, too.

15 WALT: Well, I might as well drink with strangers rather than
drink alone. After all, it is my birthday.

[Walt gets up and walks with Sue towards her house.]

SUE: Really? Happy Birthday, Wally.

WALT: Don't call me Wally.

20 [Inside the Lors' house.]

WALT: What am I doing wrong? Everytime I look at somebody
they look on the ground. [...]

PHONG: [speaking enragedly in Hmong language and pointing
towards Walt]

25 WALT: What's she saying?

SUE: She said welcome to her home.

WALT: Oh, No, she's not.

SUE: Yeah, no, she didn't.

WALT: She hates me. Come on!

30 SUE: Yes, she hates you.

[A little Hmong girl walks past and Walt pats her on the
head. Everyone in the room looks in horror at Walt and starts
murmuring.]

WALT: What are you fish heads looking at anyway? [...]

35 SUE: A lot of people in this house are very traditional. Number
one, never touch a Hmong on his head, not even a child. Hmong
people believe that the soul is on the top side of the head. So,
don't do that.

WALT: It sounds dumb, but fine.

40 SUE: Yeah. A lot of Hmong people consider looking someone in
the eye very rude. That's why they look away when you look
at them.

WALT: Anything else?

SUE: Yeah, some Hmong people tend to smile and grin when

45 being yelled at. It is a cultural thing. It expresses embarrassment

a) Explain why Walt accepts Sue's invitation.

_____

_____

_____

_____

_____

_____

_____

b) Describe how Walt feels at the Lors' house
and what he learns about the Hmong rules of
conduct.

_____

_____

_____

_____

_____

_____

_____

_____

or insecurity. It's not that they're laughing or anything.

WALT: You people are nuts. [...]

SUE: Kor Khue [the Lor family shaman] is interested in you, he heard what you did. He would like to read you. It'd be rude not
50 to allow him this, it's a great honor. [...]

WALT: Yes, sure. Fine by me.

SUE: [Sue translates what the Shaman says]

Kor Khue says people do not respect you. They don't even wanna look at you. He says the way you live with your food has
55 no flavor. You're worried about your life. You made a mistake in your past life, like a mistake that you did, you're not satisfied with. He says you have no happiness in your life. It's like you are not at peace.

[Walt stands up without replying anything and looks into the
60 living room at all the Hmongs eating and carrying on. Walt sees a young woman go to each of the older folks and offer tea and cookies from a tray. He also sees a young Hmong assisting an elderly person coming down the stairs. Walt coughs hard. He wipes blood from his lips.]

65 SUE: Are you alright?

WALT: Yeah, I'm fine. I'm fine.

[Walt brushes past her and goes into the bathroom.] [In the bathroom Walt washes his face in the sink and dries his hands. He looks long and hard in the mirror.]

70 WALT [to himself]: God! I've got more in common with these goddamned gooks than my own spoiled-rotten family! Jesus Christ! Happy Birthday!

[Walt opens the bathroom door, where Sue is waiting for him]

SUE: Are you okay?

75 WALT: Yeah, yeah, I'm fine.

[...] I bit my tongue. It's nothing. Why don't we go down and get some of that good gook food? You know, I'm starving. [...]

[Walt sits amongst several old Hmong women, who take great delight in feeding him different Hmong dishes which he's
80 obviously never tasted before. Walt reacts with great enthusiasm to the food, occasionally making jokes like he's choking, etc.]

This corny stuff goes over like gangbusters with the Hmong ladies. [Sue comes in and rolls her eyes at Walt.]

16

At the start of the film, Walt was a desperately lonely and isolated old man feeling alienated by his family.

Explain his change in behaviour by

a) describing his statement "We miss mama, don't we, Daisy?"

b) giving reasons for his sense of belonging to Hmong community, shown in the statement "I've got more in common with these goddamned gooks than my own spoiled-rotten family!"

17   CHALLENGE

Read Walt's horoscope from the beginning of his birthday scenes and analyse how it foreshadows the events to come.

c) Analyse the sequence from 44:15 to 46:42. How and why does Walt's relationship to the Lor family/the Hmong community start to change?

_____

_____

_____

_____

_____

_____

_____

_____

_____

_____

_____

_____

_____

Walt's birthday horoscope:

This year you have to make a choice between two life paths. Second chances come your way. Extraordinary events culminate in what might seem to be an anti-climax. Your lucky numbers are: 84, 23, 11, 78 and 99.

A tender breeze blows

18 Pair work

a) Read the following quote by John Heitmann.
Explain its meaning and analyse how far this "life-defining moment of a symbolic act of automobility" is represented in the closing scene. Think of the mise en scène of the car itself. Take a look at the lyrics, too.

"In the closing scenes of Clint Eastwood's 2008 film 'Gran Torino' the stories of one man's personal redemption and another's dream of achieving independent manhood come together in two life defining moments: one of self-sacrifice, and the other, a symbolic act of automobility."

b) Analyse the cinematographic techniques employed in the final scene and the effects they contribute. Use p. 113.

Lyrics *Gran Torino*
[...] Gentle now
A tender breeze blows
Whispers through a Gran Torino
Whistling another tired song
5   Engines hum and bitter
Dreams grow
Heart locked in a Gran Torino
It beats a lonely rhythm all
Night long
10   These streets are old
They shine with the things
I've known
And breaks through the trees
Their sparkling
15   Your world is nothing more
Than all
The tiny things
You've left behind

Camera angle	
Field size	
Colours/lighting	
Music/songtext	

Walt and Sue – a culture clash?

19

Read the info box on the "Hmong Culture" (p. 120). Transfer the most important pieces of information into a suitable graphic organizer. Think of categories like way of living, gender roles, religion, etc.

20 Pair work

After Walt "rescues" Sue from the clutches of the black gang, Walt gives her a ride home.
Watch the scene again (36:16-38:23) and examine how Walt's mindset about the Hmong clashes with Sue's explanations (script: see p. 120 f.). In doing so:
a) Outline what Walt states about the Hmong.
b) Point out what Sue answers to clarify Walt's misconceptions.
c) Comment on Sue's reactions: Would you have acted the same way? Why or why not?
Discuss with a partner.

Hmong culture

The Hmong, meaning "free man" or "free people" in the Hmong language, are an Asian tribal ethnic group, which used to live in remote mountainous areas[1] of Southeast Asia, primarily in China, Laos, North Vietnam, and Thailand. The Hmong used to lead a farming life as communal self-supporters using slash-and-burn agriculture[2] to cultivate crops like rice, yams, potatoes, corn, and squash. However, hemp[3] and cotton have also been grown for textile production. The Hmong village community can be regarded as a vast extended family, in which everyone collaboratively supports each other. Entire Hmong villages have to relocate at times, due to shifting agriculture causing soil to loose its fertility.

There are distinct gender roles. Men go hunting or fell trees, whereas women are responsible for household chores, childcare, and some farm work. Hmong women are very good at needlework and embroidery[4]. Not only have they produced colourful clothes, but also *paj ntaub* ("flower cloth"), which not only expressed and passed on the religious beliefs of the Hmong from generation to generation but also their cultural stories. This was important because the Hmong had no written language until the 1950s and so these cloths were a means to preserve their culture. Hmong beliefs can be traced back to Taoism and Buddhism. Believing in a variety of spirits, associated with the house, nature or ancestors, most Hmong are animists[5] believing that illnesses are caused by spirits and can be healed by Hmong shamans. As shamans are capable of bridging the natural and spirit worlds, they also carry out ceremonies to renew the general protection of the household. For these spirit ceremonies, animal sacrifices (e.g. chicken, pigs) are made. It is believed that the spirit takes the soul of the sacrifice and the meat is eaten by the participating Hmong. The Hmong have now spread out through immigration worldwide including to Western countries like the U.S. Some push factors behind their immigration were their persecution in China and the Laotian civil war as well as the Vietnam War in the 1960s and 1970s. During the Vietnam War, many Hmong fought alongside the United States against the Communists. However, after the Communists took control of Laos in 1975, many Hmong were forced to flee their homeland in Southeast Asia. While adapting to new cultures, traditional beliefs, values, and norms are still maintained and practiced.

Annotations

[1] **remote areas** = areas far away from cities and places

[2] **slash-and-burn agriculture** = a method of farming that involves clearing land by destroying and burning all the trees and plants on it, farming there for a short time, and then moving on to clear a new piece of land

[3] **hemp** = a plant which is used for making rope and cloth, and also to make the drug cannabis

[4] **embroidery** = needlework, designs stitched into cloth

[5] **animists** = a person who believes that plants, objects and natural things such as the weather have a living soul

---

WALT: What's the matter with you, for Christ sake? Trying to get yourself killed? I thought you Asian girls were supposed to be smart. Hanging around in the neighborhood like that is the fast way to get you in the obituaries.

5 SUE: I know, I know. Take it easy.

WALT: And what about that goofball guy you were with. Is that a date or something?

SUE: Yeah, kind of, his name is Trey.

WALT: You shouldn't be hanging out with them. You should be

10 hanging out with your own people. The other Hummongs.

SUE: You mean, Hmong?

We're Hmong, not Hu-mung.

WALT: Whatever. What the hell is Hummong, I mean Hmong, anyway?

15 [She laughs.]

SUE: Wow, you so enlighten you know that? No, Hmong is not a place, it is a people. My people come from different parts of Laos, Thailand and China.

WALT: Well how did you end up in my neighborhood? Why didn't

20 you stay there?

SUE: It's a Vietnam thing. We fought on your side and when the Americans quit, the Communists started killing all the Hmong, so we came over here.

WALT: Yeah, well I don't know how you ended up in Midwest.

25 Snow on the ground six months over in the year. What is it? Jungle people wanted to be on great frozen tundra?

SUE: Hill people. We are hill people, not jungle people. Boo-ga, booga, boo-ga.

WALT: Yeah ... Whatever.

30 SUE: Blame the Lutherans. They brought us over here.

WALT: Everybody blames the Lutherans. Well, you'd think the cold will keep all the idiots out.

SUE: Thanks for the ride.

WALT: You know something kid, you are all right. But what about 35 that dimwit brother of yours? He is little slow or something?

SUE: Thao is actually really smart, he just doesn't know what direction to go in.

WALT: Poor Toad.

SUE: It is really common. Hmong girls over here fit in better. The 40 girls go to college and the boys go to jail.

21

During the course of the film, Walt overcomes his hostility towards the Hmong family and its community. A website names the following steps to deal with cultural clashes. Discuss how well Walt and Sue use these strategies to overcome their cultural conflict and think of more strategies they could have put into action.

Keep an open mind. Do not automatically perceive anything that is different to be "wrong". Withholding[1] judgment will allow you to be an objective observer and will facilitate the process of cross-cultural understanding. Also, if you are going to a country that you know close to nothing about, do a little background research. Keeping an open mind is necessary as you learn about the country you're going to. And who knows? You may learn to understand some things you didn't previously.

Make an effort to learn the language. This increases your communication skills and it will help you to integrate with the local community. It also demonstrates your interest in the new country.

Get acquainted with[2] the social conduct of your new environment. Do not assume or interpret behavior from your own cultural perspective or "filter". Behavior is not data. For example, Americans often use the phrase "How are you?" to mean "hello" or "I acknowledge your presence as I pass you in the hall". A foreigner may wonder why Americans don't respond in detail to this question about one's well-being. Thus they may interpret the behavior of walking away before one has a chance to respond to the question to be "uncaring", "superficial" or even "rude". An American knows otherwise and would probably not be offended that someone did not take the time to respond to this question. Remember: If in doubt, check it out!

Do not take cultural familiarity or knowledge at face-value. Even as you become savvier[3] about rituals, customs and protocol in your new environment, be careful not to attribute an explanation or rationale to what you now believe you know. A little bit of knowledge can be misleading. Psychologist Geert Hofstede wrote that 'culture' is like an onion that can be peeled, layer by layer, to reveal the content. It takes a long time to really understand a culture in its social and historical context.

Make sure you get to know people in your new environment. Respectfully ask questions, read newspapers, and attend a variety of festivals and events.

[...] Maintain a sense of humor – this is crucial! Don't be too hard on yourself if you make a cultural gaffe[4] or don't know what to do in a social situation. Laugh at yourself and others will laugh with you. Most individuals will admire your tenacity[5] and effort to understand their ways, especially if you avoid judgment and cultural comparisons that subtly and perhaps unconsciously convey a sense of superiority.

Annotations

[1] to **withhold** = to refuse to give someone something
[2] to **get acquainted** = to become more familiar with
[3] **savvy** = understanding
[4] **gaffe** = a stupid or careless mistake, for example when you say or do something that offends or upsets people
[5] **tenacity** = determination to do something , unwilling to stop trying even when the situation becomes difficult

Racism – now and then

Walt shows some examples of obvious and hidden racism towards other ethnicities.

22 Pair work

a) Before reading the text by Eduardo Bonvilla-Silva, talk to your partner about examples of racism in daily life that you either experienced yourself or that you have witnessed. How did you react? What could one do against it?

b) Read the following text about racism in former and current times by Euardo Bonvilla-Silva. Outline aspects that characterize racist mechanisms now and then using the table. Discuss in class what has changed and which practices of racism you consider more problematic. Fill in the grid.

—— Info ——

Jim Crow Laws

In the 19th century, Jim Crow was a racist theater character created by Thomas D. Rice. In the following years, it became a white expression for a stereotypical dancing and singing black person. Thus, it is also another word for "negro". At the end of the 19th century, the so-called Jim Crow laws were passed to segregate white and black people in public life. Segregation was described as the policy of keeping black and white people 'separate but equal'. In reality black and white people had very different rights; for example black people were not allowed to vote, to go to the same school as white people or to marry outside their race. These laws were finally abolished in 1965.

M.ʳ T. RICE
as
THE ORIGINAL JIM CROW

Jim-Crow racism of former times	'Colour-blind' racism ("lite racism") of current times

The New Racism
by Eduardo Bonvilla-Silva

[....] The white common sense view on racial matters is that racists are few and far between, that discrimination has all but disappeared since the 1960s, and that most whites are color blind. This view, which emerged in the 1970s, has gone viral with the election of Barack Obama as president in 2008. Whites seem to be collectively shouting, "We have a black president, so we are finally beyond race!"[...]. This new common sense is not totally without foundation (e.g., traditional racial practices and exclusion as well as Jim Crow-based racist beliefs have decreased in significance), but it is ultimately false. What has happened is that white supremacy in the United States (i.e., the racial structure of America) has changed. Today "new racism" practices have emerged that are more sophisticated and subtle than those typical of the Jim Crow era. [...] Blacks and dark-skinned racial minorities lag well behind whites in virtually every area of social life; they are about three times more likely to be poor than whites, earn about 40 percent less than whites, and have about an eighth of the net worth that whites have. They also receive an inferior education compared to whites, even when they attend integrated institutions. [....] Blacks receive impolite treatment in stores, in restaurants, and in a host of other commercial transactions. [...] How is it possible to have this tremendous degree of racial inequality in a country where most whites claim that race is no longer relevant? [...] I contend that whites have developed powerful explanations – which have ultimately become justifications – for contemporary racial inequality that exculpate[1] them from any responsibility for the status of people of color. These explanations emanate from a new racial ideology that I label color-blind racism. This ideology [...] explains contemporary racial inequality as the outcome of nonracial dynamics. Whereas Jim Crow racism explained blacks' social standing as the result of their biological and moral inferiority, color-blind racism avoids such facile arguments. Instead, whites rationalize minorities' contemporary status as the product of market dynamics, naturally occurring phenomena, and blacks' imputed[2] cultural limitations. For instance, whites can attribute Latinos' high poverty rate to a relaxed work ethic ("the Hispanics are manana, manana, manana – tomorrow, tomorrow, tomorrow") or residential segregation as the result of natural tendencies among groups ("Do a cat and a dog mix? I can't see it. You can't drink milk and scotch. Certain mixes don't mix:"). Color-blind racism became the dominant racial ideology as the mechanisms and practices for keeping blacks and other racial minorities "at the bottom of the well" changed. I have argued elsewhere that contemporary racial inequality is reproduced through "new racism" practices that are subtle, institutional, and apparently nonracial. In contrast to the Jim Crow era, where racial inequality was enforced through overt means (e.g., signs saying "No Niggers Welcomed Here" or shotgun diplomacy at the voting booth), today racial practices operate in a "now you can see, now you don't" fashion. For example, residential segregation, which is almost as high today as it was in the past, is no longer accomplished through overtly discriminatory practices. Instead, covert behaviors such as not showing all the available units, steering minorities and whites into certain neighborhoods, quoting higher rents or prices to minority applicants, or not advertising units at all are weapons of choice to maintain separate communities. In the economic field, "smiling face" discrimination ("We don't have jobs now, but please check later"), advertising job openings in mostly white networks and ethnic newspapers, and steering highly educated people of color into poorly remunerated jobs or jobs with limited opportunities for mobility are the new ways of keeping minorities in a secondary position. [...] Whether in banks, restaurants, school admissions, or housing transactions, the maintenance of white privilege is done in a way that defies[3] facile[4] racial readings. Hence, the contours of color-blind racism fit America's new racism quite well. Compared to Jim Crow racism, the ideology of color blindness seems like "racism lite". Instead of relying on name calling (niggers, spics, chinks), color-blind racism otherizes softly ("these people are human, too"); instead of viewing interracial marriage as wrong on a straight racial basis, it regards it as "problematic" because of concerns over the children, location, or the extra burden it places on couples. Yet this new ideology has become a formidable political tool for the maintenance of the racial order. Much as Jim Crow racism served as the glue for defending a brutal and overt system of racial oppression in the pre-civil rights era, color-blind racism serves today as the ideological armor for a covert and institutionalized system in the post-civil rights era. And the beauty of this new ideology is that it aids in the maintenance of white privilege without fanfare[5], without naming those who it subjects and those who it rewards. [...] Shielded by color blindness, whites can express resentment toward minorities; criticize their morality, values, and work ethic; and even claim to be the victims of "reverse racism[6]" [...].

Annotations
[1] to **exculpate** = to free sb of sth
[2] **imputed** = supposed/implied
[3] to **defy** = to challenge
[4] **facile** = effortless, easy
[5] **without fanfare** = here: without sensation
[6] **reverse racism** = whites who claim to be discriminated against

23

Having read about the differences between the more overt *Jim-Crow racism* and the more covert *new colour-blind racism*, describe Walt's racist behavior in relation to that. Point out how he expresses his racism (language; actions).

language	actions
_____	_____
_____	_____
_____	_____
_____	_____
_____	_____
_____	_____
_____	_____
_____	_____

24 Pair work

Not only Walt shows his dislike for the Hmong family. Sue's grandmother is equally hostile towards Walt. Watch the veranda scene again (11:50 – 12:20) and write a dialogue between the two in which both of them explain their point of view. Think about how such an open dialogue could change their relationship.

Walt: "Oh, Jesus ... Polarski (Walt's former neighbour) would roll over in his grave if he could see his lawn now. What the hell the chinks had to move in this neighborhood for?"

Grandma Lor: [in Hmong] "Why does that old white man stay here? All the Americans have moved out of this neighbourhood. Why haven't you gone? Why don't you strut away, you dumb rooster?"

_____

_____

_____

_____

_____

Walt Kowalski – an angry white male?

25

The idea of the Angry White Male emerged in the 1990s, promoted by several publications. Read the following informative text and compare Walt Kowalski with the image of the Angry White Male.

The Angry White Male

The idea of "The Angry White Male" came into being around the 1990s and has meanwhile taken root as a stereotype in the U.S. These men consider themselves as true, white Americans that ought to
5 be privileged due to their sex, contribution to the country, and race. In America's culturally diverse and colorful society they consider themselves to be less visible, as if they are no longer on a level playing field. Believing that America has lost its unique
10 greatness, Angry White Men are disillusioned by American politics and developments within society and feel screwed over and betrayed. They don't believe the American Constitution to be a 'living document', but rather think that it must be
15 read and implemented literally. As such they reject the unlimited power of the government, especially when it comes to economic policies that they perceive to be communist. The Angry White Man believes in the constitutional right to bear arms
20 and is ready to defend his home and country at any time, which is the reason for his possession of a weapon and his affiliation with the National Rifle Association.
Angry White Males are aware that their American
25 Dream won't come true and turn into bitter patriots believing in and following President Trump's slogans, "America First!", "American people first!", and, of course, "Make America great again!". As a result, Angry White Males have a rather
30 conservative sentiment, opposing any liberal anti-discriminatory policies and attitudes such as affirmative action or feminism. The concept of the Angry White Male is like a collective identity crisis of white males feeling betrayed and emasculated,
35 which frustrates them and makes them angry. To address that anger and to identify its causes, Angry White Males look for scapegoats and find them in people, institutions, or movements that are "different" to them.
40 Most of the Angry White Men come from once flourishing industrial core regions and economically and educationally poor backgrounds. For those affected, demographic changes like outsourcing have led to economic demise.
45 However, the phenomenon of the Angry White Male has spread and can be found within all economic backgrounds and geographic areas in America. The Angry White Male is an autonomous handyman who takes care of all situations himself.
50 In doing so, he is far more rational than emotional. Women do know about their quintessential tough manliness and either love or hate him. Although his language tends to be harsh and includes some racist expressions, he is not necessarily a racist, but
55 is very frustrated by non-American immigrants, practicing their culture without adapting to the American way of life. However, he is willing to give everybody a fair chance if they work hard, play by the rules and learn and speak English.

_____

_____

_____

_____

_____

_____

_____

26

Walt Kowalski develops during the course of the film from being a rather racist lone wolf veteran to a more or less helpful, caring and more open-minded father figure, who gives up his life for the Hmong family next door. Choose five central scenes which lead to this development and represent this progress by drawing a corresponding graph. Think about the role of Walt's contact to the Hmong family in particular.

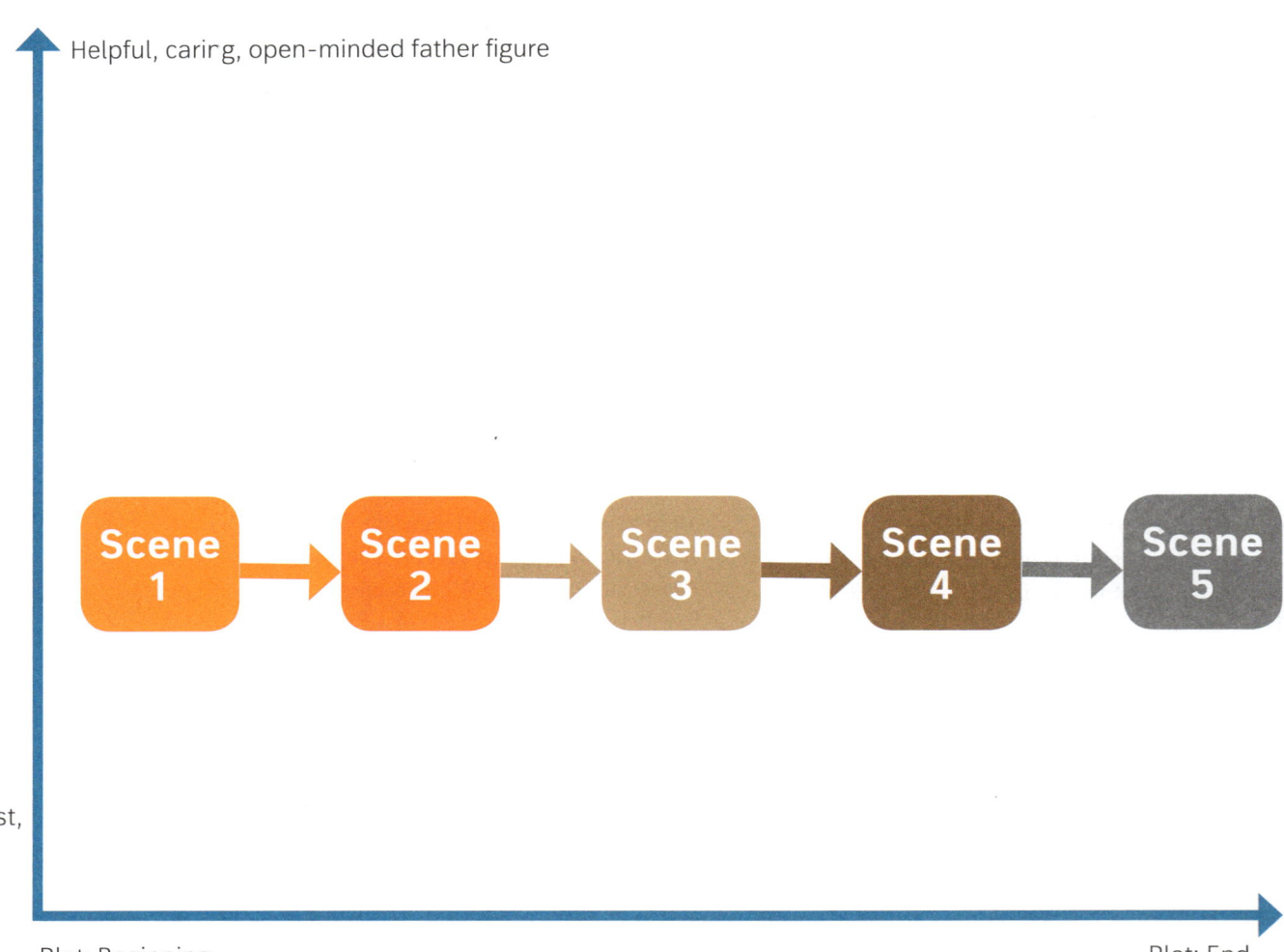

Helpful, caring, open-minded father figure

Scene 1 → Scene 2 → Scene 3 → Scene 4 → Scene 5

Racist, lone wolf

Plot: Beginning   Plot: End

POST-VIEWING: IS WALT A HERO?

Walt Kowalski seems to have many different faces: Angry white male, lone wolf, racist, father figure or a hero?

27 **Pair work**

Read the info box on what makes a hero.

a) First, on your own, state more aspects that come to your mind when thinking of a hero/heroine.

b) Compare your results with a partner and add more aspects if necessary.

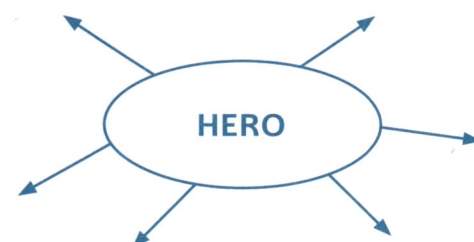

HERO

Info

What makes a hero/heroine

A **hero/heroine** can be defined as someone who has a concern for other people in need. Knowing that there is a personal risk to get hurt (physically, socially, or in terms of quality of life), a hero/heroine defends, helps or even saves these often defenseless people without any expectation of reward. His/her actions are always voluntary and intentional. Self-sacrifice is sometimes seen as the climax of a heroic act as it is highly courageous and selfless.

28 **Group work**

Watch the scene of Walt's self-sacrifice again (1:45:20 – 1:46:33).

– Describe how you feel watching Walt being shot down.

terrified | nervous | worried | frightened | threatened | sad | aggressive | tense | shocked | frustrated | upset

– Discuss in your group why Walt seeks the fatal confrontation in front of witnesses.

– Afterwards analyse in groups how cinematic techniques (camera angle and movement, sound, color and lighting) (cf. p.111) evoke these feelings. → **S16:** Checklist: Analysis of a film scene

29 CHOOSE

a) Read the following quote by Antonio Machuco:

"Walt understood that the stupidity and brutality of violence only generate more lethal and indiscriminate violence. And he understood that his actions had also contributed to the unfolding of the cycle. He then made his decision. [...] Walt clearly shows that his decision is an objective response to the objectivity of the situation: either the continuation of violence that will eventually devour[1] everybody, or – what? The sacrifice of himself, by which he puts an end to the cycle of violence. This is the only and truly radical solution to the problem. [...]"

Annotations

[1]to **devour** = to destroy

b) Discuss whether you agree or disagree with this statement. Illustrate reasons for Walt's self-sacrifice. **OR**

c) What would have happened if ...? Together with a partner, think of an alternative solution to Walt's self-sacrifice and write a letter to Walt in which you present to him an alternative to his self-sacrifice plan (e.g. calling the police, not acting at all ...)

30 **Pair work**

Whereas the definition of heroism would see Walt as a hero, in conventional Christian wisdom self-sacrifice ending in death is considered to be suicide, and suicide is considered to be an immoral act. Therefore Father Janovich would probably disagree with the statement that Walt is a hero. The website "Hollywood's Heroes" has a forum, in which the viewers of films can vote on a scale to which degree certain characters are heroes or not.

Not a Hero ◄─────────────────────────────────────► **Hero**

Do the same with Walt: Discuss with a partner where you would put Walt on this scale and write a forum entry for the website in which you justify whether or not Walt is a hero for you.

POST-VIEWING: DEALING WITH THE FILM AS A WHOLE

31

Pick one of the following topics regarding the film *Gran Torino* and prepare a 5-minute presentation. You may use a graphic organizer or cue cards, but you have to present your findings freely.

- From funeral to funeral (The film starts and ends with a funeral.)
- Daisy – from porch to porch (In what way does Daisy connect the two worlds?)
- Walt's Gran Torino – from "hidden in the garage" to "out into the open"
- Violence inevitably leading to violence
- Thao's transition from a Hmong boy to an American man
- Sue – the unfailing heroine in *Gran Torino*
- The meanings of "life" and "death" in *Gran Torino*
- The biological and the other, chosen family
- (...)

Language support

Giving a presentation		
Introduction	**Body**	**Conclusion**
• I will begin by describing/ explaining ... and continue with ... Finally, I will ... • I'm going to take a look at/ examine ... • My topic today is ... • My presentation is concerned with ... • The issues I want to mention/ discuss ... • This presentation focuses on the issue of ... • There are a number of things to consider when looking at the issue of ... • Have you ever thought/been in a situation where ... • You are certainly aware .../ As you know ... • I shall be looking at the following areas ...	• Firstly .../Secondly .../Thirdly ... Finally ... • First of all, I will ... and then I will go on to ... Then/Next .../Finally/ Lastly ... • To begin with I'd like to say a few things about ... • An important point to consider is ... • In addition • Now I'd like to look at ... • Let's consider this in more detail ... • The significance of this is ... • This leads me to my next point ... • Turning our attention now to ... • For example ... • A good example of this is ... • As an illustration, ... • To give you an example ... • To illustrate this point ... • Simply put/In other words ... • So, what I am saying is ...	• So, what we have learned today is .../To summarize, the most important points are ... • So, we have covered ... I would like to recap ... • I think it is fair to say ... • I'd like to stress/highlight/ emphasize the following points ... • Does anyone have any questions? • I am happy to answer any queries/questions ... • If you would like me to elaborate on any point, please ask.

32   CHALLENGE   → **S9:** How to structure a text   → **S8:** How to improve your text

Pick one of the topics from above and compose and write an expository essay. Your essay should be at least five paragraphs long including an introduction, a body with topic sentences and a conclusion.

33

After having dealt with Clint Eastwood's *Gran Torino* in detail, write a film review for an online audience. Use the following guidelines to structure your text.

How to write a film review

A film review offers information on a film. It is usually a recommendation for a film or informs its readers why it might not be worth watching.

– Start with a catchy introduction in which you give essential information about the film (title, director, genre, release date, actors, characters, setting and plot).
– Then, give a brief summary of what the film is about, but avoid spoilers.
– Afterwards, state your personal impression of the film.
– Finally, point out the purpose of the film and come up with a convincing conclusion as to why the reader should or should not watch the film.

Language support

Writing a film review	
Useful phrases: • The film "…" is a drama/action film/thriller/… • The film was directed/produced by … and released in … • The film was well-directed by … • Starring … (actor's name) • The main character is played by … • … is absolutely remarkable as … • The acting is remarkable/convincing/too melodramatic/… • The film won/The film was awarded …	**Characters/plot:** • The main character is called … • The story is about/deals with/focuses on … • The film tells the story of … • The film opens/begins with … • As the story continues/unfolds/develops … • The plot is multi-dimensional/complicated/thrilling captivating/arouses curiosity/is full of tension … • The plot hast a surprising twist./ The plot is incoherent/mediocre/appalling. • One of the best moments in the film is when … • It's a non-linear/fragmented narrative. • The characters give an exceptional performance when … • The characters are believable/shallow/ unconvincing.
Setting: • It is set in … • The story takes place in/unfolds in … • The film begins in … • The film creates a … atmosphere/mood …	**Cinematography:** • The camera work is impressive/spectacular./ unrealistic/confusing. • The camera operations draw attention to … • The special effects are stunning/impressive/poor/ amateur. • The music is profound/clichéd/conveys a … atmosphere. • The music underlines emotions/connects scenes …

Opinion
• I believe …
• He/She does a very good job as …
• I (highly/strongly/definitely) recommend/don't recommend this film because …
• A 'must-see'!/A box-office succes/failure!/Don't miss it!
• A very impressive portrayal of …
• On a scale of 1-10, I give this film a …
• The best/worst thing is …
• If you like … this film is for you.
• The film is a worthwhile watch./I'm afraid the film is a complete waste of time and money. Only watch this film if you have plenty of time to spare.
• … is well worth seeing/not to be missed/a truly great piece of filmmaking.
• The film is exciting/moving/realistic/over-complicated/confusing/far-fetched.
• The film is thought-provoking/touching/moving.

Violence: gang culture

Gangs have contributed to Detroit's decline and high crime rate. In the following tasks, you will deal with gang culture.

1 → **S20: How to listen/watch effectively**
Watch the first minute of the YouTube documentary on gangs in Detroit. **Webcode** WES-73652-12
Exchange your first impressions with a partner:
- How did you feel while watching this clip?
- What do you think it is like to live in gang-controlled areas of Detroit?
- Can you think of similar problems in any German city?

GANGS

Gangs are a society within the society, making them a subculture to the dominant cultural society. Its members live in and follow an alternative belief and value system, which dictates acceptable and unacceptable behaviour.
5 Although each gang has a name and a culture of its own, they show common structures. A gang is a group of people who have adopted a group identity based upon race, ethnicity, territory, or money-making activities. A member of a gang is referred to as a "gangster", "gang
10 banger", or "thug". Gangsters share a common group name, symbols (e.g. tattoos), gang-related clothing style (e.g. hats, bandanas, scarves of certain colors), and signs (e.g. graffiti). They have their own verbal (e.g. jargon) or non-verbal language (e.g. greeting rituals), customs
15 and rules, and are linked to specific territories (e.g. cities, neighbourhoods, parks), which they control and defend against other rival gangs. They often make money through illegal activities within their claimed territory. Gangs are internally organized and have a hierarchy
20 and members have specific roles (e.g. leader, respected original gangsters, look-outs, recruiter, dealer). Any violation of gang conduct may lead to varying degrees of sanctions. Disloyalty usually ends in death, which means that walking out on gangs is practically impossible. The
25 features of gang culture are passed on from generation to generation leading to their growth and maintenance. Gangs tend to recruit new members by offering them the benefits of being in a gang like a sense of belonging and ownership of an area, social deviation from society,
30 the image of tough manliness, prestige status, physical protection by numbers, excitement, and autonomy. Often family conflicts in problematic homes, poverty, academic failure, the availability of drugs and weapons, links to current gang members or a lack of belonging to
35 a greater community drive potential novices towards gangs. An additional reason might be glorified gangster rap music by artists such as Ice T or 2Pac, who publically and successfully promote gang values, attitudes and behaviour. To become a gang member, new aspirants
40 usually have to complete initiation rites to prove their worthiness, which is often violent crimes that can include theft, murder, gang rape, or drive-by shootings. However, gang life includes high-risk issues: Withdrawal from family and friends, drug-taking, unending exposure
45 to threats and offences, the permanent risk of arrest, a loss of opportunities, and the danger of injury or even death. Gangs cause significant problems in the US due to vandalism, dangerous conflicts between rival gangs, drug and weapon crimes and drive-by shootings.

2

Look at the pictures, read the info text on gangs and try to describe what makes a gang. Discuss with a partner why people might want to be part of a gang. Think of these aspects.

Features of gang culture

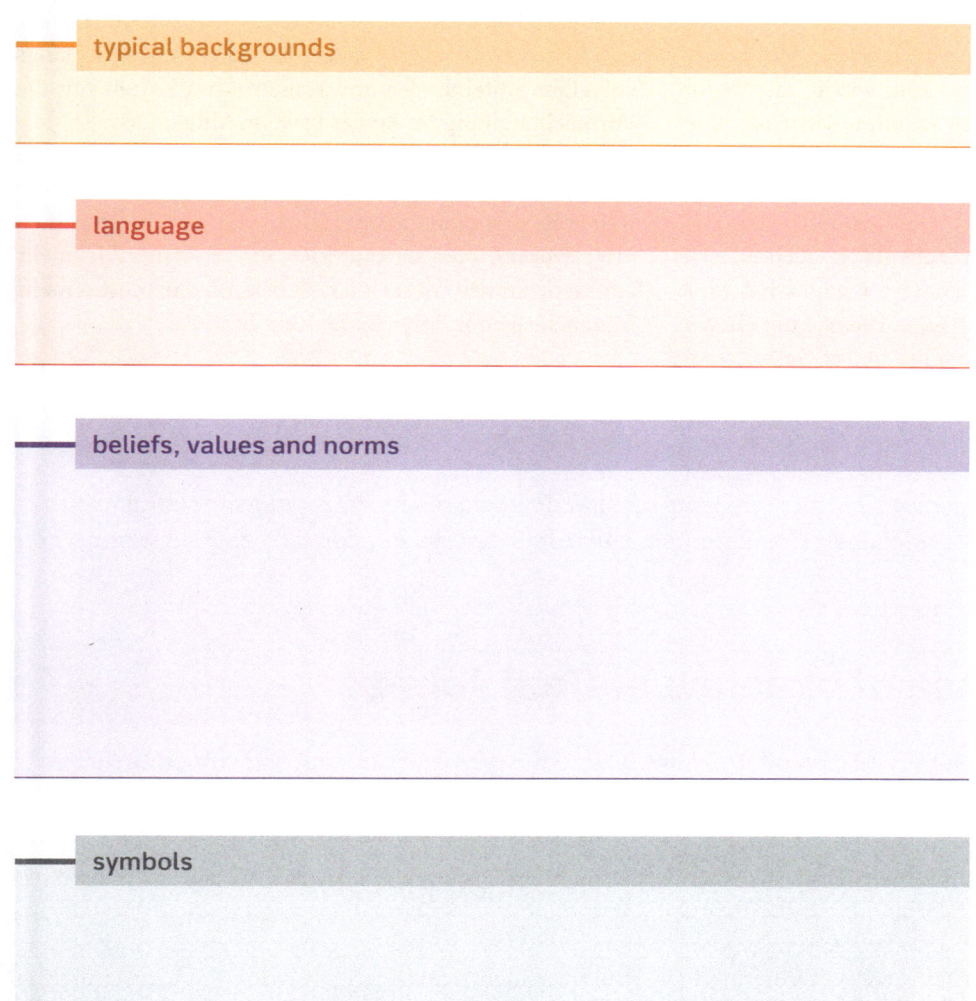

typical backgrounds

language

beliefs, values and norms

symbols

Mediation

3 → **Workshop:** Mediation → **S19:** How to improve your mediation skills

An American friend of yours is currently working on a paper about street gangs. She has heard about the German street gang "Black Jackets" and wants to know what makes young people join them. Having found the following article, you answer your friend's question in an e-mail.

Die Gang als Familienersatz
von Matthias Korfmann

Was bietet die Gang den Jugendlichen?

Reich: Sie ist eine Art Ersatz-Familie. Junge Menschen wünschen sich eine Familie, Geborgenheit, Zugehörigkeit und feste Regeln, die orientierend sind. Bei den Black
5 Jackets bekommen sie das, was sie sich wünschen. Sie sind Teil einer Gruppe, sie müssen Autorität akzeptieren, sie müssen zuverlässig sein und können sich auf andere verlassen. Das ist die Erfüllung jugend-typischer, essenzieller Bedürfnisse. Nur leider ist es in diesem Fall keine
10 gute Ersatzfamilie, sondern eine, die Straftaten verübt.
Welche Werte werden in dieser Gruppe besonders geschätzt?
Reich: Es geht immer um Respekt und Ehre. Damit machen sie es sich sehr leicht, denn im Namen der Ehre ist ja quasi alles legitim. Mit Ehre ließe sich sogar ein
15 Mord begründen. Und der Respekt ist genauso wichtig.

Die meisten jungen Menschen schaffen es, sich über Leistung Respekt zu verschaffen. Wenn einer aber benachteiligt ist oder sich so fühlt, dann ist das nicht so leicht. Der versucht vielleicht, sich durch Gewalt und
20 durch die Zugehörigkeit zu einer starken Gruppe Respekt zu verschaffen.

Wie alt sind die Mitglieder?

Reich: Das geht im Jugendalter von 14 oder 15 Jahren los. Die meisten steigen aus der Gang wieder aus, bevor
25 sie erwachsen sind. Aber einige schaffen den Absprung nicht und machen weiter. Wenn dann noch harte Drogen dazukommen, wird es richtig ernst. Je älter die Mitglieder, desto schwerer der Ausstieg. Das kann verheerend enden. Ich betreue im Maßregelvollzug auch solche
30 jungen Männer. Stellen Sie sich vor, jemand hat eine hohe Position in der Gang erreicht. Das ist ungeheuer faszinierend für jemanden, der sonst in der Gesellschaft zu den Benachteiligten zählt. Nur in diesem System, nur in einer solchen Gang hat dieser Mensch Macht. Also
35 versucht er, dieses Regelwerk wenn möglich auch im Maßregelvollzug durchzusetzen. Es ist ungemein schwer, so etwas noch zu korrigieren.

Sind Straßengangs wie die Black Jackets eine Gefahr?

Reich: Sicher. Aber nicht so sehr für normale Bürger
40 und Unbeteiligte. Oft streiten die verschiedenen Gangs vor allem miteinander und tragen ihren Kampf um die Vormachtstellung im Revier bzw. im Milieu aus.

Was kann man tun? Sollten sich Streetworker um diese Jugendlichen kümmern?

45 **Reich**: Es gibt einen alten Spruch: Gib der Gruppe einen Streetworker, und sie hält sich um so länger. Je mehr Aufmerksamkeit diese Gangs bekommen, desto mehr fühlen sie sich in ihrer Bedeutung bestätigt.

4

After you have gained some general insights into gang culture, do some research on gangs in Detroit. You can also watch the documentary (cf. task 1) and prepare a two-minute presentation (cf. Language support on p. 128).

The omnipresence of violence in *Gran Torino*

During the film, violence is omnipresent on different levels. Use the provided material and complete the following tasks.

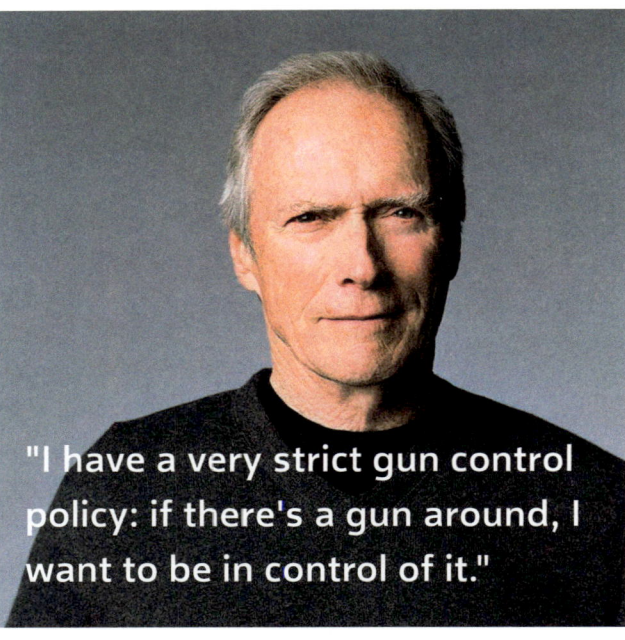

"I have a very strict gun control policy: if there's a gun around, I want to be in control of it."

Info

Civilian gun ownership in the US

The Second Amendment to the United States Constitution gives each person in the US the right to keep and bear arms. Thus, civilian gun ownership is almost three times higher in the US compared to Germany. In the US, there are 89 guns per 100 people, whereas in Germany there are only 30 guns per 100 people. Gun control is a highly debated topic in the US – especially between Democrats (as opponents) and Republicans (as proponents). However, school shootings and a high amount of armed conflicts increasingly lead people to demand a stricter gun control policy.

5

Read Clint Eastwood's quote about gun control policy. State what you think about his statement.

6

While doing some research on gun control in the US, you came across the following web discussion. Read the opinions.

We need gun control. We have way too many guns on our streets, in our homes, and in our schools. How can we feel safe? Something needs to change to stop the spread of these deadly weapons. Otherwise, it will be too late to make a change at all. This is obvious to me.

Mostly good. Honestly, I think there is not just one answer to this question. Of course, I think gun control is great if it ends all the violence, especially school shootings. However, people argue that it is taking away an important right from us which could be problematic.

No, gun control is bad. In my opinion, gun control does more harm than good. It keeps law abiding citizens from owning a gun and using it for things such as hunting or self protection. It's these good people's constitutional right to do that. Why would we take it away? Criminals will obtain guns regardless of any gun control.

Mediation

7 → **Workshop:** Mediation → **S19:** How to improve your mediation skills

Additionally, you found a German article on gun violence in the US. Mediate this article to write another "yes" entry for the website.

In der Schule, an der Uni – 21 Tote in 45 Tagen
Von Silke Fokken Fabian Melker/DER SPIEGEL

Ein 19-Jähriger feuert in Florida auf Schüler und Lehrer. 17 Menschen sterben. Es ist das 18. „School Shooting" in den USA in diesem Jahr – und das mit der höchsten Opferzahl.

5 Nach dem tödlichen Angriff auf eine Schule in Parkland, Florida, herrscht in den USA Entsetzen – nicht nur, weil ein 19-jähriger Ex-Schüler 17 Menschen erschossen hat. Sondern auch, weil sich Fälle dieser Art an Schulen in den USA häufen. Als Nikolas Cruz in Parkland um sich
10 schoss, war das Jahr 2018 gerade einmal 45 Tage alt. In diesen knapp sieben Wochen gab es – die Tat in Parkland inbegriffen – 18 „School Shootings" in den USA, wie die „Washington Post" unter Berufung auf „Everytown for Gun Safety" berichtet. Die Organisation setzt sich für strengere
15 Waffengesetze ein. Diese Zählung umfasst auch Unfälle mit Schusswaffen, bei denen sich versehentlich Schüsse lösten. In der Liste tauchen außerdem Fälle auf, in denen Universitäten Tatorte waren, sowie Angriffe mit Schusswaffen, bei denen niemand verletzt wurde.
20 **US-Bundesstaat Florida: Schüsse an der Marjory Stoneman Douglas High School**
Doch selbst wenn man nur die Vorfälle zählt, bei denen Menschen verletzt oder getötet wurden, weist die Statistik für dieses Jahr im Schnitt immer noch jede Woche mehr
25 als einen Vorfall mit Schusswaffen an Schulen oder Universitäten in den USA auf. Inklusive der Toten von Parkland starben laut „Everytown for Gun Safety" und „Gun Violence Archive" an US-Schulen oder Universitäten seit Jahresbeginn 21 Menschen durch Schüsse anderer
30 Personen. Sechs Beispiele:

22. Januar, Gentilly, Louisiana: Aus einem Pick up-Truck feuerte ein Unbekannter auf Schüler der NET Charter High School. Ein 14-Jähriger wird laut „Everytown" verletzt. Die Polizei nimmt später zwei weitere Schüler fest, von denen
35 einer Schmauchspuren an den Händen hatte. Der andere trug Munition bei sich.
22. Januar, Italy, Texas: Ein 16-Jähriger feuert in der Mensa der Italy High School Schüsse ab, wie „Time" berichtet. Dabei verletzt er ein 15-jähriges Mädchen, das
40 ins Krankenhaus gebracht wird. Als er auf einen weiteren Schüler schießen will, wird er gestoppt. Die Polizei nimmt den Jungen fest.
23. Januar, Benton, Kentucky: Ein 15-jähriger Schüler stürmt mit einer Waffe an die Marshall County High School
45 und schießt um sich, wie der Guardian berichtet. Ein 15-jähriges Mädchen stirbt noch in der Schule. Eine zweite 15-Jährige erliegt ihren Verletzungen im Krankenhaus. 17 Menschen werden verletzt, die meisten durch Kugeln, andere im Gedränge. Der Schütze wird festgenommen.
50 **31. Januar, Philadelphia, Pennsylvania:** Auf dem Parkplatz der Abraham Lincoln High School fallen Schüsse. Ein 32-Jähriger wird zweimal ins Bein getroffen und erliegt später im Krankenhaus seinen Verletzungen, wie der Sender ABC berichtet.
55 **1. Februar, Los Angeles, Kalifornien:** Eine 12-Jährige bringt eine Waffe mit in die Salvador Castro Middle School. Wohl ohne Absicht löst sich ein Schuss. Die Kugel verletzt einen 15-Jährigen lebensgefährlich am Kopf, vier weitere Personen erleiden Verletzungen.
60 **5. Februar, Oxon Hill, Maryland:** Ein 17-Jähriger wird an der Oxon Hill High School von zwei Schüssen in

die Brust getroffen. Die Polizei nimmt seine 17-jährige Ex-Freundin und einen 18-Jährigen fest. Sie vermutet, dass die beiden räuberische Absichten hatten. Das
65 Opfer überlebt. Die Folgen der Schusswaffenvorfälle an Schulen sind nicht immer so gravierend wie in Parkland. Aber die Taten häufen sich seit Jahren. Seit 2013 zählte „Everytown for Gun Safety" 290 „School Shootings". Über viele der Vorfälle wird wegen dieser Häufung kaum
70 mehr berichtet. Kritiker fürchten, dass ein gefährlicher Gewöhnungs- und Abstumpfungseffekt einsetzt: „Werden diese Massenerschießungen jetzt zur Routine? Sagen wir jetzt jedes Mal danach ‚genug ist genug', und dann geht es einfach so weiter?", empörte sich etwa Bill Nelson,
75 Senator der Demokraten aus Florida, nach der Tat in Parkland. Dazu kommt, dass nach quasi jedem größeren Vorfall eine wie ritualisiert geführte Debatte einsetzt: Kritiker fordern eine Verschärfung der Waffengesetze in den USA, ihre Gegner lehnen dies ab – so geht das seit
80 Jahren. Die Amerikaner sind seit Jahrzehnten gespalten in der Frage, ob ihr vergleichsweise laxes Waffenrecht strenger werden soll.

„Schwieriger, ein Bier zu bekommen als eine solche Waffe"
85 Nicht zuletzt US-Präsident Donald Trump verteidigt den freien Besitz von Waffen, flankiert von einer starken Waffenlobby im Land, allen voran die National Rifle Association (NRA). Der Kongress hatte auch nach dem Massaker 2012 in Newtown, Connecticut, die
90 Waffengesetze in den USA nicht verschärft. Damals starben an der Sandy Hook Grundschule 20 Kinder und sechs Lehrer; der Amokläufer hatte zuvor bereits seine Mutter erschossen. Nach der Tat beging er Suizid. Nach Informationen der Nachrichtenagentur AP hatte
95 der 19-jährige Schütze in Florida die Tatwaffe, eine AR-15, vor einem Jahr legal gekauft. Solche Waffen sind ab einem Alter von 18 Jahren erhältlich. Der Rechtsprofessor Richard W. Painter sagte: „Für einen 19-Jährigen in Florida ist es wahrscheinlich schwieriger, ein Bier zu bekommen
100 als eine solche Waffe." Nach jüngsten Berechnungen der „New York Times" stellen Amerikaner etwa 4,4 Prozent der Weltbevölkerung, ihnen gehören inzwischen aber 42 Prozent aller Schusswaffen auf der Erde. Die hohe Zahl von Waffen im ganzen Land und ihre ständige
105 Verfügbarkeit lässt die Zahl der Attacken nach Ansicht von Kritikern immer weiter ansteigen. Statistiken untermauern diese Vermutung. 2017 erreichte die Waffengewalt in den USA ein besonderes Ausmaß. Fast 16.000 Menschen starben durch Schusswaffen, rund doppelt so viele
110 wurden verletzt.

8

Read through some more arguments against gun control.

Gun control doesn't stop bad people from having guns. It just stops good citizens from using them to defend themselves, their family and fellow citizens.

Gun control does not stop criminals from having guns, but it does leave good people defenseless. Do you really think someone who wants to shoot people will have a problem with stealing a gun? However, gun control will leave good people without a chance to defend themselves or their fellow citizens.

Two banks, no guards, tons of money. Imagine: You are a criminal and you want to rob a bank with a gun - which bank would you rob? The bank with armed, trained, and committed citizens that are ready to defend themselves and others? Or the one with unarmed citizens who have only seen guns in movies? If someone decided to rob the "unarmed bank", there would be tons of dead, innocent people. If someone decided to rob the "armed bank", the shooter would be dead or disabled after maybe 1, or 2, shots! There would maybe be 3 casualties, max. If you were a "bad guy", would you pull out your gun in a police station or in a "no gun zone"?

Jack B.

It makes us unsafe.

No, there's nothing good about gun control. It makes us less safe. Throughout history, many governments have turned on their own people. Some have even killed them in the name of societal good. We need to be able to fight back. We will not be better off with gun control. Gun control does not prevent gun crime. It just takes away people's ability to defend themselves. Gun bans already exist and do not work. Banning weapons makes good people easy targets for criminals. It does not make a difference. Criminals will always figure out a way to get a gun. Even without a firearm, they will always commit crimes (only with other weapons). Also, bombs and resultant fires have caused way more deaths than guns. Gun control does not work. If the founding fathers of the U.S. knew the country was giving up their protection, they would turn over in their graves.

Melissa B.

9

After another school shooting in New York, the morning show "Wake up, New York" initiates an open discussion about gun control. In addition to the host of the show, the following people are invited:

- Tom Herford, Republican and defender of the Second Amendment
- Ivanka Trump, Republican and daughter of former US President Donald Trump, defender of the Second Amendment
- Michelle Obama, Democrat and former First Lady, pleads for stricter gun control
- Gerald Smith, police officer, experienced three school shootings, pleads for stricter gun control
- Caroline Geiger, victim of an armed robbery, suffers from severe post-traumatic stress disorder, pleads for stricter gun control
- Adam Kowalski, archer, defender of the Second Amendment

In class, assign the different roles and think of at least three arguments you want to share during the discussion. The rest of the class will represent the audience, who can also participate in the discussion. Think about different arguments for both sides. You could think about the following guiding questions: Do you think it is reasonable to own a gun for self-defense? Is vigilantism[1] legitimate? What is the situation like in Germany? [1] **vigilantism** = lawless spirit

10 → **S9:** How to structure a text → **S8:** How to improve your text

An American friend of yours who lives in Detroit wonders whether gang conflicts are also a problem in Germany. Not knowing about that issue yourself, you have researched on the Internet and come across the following newspaper article. Write an e-mail to your friend in which you describe the German gang issues presented in the article.

Bandenkrieg im Kölner Rockermilieu: „Hier wird wie im Wilden Westen rumgeballert"

In Köln eskaliert ein Streit im Rockermilieu, Bandidos und Hells Angels bekämpfen sich mit Schusswaffen teils auf offener Straße. Kölns Polizeipräsident spricht von Wildwest – und will durchgreifen. Auseinandersetzungen 5 zwischen Rockerbanden gefährden nach Einschätzung der Polizei derzeit die öffentliche Sicherheit in Köln. „Mitten auf Kölner Straßen wird mit hochkarätigen Waffen geschossen", sagte Polizeipräsident Uwe Jacob am Mittwoch. „Als wären wir hier im Wilden Westen 10 wird hier rumgeballert." Auf Außenstehende werde bei den Schießereien keine Rücksicht genommen. Es sei ein „glücklicher Zufall, dass bisher noch niemand zu Tode gekommen" sei, sagte Klaus-Stephan Becker, Leiter Direktion Kriminalität. Zuletzt war es in Köln immer 15 wieder zu Auseinandersetzungen auf offener Straße gekommen. Es gehe dabei um einen sich immer weiter aufschaukelnden Konflikt zwischen Bandidos und Hells Angels. Dies seien keine Rocker im eigentlichen Sinne, sondern kriminelle Banden, die handfeste wirtschaftliche 20 Interessen verfolgten. Die Banden seien „von Migranten deutlich dominiert". Die Mitglieder stammten zum Teil aus der Türkei, aus dem Kosovo und Nordafrika.

Kölner Polizei will härter gegen Rocker vorgehen

25 Künftig will die Kölner Polizei härter gegen die rivalisierende Rockerbanden vorgehen. Am Mittwoch habe es bereits erste Durchsuchungen gegeben, sagte Polizeipräsident Jacob. Zudem werde man verstärkt kontrollieren. Es würden Zivilfahnder und 30 erfahrene Ermittler aus dem Bereich der organisierten Kriminalität eingesetzt. Ein wichtiger Punkt sei auch die Finanzermittlung. Dabei gehe es etwa um die Gelder und teuren Autos der Bandenmitglieder. „Wir werden sehr robust gegen diese Vereinigungen vorgehen", versprach 35 Jacob. „Wir werden es nicht dulden, dass es in Köln so weitergeht wie bisher."

_____

_____

_____

_____

_____

Gang culture in film

11

In *Gran Torino*, the audience is confronted with three different gangs. On page 131, you defined some features of gang culture (typical backgrounds, language, beliefs, values and norms, symbols). Watch the following scenes of *Gran Torino* again and describe the gangs in the film with regard to these categories. Compare your results with the theoretical features identified earlier.
(Scenes: 13:13 – 18:08; 24:26 – 25:36; 31:48- 33:33; 1:20:26-1:21:34)

Features of Gang culture

typical backgrounds

language

beliefs, values and norms

symbols

12

Although Thao's cousin puts him under so much pressure (he even hurts him with a cigarette), Thao does not want to be part of his gang. Explain Thao's position against the setting of your knowledge about why gangs hold such an attraction for young people.

13 CHALLENGE

Assess why his cousin might think that Thao is the ideal victim for a gang.

14

In contrast to Thao, Sue's boyfriend desperately wants to be part of the black gang. Analyse the scene transcript and illustrate how Trey tries to "fit in" language-wise and how the black gang shows that Trey cannot be accepted.

[Sue walks with her ridiculous Wigger (urban white kid) boyfriend, TREY. Trey wears big baggy pants, a sports jersey and an Oakland Raiders visor upside-down and backwards.
5 They walk past three BLACK GUYS leaning against a building. The TALL BLACK GUY spots Sue and smiles.]

TALL BLACK GUY: Hey, girl, you come over here and talk to me. Come on, baby, don't be shy.
[Trey and Sue move as far over on the sidewalk as they can
10 to avoid the black guys. They try to ignore them.]

TALL BLACK GUY: Come on, sweetie, don't be like that. You talk to me, don't be all stuck up and shit.

[ACROSS THE STREET
Walt waits at a stoplight. He watches Sue and Trey and
15 the three black guys who block their path.
One black guy flips Trey's VISOR onto the ground. The Tall Guy makes "kissy faces" at Sue as he touches his crotch.
Walt sits there for a second; he shouldn't help, but Walt
20 solves every situation by being aggressive.
Walt drives off, then makes a U-turn.
The Tall Black Guy now focuses on Trey.]

TALL BLACK GUY: What are you 'sposed to be?
[Trey puts up his hand to "hi-five." The Tall Black Guy
25 just looks at him.]

TREY: Yo, it's cool, dog.

TALL BLACK GUY: What the fuck are you doing in my neighborhood, boy?

TREY: Nothing. We're going to Red Roost
30 to get some CDs. That place is trippin', bro.

TALL BLACK GUY: What you call me, you fucking with me, bitch? You think you're funny?

TREY: Nothing. No.

TALL BLACK GUY: I'm warning you, boy. What you
35 all come up in here for? You here to bring me this present?

TREY: Huh?

TALL BLACK GUY: This Oriental yummy for me? Don't worry, I'll take good care of her.

The word "boy"

The word "boy" has a particular meaning for black people, resulting from the history of slavery. In the days of slavery, white masters would refer to black enslaved people as "boy" in order to stress their inferiority. Thus it is a strong sign of disrespect in black communities to refer to someone as "boy"

15

Throughout the film a spiral of violence between Walt and the Hmong gang becomes evident. Take a look at the theoretical spiral of violence on the left. Relate it to the key events that finally led to Walt being shot by the Hmong gang and fill out the spiral of violence on the right.

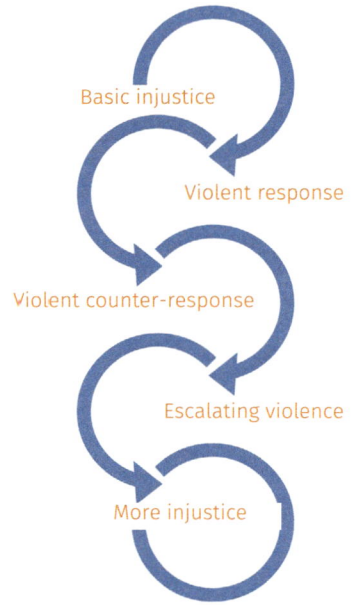

Basic injustice

Violent response

Violent counter-response

Escalating violence

More injustice

16

Discuss Walt's behavior towards the Hmong gang. Do you think it is legitimate to meet force with force or can you think of other options to solve such a conflict?

17   CHALLENGE

Illustrate one central event in the spiral of violence and write an alternative, non-violent screen-play script. How would this have influenced the actions to follow?

Info

Writing an alternative script

Script
– Write the screenplay based on fact and plausible deductions, asking yourself several questions:
   Who? What? When? Where? Why?
– Indicate the setting, camera operations, stage directions, requisites and write the dialogue

Dialogue
– The dialogue should seem authentic to the reader/viewer
– Write the dialogue according to the characters' language and tone as known from the materials

_____

_____

_____

_____

18 CHALLENGE
Father Janovich's recruitment – Does religion use strategies similar to gang recruitment? Write down your thoughts.

_____

_____

_____

_____

_____

_____

19
Father Janovich and Walt meet six times during the plot of the film.
a) Briefly summarize each scene and state the reasons for their encounters.

_____

_____

_____

_____

_____

_____

b) Examine how Father Janovich tries to get Walt to confess.

_____

_____

_____

_____

c) Compare the encounters with gang recruitment (cf. Gang Culture). Use the table on the following page.

_____

_____

_____

_____

Topic **Ethnic and cultural diversity:** Gran Torino

	scene summary and reason for encounter	Father Janovich: strategies	comparison with gang recruitment
#1 (07.25–08.20)			
#2 (11.55–12.40)			
#3 (17.30–20.02)			
#4 (27.38–29.43)			
#5 (1.26.30–1.29.40)			
#6 (1.32.35–1.34.37)			

	scene summary and reason for encounter	Father Janovich: strategies	comparison with gang recruitment

Pre-reading

1

Hamlet is one of William Shakespeare's later tragedies, written around 1600-1602. It is set at the Danish royal court.

To get some ideas about the setting and atmosphere of the play, carefully study the photos below. Then choose the adjectives or expressions from the box that best describe the atmosphere the photos convey. Give reasons.

> cold | spooky | vast | remote | fortified | belligerent | grand | on the brink of war | gloomy | depressing | wintry

2

As you have gained some insight into the setting, find out about the characters in *Hamlet*.

a) Read the short descriptions of the characters below and on page 142. Then start a character map in which you show the relationships between them. Add additional information to your map while you read the play.

Hamlet

the son of the late king Hamlet and the nephew of the present king; a student at the University of Wittenberg

Claudius

King of Denmark and brother of the former king. He has killed his brother.

Gertrude

Queen of Denmark, Claudius' wife and Hamlet's mother; after the death of her first husband, the former king, she recently married his brother

Polonius

Claudius' counsellor, father of Ophelia and Laertes

Ophelia

Hamlet's true love, Polonius' daughter. She drowns later on in the play.

Laertes

Polonius' son and Ophelia's brother, a student in France

Horatio	Fortinbras
Hamlet's best friend and fellow student at Wittenberg Un versity	the young Prince of Norway, whose father (also called Fortinbras) was killed by Hamlet's father (also called Hamlet)

The Ghost	Rosencrantz and Guildenstern
An other-worldly presence who has taken on the form of old King Hamlet. He tells Hamlet that his father was murdered by Claudius and he should avenge him.	two of Hamlet's former friends from Wittenberg, summoned by Claudius and Gertrude to find out about the reasons for Hamlet's melancholy

Voltemand and Cornelius	Marcellus and Bernardo
Danish ambassadors who are sent to Norway to negotiate peace	Danish military officers and casual friends of Hamlet who first see the ghost walking the ramparts of Elsinore Castle

Francisco	Reynaldo
a soldier and guardsman	Polonius' servant who is sent to France by his master to spy on Laertes

Players	Osric
a group of actors who come to Elsinore to perform a play partially written by Hamlet	a foolish courtier who, on Claudius' order, summons Hamlet to take part in a duel with Laertes

Two clowns
gravediggers who discuss various issues while digging a grave

b) Having caught a first glimpse at the characters involved, outline what you expect from the play.

Language support

I expect the play to be full of intrigue/corruption/revenge/…
I think that … will try to plot against …/avenge …/commit murder/…
From what I have read, I assume the play will be fast-paced/action-packed/a romance/…

3

There is no evidence to be found in Shakespeare's biography that he ever visited Denmark. So where did he get his idea of a Danish prince avenging his father's death from?

a) Watch an extract from a video and tick the correct answers. Before watching the extract (00:00–02:00), read the questions carefully. **Webcode** WES-73652-13

1   Where does the recording take place?
   ☐ in Denmark
   ☐ in a London loft
   ☐ at the Danish Embassy in London

2   Why did Shakespeare choose Kronborg Castle for the setting of Elsinore in *Hamlet*?
   ☐ He liked the castle very much.
   ☐ There are a lot of explanations for it.
   ☐ He read about it.

3 When did a troupe of English actors come to Kronborg Castle?
☐ in 1518
☐ in 1568
☐ in 1586

4 How do people know about this visit?
☐ There are records of the payment the actors received.
☐ Shakespeare mentions it in his work.
☐ It was commonly known in London at the time.

5 Where did the theatre players come from?
☐ London
☐ Leicester
☐ Copenhagen

6 What was the name of the actors' troupe?
☐ The King's Group
☐ London Group
☐ Leicester Group

7 What was special about Kronborg Castle?
☐ It was the biggest Renaissance castle in northern Europe.
☐ It had the highest tower in Denmark.
☐ It was the Danish king's main residence.

8 How did Shakespeare know about the castle?
☐ He was one of the three actors visiting the castle.
☐ The three actors told Shakespeare about the place.
☐ Ambassadors told him about the castle.

9 Did Shakespeare really visit the castle?
☐ Yes, he did.
☐ No, he did not.
☐ It is not certain.

b) It is widely believed that Shakespeare was inspired by a version of the Scandinavian legend of *Amleth* by the Danish author Saxo Grammaticus (1150-1220). Research this legend and then show the characters' relationship in the character map below.

Gervendill   Koll

Horvendill   Feng

Gerutha   young girl

Amleth

Rørik Slyngebond   princess of England

King of England   Wiglek

Hermuthruda

4

While reading: Act I

SCENE I: THE OPENING SCENE OF THE PLAY

1

The play opens with a changing of the guard at the royal court of Elsinore Castle in Denmark. Francisco, who is on sentry duty, is relieved by Bernardo. Horatio and Marcellus arrive to join Bernardo. The country is on the brink of war with Norway.

a) Read the first part of the opening scene of the play (ll. 1-107) and try to understand as much as possible. Then answer the following questions:

1. What time is it when Bernardo relieves Francisco? _____

_____

2. How does Francisco feel and why? _____

_____

3. What was his guard duty like? _____

_____

4. What did Marcellus and Bernardo witness on their guard duty the previous two nights? _____

_____

5. What does Horatio think about their report at first? _____

_____

6. Why has Marcellus asked Horatio to join them on their guard duty? _____

_____

7. How does Horatio react when he sees what the soldiers told him about? _____

_____

_____

b) In the opening scenes of his plays, Shakespeare uses language to attract the audience's attention and to make them curious about what will happen next. Bear in mind that in Elizabethan theatres there were hardly any props or scenery to indicate the setting. All this has to be done through language. Identify the means Shakespeare uses for these different purposes and analyse them.
Use a grid like this one.

lines	text	analysis
1	Who's there?	*question suggests that Bernardo can't see anything → shows it is dark and that Bernardo is nervous*
...	...	...

c) In class, talk about why Shakespeare opens his play in such a manner.

2

Horatio believes his friends now and tells them why Denmark is preparing for war.
a) Read lines 134-174 of the first scene of Act I and retell Horatio's story using the cues in the box below.

> to reach an agreement | sealed contract | to reclaim land | a bunch of outlaws | to wage war against |
> to die in combat | to lose territories | to stand guard | to prepare for war

b) **Group work (5)** While one student reads the lines slowly, the other members act out the lines.

3

Many plays open with a scene that sows the seeds of a catastrophe that will follow.
a) Speculate what disastrous events may occur during the course of the play.
b) Explain how the first scene foreshadows these events.

4   CHOOSE **Group work (4-5)**

Talk about how you would stage the opening scene.
Consider

- the first thing the audience sees.
- how you bring across the atmosphere and how the short sentences or questions contribute to the overall atmosphere.
- how each character speaks (nervously, clearly, calmly, forcefully, boldly, etc.).
- how you bring the setting across: In Shakespeare's time the play would have been staged at broad daylight. Which words or phrases help to create the impression of night and darkness?
- whether the audience sees the apparition?

Present your ideas to the class.

OR

Hamlet has been turned into a film many times. Here are some examples of the opening scenes:
- battle scenes between Denmark and Norway with old King Hamlet wounded
- old King Hamlet's funeral procession
- flags on the walls of Elsinore Castle signifying the death of old King Hamlet
- the queen crying at the tomb of her husband
- a chef peeping around a curtain to see if the next course can be served at a banquet

Assess the examples listed above. Then devise your own version that accompanies the credits and leads to the first line of text spoken by a character.

SCENE II

5

Claudius, recently crowned King of Denmark, enters the stage, addressing his courtiers.

a) Read his address (ll. 1-43). Then decide whether the statements below are true or false. Correct them if necessary.

	Statement	Evidence	true	false
1	Despite King Hamlet's recent death and the nation's mourning, Claudius needs to consider his own position.			
2	In a very joyful ceremony, Claudius has married his brother's widow.			
3	His courtiers advised him against marrying Gertrude.			
4	Fortinbras holds a poor opinion of Claudius.			
5	Fortinbras seems to think that Denmark is in a chaotic state after King Hamlet's death.			
6	Fortinbras wants to reclaim the lands his father lost to the late Danish king.			
7	Claudius has written a letter, asking the powerful King of Norway to stop his nephew's activities.			
8	Claudius sends two ambassadors to Norway.			

b) **Pair work** Talk about how Claudius comes across. Does he seem devious or honest, resolute or weak?

c) **Pair work** Talk about what words you would particularly stress in the speech. Then read out the King's address.

6

Claudius and Gertrude are worried about Hamlet and talk to him.

a) Read the extract (ll. 79-143). Then match the following statements to the characters Gertrude, Hamlet and Claudius and give the line reference.

Statement	Lines	Character
Your behaviour is a sin against God's will and against nature.		
Stay with us and do not go back to Wittenberg.		
Stop wearing black clothes.		
You are the next in line for the throne.		
Stop mourning for your father's death.		
It is unmanly for a son to grieve so long for a dead father.		
The sighing, the weeping, the downcast eyes – other people may use all this to put on a show.		
It is normal for people to die. So why are you so extremely sad, nonetheless?		
My clothes hint at the real grief I feel.		

b) Analyse the relationship between Hamlet, Gertrude and Claudius.

c) **Group work (3)** Act out the extract. Use emphasis and intonation to convey the characteristics of the relationship between the three characters.

7

After talking to his mother and uncle, Hamlet remains alone on stage. Read his following soliloquy below.

a) Structure the soliloquy and label the different parts. The first one has been done for you.

Text	Annotations	Notes
O, that this too, too solid flesh would melt, Thaw and resolve itself into a dew, Or that the Everlasting had not fixed His canon 'gainst self-slaughter. O God, God, 5 How weary, stale, flat and unprofitable Seem to me all the uses of this world!	**to thaw** to melt **to resolve** to dissolve **the Everlasting** God **canon** divine law **self-slaughter** suicide **stale** old, tasteless **uses** business	Hamlet contemplates suicide
Fie on't! ah fie, 'tis an unweeded garden, That grows to seed, things rank and gross in nature Possess it merely. That it should come to this: 10 But two months dead – nay, not so much, not two – So excellent a king, that was, to this Hyperion to a satyr, so loving to my mother That he might not beteem the winds of heaven Visit her face too roughly. Heaven and earth, 15 Must I remember? Why, she would hang on him As if increase of appetite had grown By what it fed on. And yet, within a month (Let me not think on't – Frailty, thy name is Woman), A little month, or ere those shoes were old	**Fie on't** To hell with it. **unweeded** without the weeds (*Unkraut*) having been removed **grows to seed** becomes overgrown with undesirable plants **rank** growing without limit **gross** dense, thick **in nature** as is natural **merely** completely **to beteem** (archaic) to allow **hang on him** be so in love with him **on't** about it **frailty** weakness **ere** before	
20 With which she followed my poor father's body, Like Niobe, all tears. Why she, even she – O God, a beast that wants discourse of reason Would have mourned longer – married with my uncle, My father's brother (but no more like my father	**wants discourse of reason** does not have the ability to think	
25 Than I to Hercules). Within a month, Ere yet the salt of most unrighteous tears Had left the flushing in her gallèd eyes, She married. O most wicked speed, to post With such dexterity to incestuous sheets! 30 It is not, nor it cannot come to good. But break, my heart, for I must hold my tongue.	**unrighteous** insincere **flushing** flowing tears **gallèd** irritated **to post** to hurry **dexterity** haste	

b) Sum up what Hamlet criticizes his mother for.

c) Read the info bcx below. Use the information to discuss the function of this soliloquy.

Info

Soliloquy

Soliloquy is the act of talking to oneself. This can be done silently or aloud. In drama, the term describes the practice by which a character, alone on stage, utters his or her thoughts for the audience to hear. Soliloquies serve as a dramatic device to let the audience know about the character's intentions and state of mind, and also to give additional information about the action of the play.

Soliloquies are often used to
- set the scene
- make the audience part of the play
- explicate the character's feelings
- clarify matters
- introduce further information

SCENE III

8

Laertes is about to go back to Paris. Before he goes, he takes his leave of his sister.

a) Read the dialogue between Ophelia and Laertes (ll. 1-61). Then tick the pieces of advice Laertes really gives Ophelia and give the line reference.

Be aware that Hamlet might only toy with you.	✓	l.10: "the trifling of his favour"
Hamlet's feelings for you are sincere.		
He might love you now.		
Due to his high position, he cannot do what he likes.		
He is a virtuous prince that you can trust.		
Hamlet is powerful enough to choose his own wife.		
He cannot choose freely as ordinary people can do, as he has got a position to think of and a country to run.		
If he says he loves you, believe him.		
Consider your honour that is at stake if you now lose your virginity to him.		
Hold back in your affections.		

b) Sum up Laertes' advice to his sister in 1-2 sentences.

c) Describe Ophelia's reaction to Laertes' advice.

SCENE V

9

Horatio has informed Hamlet about the strange apparition. When one night the two friends join Marcellus on his midnight watch, the ghost appears again. Alone with Hamlet, the ghost discloses the whole story.

a) Read the extract (ll. 23-140) and answer the following questions.

1. Why is the ghost doomed to walk the earth by night? _____

_____

2. What information does he give about his life in purgatory? _____

_____

3. What was the official version of the former king's death? _____

_____

4. What does the ghost think about the queen? _____

_____

5. What was the real reason for the king's death? _____

_____

6. What troubles the ghost particularly about the end of his life? _____

_____

7. What does the ghost tell Hamlet to do about his mother? _____

_____

8. What does the ghost ask Hamlet to do? _____

_____

9. How does Hamlet react to the ghost's wish? _____

_____

b) CHOOSE **Group work (3)** You need a narrator, King Hamlet and Claudius. While the narrator reads lines 84 ("Sleeping within my orchard") to 105, the others act out what is described.

OR

Group work (3-6) Imagine you are a film crew shooting this three-minute scene.
Talk about
- what lines you want to use or leave out.
- what shots you use.
- what background music supports the atmosphere of the scene.
- what camera movement you want to employ.
- what special effects to use.

While reading: Act II

SCENE II

1

The King and Queen have sent for Rosencrantz and Guildenstern, two friends of Hamlet's.

a) **Group work (4)** Read the extract (Act II, Scene II, ll. 1-52). Outline the main purpose of the two friends' visit.

b) Discuss the following questions in your group by referring to the text.

1. Does Claudius come across as a worried stepfather and uncle?
2. How does Gertrude come across?
3. Has Claudius sent for Hamlet's friends to put him under surveillance?
4. Do the two friends come across as individual beings or rather like a double act?
5. Do Rosencrantz and Guildenstern seem like true and honest friends?

c) Act out the lines bearing in mind what you have discussed.

d) Rosencrantz and Guildenstern always appear together on stage. Talk about why Shakespeare makes them do so.

2

Ophelia has given her father a letter that Hamlet seems to have addressed to her. Now Polonius reads out the letter to the King and Queen.

a) Read Hamlet's letter (ll. 146-165) and summarize it in one sentence.

b) Read the extract ll. 142-228. In class, discuss whether you think this letter is real or simply fabricated by Polonius. If so, what could be the purpose?

c) Polonius tells the King and the Queen what advice he has given his daughter. Read his advice (ll. 188-192) and paraphrase it in your own words.

d) Polonius continues by describing the classical symptoms of lovesickness. Read lines 193-198 and attribute the modern names of the symptoms to the words from the text.

1	sadness	☐ insomnia
2	fast	☐ delirium
3	watch	☐ loss of appetite
4	weakness	☐ depression
5	lightness	☐ weakness

Info

The Elizabethans believed that lovesickness was a serious disease that could lead to madness or even death.

e) Outline Polonius' plan.

f) Analyse Polonius' character: Choose the adjectives that best describe him and find examples from the text to prove your point.

> strategic | loyal | loving | worried | cunning | duplicitous | dishonest | contemptuous

3

Hamlet welcomes his two old friends at Elsinore.

a) Read the extract (ll. 322-420), tick the topics they talk about and give evidence.

Topic	✓	Evidence
well-being		
being lucky		
sexual puns		
the reason for their visit		
their prison sentence		
ambition		
nightmares		
honesty		

b) Choose the adjectives that best describe Hamlet's relationship with Rosencrantz and Guildenstern. Find examples from the text to prove your point.

happy | difficult | strained | close | intimate | harmonious | honest | caring | dishonest | deceitful

c) Having seen his friends off, Hamlet contemplates their meeting: Write his inner monologue in which he reflects upon his friends' attitude towards him.

4

Hamlet informs his friends about his state of mind.

a) Read Hamlet's speech (ll. 422-440) and describe his state of mind.

b) Shakespeare is believed to refer to the Globe Theatre in these lines. Look at the picture and identify the allusions to the Globe Theatre in Hamlet's speech.

c) Analyse the language Hamlet uses to describe mankind. Identify the stylistic devices and explain their intended effect on the audience.

anaphora | metaphor | antithesis | alliteration | repetition | parallelism | exclamation

d) **Group work (4-5)** Which tone do you find most appropriate for delivering Hamlet's speech: sarcastic, melancholic, sincere, bitter or awe-struck? Discuss. In your group read out the extract and try out various ways of delivering Hamlet's lines.

5

A group of actors have arrived at Elsinore. Hamlet asks them to perform a play the next night that includes a speech he has written. When they have gone, Hamlet ponders upon the players' ability to feign feelings.

a) Read Hamlet's soliloquy (ll. 745-813). Then structure it and summarize each part in one sentence. The first one has been done for you.

Lines	Summary
747-754	Hamlet praises the actor's skill to feign emotions.

b) Describe Hamlet's plan to trick his uncle.
c) Read the info box and identify dramatic irony in the soliloquy.
d) **Group work (5-7)**
  1 Talk about
    • how Hamlet comes across. Is he impatient, angry or desperate?
    • the function of the soliloquy. Bear in mind what you have learned about soliloquies on p. 148.
  2 Prepare a presentation of the soliloquy, with each of you delivering a part of it.

Info

Dramatic irony

This literary device is used when the audience knows more than the characters in the scene.

153

While reading: Act III

SCENE I

1

After Rosencrantz and Guildenstern have reported back to the King and Queen, Claudius lets the Queen in on his plan to spy on Hamlet. Then Hamlet enters the stage.

a) Read Hamlet's most famous soliloquy. Then answer the questions below.

1. What are the two options Hamlet is torn between?
2. What is the advantage of eternal sleep according to Hamlet?
3. What uncertainty does Hamlet see in death's sleep?
4. What injustices does Hamlet list?
5. What explanation does Hamlet give for why people do not end their lives despite the hardships they endure?
6. What consequences does the fear of death have for man according to Hamlet?

b) Tick the synopsis that best summarizes Hamlet's soliloquy.
- ❑ Hamlet contemplates death and all its consequences.
- ❑ Hamlet meditates on the problems of living and dying.
- ❑ Hamlet is afraid of all the things that might happen after death.

c) Watch the video and describe how Hamlet comes across in this version. Is this your understanding of the soliloquy? Discuss in class.   **Webcode** WES-73652-014

d) **Pair work** CHOOSE Explore the soliloquy with a partner.
Stand back-to-back, arms linked. One of you, who can see the script, reads out a line, the other one repeats it.
OR
You share the speech, alternately speaking small units as a kind of conversation.
OR
Think of a simple every-day task, such as painting a wall, cleaning shoes or chopping wood. While you speak small units of the soliloquy alternately, carry out the task.

e) In class, discuss how the activities in d) contribute to a better understanding of the soliloquy.

f) Imagine you are a director and want to turn the soliloquy into a film. Take notes on
- cinematic devices (field size, camera angle etc.)
- the scenery and props
- the background music
- the way the actor speaks the lines.

2

The King and Polonius eavesdrop on a conversation between Ophelia and Hamlet (ll. 125–224).

a) Outline the conversation between Ophelia and Hamlet.

b) Hamlet treats Ophelia rather harshly. Explain possible reasons for his behaviour.

c) In this extract the themes sin, virtue, appearance and reality play an important role. Find lines in the extract that refer to these themes. Draw a mind map and show how the themes correlate.

d) **Group work (3)**
1. Discuss what Hamlet really thinks about Ophelia. Does he know he is being spied on? Does he trust Ophelia?
2. Act out the dialogue: After Hamlet's lines a third student voices his thoughts.

SCENE II

Two players, playing the roles of a King and Queen, act out the play in front of the Danish royal court

a) Read the extract (Scene II, ll. 206-380). Paraphrase the core ideas of the player King and Queen's conversation. Use the characters' perspective as shown in the example.

The player King	*The player Queen*
• *We have been married for 30 years.*	• *I hope we will be for another 30 years. I am worried about your health. It is typical of a woman to worry when she loves. I love you deeply and fear for you and your well-being.*
• ...	• ...

b) **Dramatic reading** Read out your results from task a) as a dialogue. Then talk about what gets lost and what becomes clearer.

c) Describe the audience's reactions to the play.

d) Explain the function of the play-within-a-play.

Info

The play-within-a-play

The play-within-a-play is a dramatic convention very popular in Shakespeare's time: a character in a story becomes the narrator of a second story.

As the first professional theatre had only been established some years before in 1567, Elizabethan authors liked to explore the new technical possibilities of the theatre and the nature of entertainment. Besides, the question of the kind of truth that can be told through plays was a focus of the playwrights' interest. As it was widely believed at the time that the theatre had a real impact on its audience, the performance of a crime was believed to force the criminal spectator to admit his or her guilt.

Thus, it is not surprising that a play such as Hamlet that evolves around the themes of performance, deception, authenticity, and reality makes use of this literary device. As it also keeps the audience at a distance from the actual crime, it also questions the reliability and the motives of the storyteller.

In general, the inset story or play may have various functions. It may simply offer entertainment, provide an example of what is told in the outer story, have symbolic or psychological significance to the characters of the outer story, or reveal the truth about something that has happened in the outer story. Finally, it may also deflect the audience's attention from a plot twist.

SCENE III

After Claudius interrupts and leaves the performance, he considers his next move: He plans to send Hamlet to England with Rosencrantz and Guildenstern accompanying him. Polonius meanwhile plans another ruse: He wants to eavesdrop on a conversation between Gertrude and Hamlet behind a wall hanging.

a) Look up the story of Cain and Abel in the Bible (Genesis 4:11-12) and outline its contents.

b) Read Claudius's soliloquy (Scene 3, ll. 50-86). Then tick the summary that best captures its content.

   ☐ Claudius is torn between the repentance for his crime and his ambition to stay in power. He tries to pray and ask God for forgiveness.

   ☐ Despite his guilty conscience, Claudius does not show any remorse and plots to get rid of his enemies.

   ☐ Claudius is sure that his secret is now revealed and is therefore very unhappy about the murder he has committed. Although he admits his guilt, he cannot show repentance as he is still in possession of Gertrude and the throne.

c) Write an analysis of the language Claudius uses to reveal his state of mind. Follow steps 1-3 and use the language support below.

1 Identify three or four stylistic devices from the box below and explain their functions within the soliloquy.

Tip Start with an introductory sentence which introduces the topic.

> alliteration | rhetorical question | accumulation | anaphora |
> exclamation | simile | antithesis | apostrophe

2 Look at the language Shakespeare uses: is it emotive, offensive, strong or crude? Analyse the choice of words.

3 Explain the function of the reference to Cain and Abel.

Language support

> Shakespeare uses/employs ...
> He repeatedly employs ...
> This can be seen in line xy when he ...
> This becomes most evident when he lists ...
> Quite a number of words/adjectives refer to ...
> The most striking example can be found in ll. ...
> It is striking that ...
> This stylistic device shows/is a typical example of/illustrates/personifies ...

d) **Group work (4-8): Echoing** Re-read Claudius' soliloquy and underline key words. While one student now reads Claudius' soliloquy the others echo the keywords. Talk about the effect this technique has on the audience. How does it contribute to the atmosphere?

e) Now read Hamlet's reaction when he sees Claudius kneeling (ll. 88-118). Sum up his thoughts in 2-3 sentences.

f) **Pair work: Good angel – bad angel** Work out what Hamlet might tell himself while contemplating his options: should he kill Claudius or not? What arguments does he weigh up? First collect arguments for and against his decision to kill Claudius. Then sit with your backs to each other and perform this conversation of Hamlet's conscience. Use the arguments you have collected as a starting point.

SCENE IV

5

While Polonius is hiding behind a wall hanging, Hamlet chides his mother.

a) Read the extract (Scene IV, ll. 1-48) and answer the following questions:

1. What is Gertrude supposed to tell Hamlet?
2. What does Hamlet accuse his mother of?
3. What does Hamlet want his mother to do?
4. What does Gertrude think Hamlet wants to do to her?

b) **Pair work: Dramatic reading** Read out lines 15-48. Before you do so, talk about how to read the lines. Is Hamlet agitated, rude or impatient? Is Gertrude angry or afraid? How do the lines each character speaks contribute to the atmosphere?

c) Do you think that Hamlet knows that he has killed someone? Share your ideas in class.

d) Read the continuation of the scene (ll. 49-155). Sum up the arguments Hamlet presents to his mother.

e) **Pair work** Gertrude only has a few lines. Write some more lines for her to show what she really thinks about Hamlet's arguments. Then present the dialogue between mother and son in front of the class. You can have a third student present the additional lines.

While reading: Act IV

SCENE III

 1

After the killing of Polonius, Hamlet disappears for a while. Rosencrantz and Guildenstern find him and bring him to the King. Read Act IV, Scene III, ll. 28-104.

a) Hamlet speaks in riddles. But Claudius knows that Hamlet means serious business with what he says. In the grid, note down what Hamlet really means. Then compare your results with a partner's.

Lines	Original text	What Hamlet really means
31	At supper.	
35	Not where he eats, but where he is eaten.	
35-36	A certain convocation of politic worms are e'en at him.	
36-37	Your worm is your only emperor for diet.	
37-38	We fat all creatures else to fat us, and we fat ourselves for maggots.	
38-39	Your fat king and your lean beggar is but variable service, two dishes, but to one table.	
39	That's the end.	
42-43	A man may fish with the worm that hath eat of a king, and eat of the fish that hath fed of that worm.	
47-48	Nothing but to show you how a king may go a progress through the guts of a beggar.	
52	In heaven.	
52	Send thither to see.	
52-53	If your messenger find him not there, seek him I' the other place yourself.	
53-55	But if indeed you find him not within this month, you shall nose him as you go up the stairs into the lobby.	

b) **Group work (4)** Act out the dialogue. One pair of students acts out the original lines. Then the other pair acts out the dialogue with Hamlet speaking the truth. Talk about the changes in atmosphere.

c) Examine to what extent Hamlet carries traits of a jester in this scene.

Info

Jesters

A jester was a popular type of character in Elizabethan drama. Jesters were also known as clowns or fools. They were employed for entertainment in royal and noble households. They usually enjoyed a high reputation and were regarded as witty and wise. In Shakespeare's plays they often function as prophets and wise men who, behind their folly, speak the truth. But there were also natural fools, who were exposed to pratfalls, misfortunes and humiliations in the plays, and whose mere function was to amuse the audience.

---

d) Talk about why Shakespeare makes Hamlet speak in riddles in this scene.

e) Explain the King's plans for Hamlet.

SCENE V

2

Laertes has stirred up a riot and wants to see the king (Scene V, ll. 157-229).

a) Outline the argument between Laertes and Claudius.

b) Describe Claudius' strategy.

c) Analyse Laertes' behaviour: choose the adjectives that best describe it, find evidence from the text and interpret it. Use a grid like the one below.

> aggressive | violent | rash | hasty | thoughtless | hot-headed | incautious | heedless | prudent | audacious | headstrong | revengeful

Adjective	Evidence (quote and line reference)	Interpretation
...	...	...

d) Use your results from task c) to write an analysis.

3

Laertes meets his sister, who has gone mad.

a) Read the extract (ll. 232-290) and describe Laertes' reaction when he sees his sister.

b) All the flowers and herbs Ophelia mentions carry symbolic associations. Explain why Shakespeare has chosen these flowers.

> fennel | pansy | violet | daisy | rue | columbine | rosemary

c) Imagine you are a psychiatrist and Ophelia is brought to you as a new patient. Analyse her state of mind, using the information from the extract, and write your medical report on her.

You may start like this:

_____, M.D.
Your name

St Bartholomew's Hospital
West Smithfield
London
EC1A 7BE

Medical report for Ophelia

Diagnosis: Ophelia shows symptoms of _____

Examination results:
Ophelia appears to be _____

_____

_____

_____

_____

_____

_____

_____

_____

_____

_____

4

Ophelia leaves a distressed brother behind.

a) Read the conversation between Laertes and the King (ll. 292-317). Explain how Claudius wants to convince Laertes of his innocence.

b) Write a soliloquy for Claudius' part after Laertes leaves. Consider
   • his present situation
   • his next steps
   • how he means to get rid of Hamlet.

c) Act out your soliloquy in front of the class.

SCENE VII

5

Claudius learns that Hamlet, whom he had sent to England, has returned to Denmark and wants to see him. He asks Laertes for advice.

a) Read the extract (Scene VII, ll. 71-218). Then decide whether the statements are true or false. Give evidence from the text.

	Statement	Evidence	true	false
1	Laertes is looking forward to meeting Hamlet.			
2	Laertes wants Claudius to make peace with Hamlet.			
3	Claudius plots against Hamlet.			
4	According to Claudius Hamlet admires Laertes for his fencing talents.			
5	Claudius wants to arrange a fencing match.			
6	Claudius lets Laertes in on his plan.			
7	Laertes does not want to poison Hamlet.			
8	Claudius suggests a backup plan to be on the safe side.			
9	He wants to manipulate the swords.			

b) Outline the two men's plot.

c) Explain how Claudius characterizes Hamlet and what part this plays in the plan.

d) Analyse Claudius' language to show how he tempts Laertes into avenging his father's death.

6

The Queen has some bad news for the King and Laertes.

a) Read the Queen's description of Ophelia's death (ll. 219-294). Imagine you are a police officer summoned to the scene. Fill in the police report on p. 161 based on Gertrude's account.

Police report

Case No. _____   Date: _____

Reporting officer: _____

Incident: _____

_____

_____

Detail of event:

1. Who was involved? _____

_____

2. What happened? _____

_____

3. Where did the incident occur? _____

_____

4. When did the incident happen? _____

_____

5. Why do you think the accused/victim did this? _____

_____

Actions taken:

_____

_____

Summary:

_____

_____

_____

b) Research the symbolic meanings of the flowers and herbs mentioned in Gertrude's account.
c) Describe the painting *Ophelia* by Sir John Everett Millais (1851-1852) on page 160.
d) Analyse the pictorial elements and their functions. Use the information on the symbolic meaning of the flowers collected in task b).
e) Discuss to what extent the painting reflects the image of nature conveyed in Gertrude's lines.

While reading: Act V

SCENE II

1

Hamlet tells Horatio what happened on his journey to England.

a) Retell Hamlet's story (Act V, Scene II, ll. 1-105) in your own words.

b) Write the letter Hamlet has manipulated.

c) Compare Hamlet's feelings about Rosencrantz and Guildenstern, Claudius, and Laertes.

Language support

> When comparing Hamlet's feelings about ... it is striking that ...
> Unlike his feelings towards ... Hamlet seems to be ...
> by comparison with/in contrast to/compared to x, y seems ...

Hamlet's feelings		
Rosencrantz and Guildenstern	**Claudius**	**Laertes**

d) **Extra** Do some research on Tom Stoppard's play *Rosencrantz and Guildenstern Are Dead* (1966). Find out about
- the main characters
- the storyline
- the themes.

2

Shortly before the fencing match with Laertes begins, Hamlet considers his options.

a) Read the extract (ll. 262-287). Tick the description that best captures Hamlet's attitude towards providence and give evidence from the text.
- ☐ Hamlet believes he can tempt providence and fend off his own fate.
- ☐ Hamlet believes in divine providence: whatever is destined to happen will happen. Man can only be prepared by meeting death with the right frame of mind.
- ☐ Hamlet has grave misgivings about the fencing match. But he does not want to appear superstitious like a woman.

b) The Queen has asked Hamlet and Laertes to chat politely before the match. Outline their chat (ll. 294-323) in 2-3 sentences.

c) Discuss Hamlet's explanation for why he has killed Polonius.

d) **Pair work** The audience knows that Laertes plans to kill Hamlet. One of you reads Laertes' lines (ll. 315-323) and pauses at each punctuation mark, the other one fills the pauses by outlining what Laertes might really be thinking. Use the grid on page 163.

Original text	What might Laertes really be thinking?
I am satisfied in nature,	
Whose motive, in this case, should stir me most	
To my revenge. But in my terms of honour	
I stand aloof, and will no reconcilement,	
Till by some elder masters, of known honour,	
I have a voice and precedent of peace,	
To keep my name ungored. But till that time,	
I do receive your offered love like love,	
And will not wrong it.	

3

The fencing match begins.

a) Read the extract (ll. 371–518) and put the events into the correct order by adding numbers to the grid.

Number	Event
7	Hamlet wounds Laertes.
8	The Queen dies.
4	The Queen takes Hamlet's cup of wine and drinks from it.
10	Hamlet wounds the King.
2	The King raises a cup of wine and offers another to Hamlet.
13	Laertes forgives Hamlet and dies.
14	Hamlet prevents Horatio from committing suicide and asks him to tell his story.
6	Hamlet and Laertes accidentally exchange their rapiers.
9	Laertes reveals the treacherous plot.
1	Hamlet and Laertes start fighting.
12	The King dies.
3	Hamlet rejects the cup.
5	Laertes wounds Hamlet.
11	Hamlet makes the King drink from the poisoned cup.

b) **Pair work**

1   Discuss why Gertrude drinks from Hamlet's poisoned cup of wine. Does she know it is poisoned? Or is it a mere accident? One partner argues that Gertrude commits suicide. The other argues that she does not know the cup is poisoned.

2   Talk about how the different interpretations change our attitude towards Gertrude.

c) **Group work (5-6)** In this final scene, the whole tragedy unfolds. Try several ways of acting out the scene:

- Have one student tell the story while the others act it out.
- Perform a mime.
- Perform a "fast-forward" version.
- Perform the scene backwards.

Talk about the different effects the ways of acting out the scene create.

4

When Hamlet is dying, he votes for Fortinbras as the next King of Denmark.

a) Read the extract. Then summarize the major events (ll. 526-598).

b) Hamlet's last words, "the rest is silence", have been widely discussed. Do Hamlet's last words imply a personal as well as a political message? Explain your interpretation.

c) Horatio lists the incidents that he will tell Fortinbras about. Explain what events he refers to.

Lines	Incident	Explanation
569	carnal [...] acts	
569	bloody [...] acts	
569	unnatural acts	
570	accidental judgements	
570	casual slaughters	
571	deaths put on by cunning [...] cause	
571	deaths put on by [...] forced cause	

d) Tell Horatio's story.

e) According to Aristotle, a famous Greek philosopher and critic (384-322 BC), the ideal tragic ending is the necessary consequence of all the action that preceded it, in other words the final outcome somehow reflects the story as a whole. Discuss to what extent this is true for this play.

Post-reading

1 CHOOSE Group work

Decide which are the most important scenes or events of the play. Use a symbol or picture to indicate what each scene is about, write a headline for the scene and summarize it in one sentence. The first event has been done for you. Then present your ideas to the class.

A ghost appears				
A ghost appears to Horatio, who then decides to inform Prince Hamlet about the apparition.				

OR

Decide which scenes or events in the play are the most important ones. Talk about how you can present them. Then act out each scene in 1 minute. One student is the timekeeper. Explain why you have chosen these scenes.

2 Group work (8)

a) Prepare a poster for each character: Hamlet, Claudius, Gertrude, Polonius, Laertes, Ophelia, Horatio and Fortinbras.
   • First find quotations typical of the character.
   • Then analyse his or her character.
   • Finally describe his or her role in the play.
b) Present your posters in a Gallery Walk.

3

Read the info box on obituaries and write an obituary for one of the characters that dies during the play. Use the information you have collected in task 2.

Info

Obituary

An obituary is a news article that announces a well-known person's recent death and informs the reader about this person's life and achievements. It has become a quite popular subgenre in British and American newspapers. It consists of a headline, a sub-heading, the name of the author, a main part and a concluding paragraph. An obituary does not always praise the person but may also show the mysterious and indecent sides of the person.

4

Hamlet raises many universal questions and deals with many universal themes that have interested people across centuries and cultures.

a) **Pair work** List as many of these questions and themes you can think of and compare your ideas with a partner's. Together, settle on one question or theme and explore it in more depth. Give evidence from the text.

b) Write an essay about your question or theme and present it to the class.

5

Choose the quote you like best. Briefly outline the context of the quote and explain your choice.

1 Frailty, thy name is Woman (Act I, Scene II, line 172)

2 Neither a borrower nor a lender be. For loan oft loses both itself and friend and borrowing dulls the edge of husbandry. (Act I, Scene III, lines 89-91)

3 Something is rotten in the state of Denmark. (Act I, Scene IV, line 134)

4 Though this be madness, yet there is method in't. (Act II, Scene II, line 291)

5 What a piece of work is a man. How noble in reason, how infinite in faculty, in form and moving how express and admirable, in action how like an angel, in apprehension how like a god – the beauty of the world, the paragon of animals. (Act II, Scene II, lines 433-437)

6 they [i.e. the players] are the abstract and brief chronicles of the time. (Act II, Scene II, lines 708-709)

7 To be, or not to be, that is the question. Whether 'tis nobler in the mind to suffer the slings and arrows of outrageous fortune, or to take arms against a sea of troubles, and by opposing end them? (Act III, Scene I, lines 90-94)

8 Our wills and fates do so contrary run that our devices still are overthrown. Our thoughts are ours, their ends none of our own. (Act III, Scene II, lines 293-295)

9 The lady doth protest too much, methinks. (Act III, Scene II, line 321)

10 This is I, Hamlet the Dane. (Act V, Scene I, lines 346-347)

6

Imagine you are a director and asked to turn Shakespeare's *Hamlet* into a modern film version. Outline this version.

1. Title: _____

2. Genre (e.g. western, thriller, horror film): _____

3. Setting (Where and when does the story take place?): _____

_____

4. Cast: actors for the main roles

_____ as Hamlet

_____ as _____

_____ as _____

_____ as _____

_____ as _____

_____ as _____

_____ as _____

7

Pair work You want to pitch your film version to a production company.

a) Prepare the pitch, in which you
  • summarize the original plot of the play
  • present your reasons for making this kind of film
  • talk about the relevance of the story for modern audiences
  • outline the main ideas of your film version.

b) Present your pitch to the class. The other students function as board members of the production company. After everyone has presented a pitch, vote for the best one.

Info

Pitch

A pitch is a short oral presentation of an idea for a film or TV series, given by a director or screenwriter to convince a film producer to fund the project. As time is money, the presentation must be short and to the point.

Fate vs. free will

FREEDOM AND RESPONSIBILITY

1

Is life determined by fate or free will? In other words, have you
ever wondered if you have control over your actions, and if so,
to what extent? Or are your actions determined by some other
forces? Philosophers have been arguing about these issues for
thousands of years.

a) **Pair work** Is the boy in the photo jumping into the water
based on his own free will? Or was his decision determined
by any exterior force? With a partner, exchange your views on
this issue.

b) Read this extract from an entry in the online *Encyclopaedia Britannica* to explore the opposing views of
free will and *determinism*. Then match the sentences on the next page to test your knowledge.

Problem of moral responsibility

by Peter Singer and Maya Eddon

Problem of moral responsibility, the problem of reconciling
the belief that people are morally responsible for what
they do with the apparent fact that humans do not have
free will because their actions are causally determined. It
5 is an ancient and enduring philosophical puzzle.

Freedom and responsibility

Historically, most proposed solutions to the problem of moral
responsibility have attempted to establish that humans
do have free will. But what does free will consist of? When
people make decisions or perform actions, they usually feel
10 as though they are choosing or acting freely. A person may
decide, for example, to buy apples instead of oranges, to
vacation in France rather than in Italy, or to call a sister in
Nebraska instead of a brother in Florida. On the other hand,
there are at least some situations in which people seem not
15 to act freely, as when they are physically coerced or mentally
or emotionally manipulated. One way to formalize the
intuitive idea of free action is to say that a person acts freely
if it is true that he could have acted otherwise. Buying apples
is ordinarily a free action because in ordinary circumstances
20 one can buy oranges instead; nothing forces one to buy
apples or prevents one from buying oranges.
Yet the decisions a person makes are the result of his desires,
and his desires are determined by his circumstances, his
past experiences, and his psychological and personality
25 traits – his dispositions, tastes, temperament, intelligence,
and so on. Circumstances, experiences, and traits in this
sense are obviously the result of many factors outside the
individual's control, including his upbringing and perhaps
even his genetic makeup. If this is correct, then a person's
30 actions may ultimately be no more the result of free will
than his eye colour.
The existence of free will seems to be presupposed by the
notion of moral responsibility. Most people would agree
that a person cannot be morally responsible for actions that
35 he could not help but perform. Moreover, moral praise and

blame, or reward and punishment, seem to make sense
only on the assumption that the agent in question is morally
responsible. These considerations seem to imply a choice
between two implausible alternatives: either (1) people have
40 free will, in which case a person's actions are not determined
by his circumstances, past experiences, and psychological
and personality traits, or (2) people do not have free will, in
which case no one is ever morally responsible for what he
does. This dilemma is the problem of moral responsibility.

Determinism

45 Determinism is the view that, given the state of the
universe (the complete physical properties of all its
parts) at a certain time and the laws of nature operative
in the universe at that time, the state of the universe
at any subsequent time is completely determined. No
50 subsequent state of the universe can be other than
what it is. Since human actions, at an appropriate level
of description, are part of the universe, it follows that
humans cannot act otherwise than they do; free will is
impossible. [...]
55 Philosophers and scientists who believe that the universe
is deterministic and that determinism is incompatible
with free will are called "hard" determinists. Since moral
responsibility seems to require free will, hard determinism
implies that no one is morally responsible for his actions.
60 Although the conclusion is strongly counterintuitive,
some hard determinists have insisted that the weight
of philosophical argument requires that it be accepted.
There is no alternative but to reform the intuitive beliefs in
freedom and moral responsibility. Other hard determinists,
65 acknowledging that such reform is scarcely feasible, hold
that there may be social benefits to feeling and exhibiting
moral emotions, even though the emotions themselves
are based on a fiction. Such benefits are reason enough
for holding fast to prephilosophical beliefs about free will
70 and moral responsibility, according to these thinkers.

1   When people make decisions   ☐   A   the necessary result of predetermined developments and conditions.

2   For the believer in free will, the individuals   ☐   B   deterministic principles.

3   When you believe in free will   ☐   C   they usually think they act and choose freely.

4   Science is based on   ☐   D   everything that happens, happens for a reason and could not happen differently.

5   Determinists believe that   ☐   E   a person's desires, beliefs and temperament.

6   According to determinism a decision made by somebody is   ☐   F   you think you are able to make choices in which the outcome has not been determined by past events.

7   Actions, in this view, are triggered by   ☐   G   they cannot be held responsible for their actions.

8   When people do not have free will,   ☐   H   make conscious choices.

c| Check your knowledge by describing the cartoon and explaining its message.

Annotations
merely = only
naught = nothing

Page 56

As you journey along the path you meet an old man.

He tells you that modern neuroscience has proved that all our actions and decisions are merely the machinations of a pre-determined universe and that our concept of 'free will' is naught but a comforting illusion.

If you agree with his hypothesis, **turn to page 72**

If you disagree, **turn to page 72**

WHAT THE ELIZABETHANS BELIEVED IN

 2

Analyse this picture, showing the *Wheel of Fortune*, which was a very widely held idea in Shakespeare's day. You can use these words and phrases.

> fate | at random | a change in fortune | to be subject to

3

Another popular conception at the time was the *Great Chain of Being*. Read the statements on the next page. Then use them to explain the picture below them.

1. A popular belief was that everything in the world had a set position in a great hierarchy. They called this belief the Great Chain of Being. If this order and positioning was upset in any way, people believed that the harmony of their whole society would be at stake.

2. Many Elizabethans believed that certain dualities existed in the Great Chain of Being. One belief they had was that the king was as important to the state as the sun was to the sky. This meant that if something seemed to be wrong in the heavens, this would worry rulers, as it could be reflected on earth.

3. Marriage could be used to help make a family wealthy or increase their social standing. Women were usually not consulted about their marriages and their feelings were not taken into account.

4. It was believed that if the structure was broken in any way – for example, if someone killed the king, if the king abdicated, or if someone married outside of their social class – then chaos would ensue and everything would fall apart.

5. It was the king's supreme responsibility to enforce and uphold this social order because he was believed to be the chosen representative of God on earth. To do something against the king, such as committing treason, was regarded as the equivalent of committing a mortal sin against God, and could lead to intense problems and chaos on earth.

4

Bearing in mind the *Wheel of Fortune* and the *Great Chain of Being*, explain how the Elizabethans regarded the issues of fate and free will.

Fate vs. free will in *Hamlet*

1

a) Read Act I, Scene V, ll. 23-116 again. Outline King Hamlet's murder in 2-3 sentences.

b) Discuss the significance of King Hamlet's murder for the state of Denmark according to the Elizabethan world view.

c) Talk about possible reasons why Shakespeare did not set his play in England.

2

a) Read the following extracts from the play and pick out aspects from these lines that underline the Elizabethan world view as described on pages 169-170. Use the right-hand column for your notes.

Extracts	Notes
His greatness weighed, his will is not his own, / For he himself is subject to his birth. / He may not, as unvalued persons do, / Carve for himself, for on his choice depends / The safety and health of this whole state, / And therefore must his choice be circumscribed / Unto the voice and yielding of that body / Whereof he is the head. / (Act I, Scene III, lines 26-33)	
Sir, in my heart there was a kind of fighting / That would not let me sleep. Methought I lay / Worse than the mutines in the bilboes. Rashly – / And praised be rashness for it – let us know / Our indiscretion sometimes serves us well / When our deep plots do pall, and that should teach us / There's a divinity that shapes our ends, / Rough-hew them how we will – / (Act V, Scene II, lines 8-15)	
I shall win at the odds. But thou wouldst not think how ill all's here about my heart. But it is no matter. [...] It is but foolery, but it is such a kind of gaingiving, as would perhaps trouble a woman. [...] We defy augury. There's a special providence in the fall of a sparrow. If it be now, 'tis not to come. If it be not to come, it will be now. If it be not now, yet it will come. The readiness is all. Since no man has aught of what he leaves, what is't to leave betimes? Let be. / (Act V, Scene II, lines 272/273, 277/278, 283-287)	

b) Explain the different attitudes towards fate and free will expressed in these extracts.

c) Is the destiny of these characters shaped by fate or by other factors, such as their personalities, chance or other people's ruses? Discuss this question in class. Take some notes beforehand in order to be able to give evidence from the play.

Polonius	Ophelia

Laertes	Claudius

Gertrude	Hamlet

Rosencrantz and Guildenstern	Fortinbras

3

Based on your findings from the previous tasks, write an essay. Here are some ideas:

- Fate vs. free will in Shakespeare's time
- Why Hamlet had to die at the end of the play
- Why Rosencrantz and Guildenstern die

4 CHOOSE

Pair work On page 168, task 1 you have learned about the philosophical concepts of free will and determinism. Imagine a modern conversation between a libertarian (representative of the concept of free will) and a determinist arguing about the question whether Hamlet was free in his decisions and actions. Carry out this discussion.

OR

Group work Discuss how our view of the world has changed in comparison to the Elizabethan world view.

The role(s) of women

ROYAL WIVES TODAY

1

What role does the British royal family play in modern society? Haven't the royals become something of the past? And what part do the women play in all this?

a) Identify the women in the photos and find out what role they play or used to play in British society.

b) Discuss to what extent they can be seen as role models. → **S6:** How to write a discussion/comment

THE ROLE(S) OF WOMEN IN SHAKESPEARE'S TIME

2 Pair work

What role did women play in Shakespeare's time? Don't forget that a woman, Elizabeth I, ruled England.

a) Read the articles about women in Shakespeare's time below. One of you reads text A, the other one text B. Sum up the main arguments of your text and then present them to your partner.

b) Compare the role of women in Shakespeare's time to that of women in Britain today. You can use some of these words and phrases

> as to | whereas | while | similarly | in contrast to | unlike | compared to | in comparison with

A Audience and social attitudes: Women

In Elizabethan times women belonged to their fathers (or their brothers if their father died), and then to their husbands. Women could not own property of their own. This is one of the reasons Queen Elizabeth never
5 married – she did not want to give up her power to a man.
The only exceptions were widows – women whose husbands had died. A widow was in charge of her own life and property, but would be likely to marry again to
10 find someone to protect her and to be the legal guardian to her children.
Women were allowed to marry from the age of 12 in Shakespeare's time, but often only women from wealthy families would marry so young. In the play *Romeo and*
15 *Juliet*, Juliet is 13, but her mother says by that age she was already married with a child. Many marriages were arranged for the good of the family and small children might be "betrothed"[1] to each other in order to join the families together before they were old enough to get
20 married. Many women did not marry until their mid-20s. Men had to be able to support a household when they married. [...]

Annotations
[1] **betrothed** = promised

B Shakespeare's presentation of women
by Lee Jamieson , 4 August 2017

Shakespeare's presentation of women in his plays demonstrates his feelings about women and their roles in society. [...]
It's well known that women weren't allowed on the stage
5 during Shakespeare's active years. All of his famous female roles like Desdemona and Juliet were in fact once played by men!
Women in Shakespeare's plays are often underestimated. While they were clearly restricted by their social roles, the
10 Bard showed how women could influence the men around them. His plays showed the difference in expectations between upper and lower class women of the time. High-born women are presented as "possessions" to be passed between fathers and husbands. In most cases, they
15 are socially restricted and unable to explore the world around them without chaperones[1]. Many of these women were coerced[2] and controlled by the men in their lives. Lower-born women were allowed more freedom in their actions precisely because they are seen as less important
20 than higher-born women.

Annotations
[1] **chaperone** = older woman who accompanies a younger unmarried woman to keep an eye on her
[2] **to coerce** = to force

The role(s) of women in *Hamlet*

1

Some critics claim that Gertrude's character raises more questions than it answers.

a) **Group work (4)** Study the extracts labelled *The role(s) of women* on pages 20/21, 22, 40/41, 58-60, 81, 93-97, 110-116, 121, 150 and 182/183 of your *Hamlet* edition. Choose one of the questions below and discuss it in your group. Try to find evidence from the play to prove your ideas. Then present your results in class.

   1. Did Gertrude have an affair with Claudius before her first husband's death?
   2. Did she love her first husband?
   3. Does she know about the plots Claudius is involved in?
   4. Did she marry Claudius for love, or did she just want to keep her social position?
   5. Does she believe her son, or does she think he is mad?
   6. Does she think critically about her own actions and situation?

b) Pair work One of you takes Gertrude's role shortly after she got married to Claudius. The other one is the psychiatrist who wants to find out about her feelings, desires and fears. Use the questions below to prepare a scene showing this meeting between Gertrude and her psychiatrist.

- What is Gertrude's present situation like?
- What does Gertrude know about Claudius?
- How does she feel about him?
- Does she love or loathe him?
- What does this feeling mean to her?
- How does she envision her future life with Claudius?
- What kind of relationship does she have to her son?
- What are her greatest hopes and fears?

c) Act out the scene in front of the class.

2

Hot seat Study the extracts labelled *The role(s) of women* on pages 20/21, 22, 58-60, 81, 110-116, 121, 150 and 182/183. Then prepare a hot seat: One student steps into the role of Gertrude, another into the role of Hamlet. The other students ask them questions about their relationship.

3

Ophelia is often portrayed as a passive victim, whom men tell what to do.

a) Study the extracts labelled *The role(s) of women* on pages 29/30, 31/32, 51/52, 58-60, 81, 82-34, 93-97, 136-138, 141/142 and 154/155 of your *Hamlet* edition. Then analyse Ophelia's relationships to the three men. Use the grid for your findings.

Language support

obedient | passive | to keep quiet about | submissive | patient | meek | lamblike | deferential | docile | long-suffering | affectionate | grief-stricken | hurt | dutiful

Polonius	
Laertes	
Hamlet	

b) Study the photos carefully. Choose an actress that fits your idea of Ophelia best. Explain your decision.

Helen Mirren (1970)

Joanne Pearce (1992)

Daisy Ridley (2018)

Natalie Simpson (2016)

c) **Pair work** Imagine you were a director and had to re-interpret Ophelia's role for today's audiences. Would she still be passive and obedient or rather emancipated and self-confident? Rewrite a scene with Ophelia, in which her more modern personality comes across. Then act out the scene.

4

Some scholars claim that the women in *Hamlet* are all powerless victims. Considering your findings from the previous tasks, discuss this claim.

Questions of morality

1   CHOOSE   **Pair work**

1   Have you ever thought about taking revenge? Where does revenge still take place? Can taking revenge ever be justified? Discuss these questions with a partner.
2   Find out what different legal systems and holy books of different religions say about taking revenge.
3   Present your findings to the class.
4   Is your motto "An eye for an eye" or rather "Turn the other cheek"? Explain.

OR

1   Have you ever thought about deceiving someone? In which areas does deception play a role? Is deception always negative? Discuss these questions with a partner.
2   Find out what different legal systems and holy books of different religions say about deceiving people.
3   Present your findings to the class.
4   Can a white lie be justified? Explain your view.

2

Although the Elizabethans regarded revenge as a crime and a sin and the revenger's soul was believed to be condemned to eternal torment, the genre of revenge tragedy was immensely popular during Shakespeare's lifetime.

a) Read the info box about revenge tragedies and apply the characteristics to *Hamlet*. Give evidence from the play.

Info

Revenge tragedy

The earliest English revenge tragedy, *The Spanish Tragedy*, was written by Thomas Kyd around 1582. Other well-known revenge tragedies are Christopher Marlowe's *The Jew of Malta* (1589–90), William Shakespeare's *Titus Andronicus* (1588) and Thomas Middleton's *The Revenger's Tragedy* (around 1606).
The most common characteristics of a revenge tragedy are:

1. a play-within-a-play
2. madness
3. the supernatural (e.g. a ghost who forces the protagonist to avenge his death)
4. disguises
5. violent murders
6. a once-noble protagonist who degenerates
7. complex plotting
8. hesitant behaviour
9. the display of melancholy
10. a fifth act in which many characters are killed

---

b) EXTRA Research the revenge tragedies mentioned in the info box. Give a brief outline of the respective plays and compare them to Hamlet: Where do they show similarities and where do they differ?
c) Talk about how the different characteristics of a revenge tragedy can be used to explore the questions of morality in Hamlet.

3

Use the information from the info box to show to what extent Hamlet or another character from the play can be called a tragic hero. Give evidence from the play.

Info

Tragedy

According to the Greek philosopher Aristotle (384–322 BC), a tragedy is a play that possesses magnitude and imitates events that evoke pity and fear. Its plot is complex, involving reversal (a changing situation) and recognition (a change from ignorance to knowledge).
The tragic hero is not of outstanding moral excellence but is held in great esteem and enjoys great fortune. He is nobler and more refined than ordinary people. The change to bad fortune that he must undergo is the result of an error of some kind (Greek: *hamartia*). This error has been interpreted in different ways. Some modern scholars call it a moral flaw or tragic flaw, others, however, interpret it as an intellectual error made in ignorance or through misjudgement, a misinterpretation of the circumstances.

4

a) Read the extracts of the play that are labelled *Questions of morality* in your *Hamlet* edition. You find them on pages 19, 22, 39-42, 55/56, 62-64, 71/72, 82, 107/108, 110-113, 114-116, 132/133, 139-141, 151/152, 153/154, 173-175, 179/180, 180/181 and 182-185. Then use the grid to collect information on the different characters regarding the various aspects of morality of the play. Use the last column to analyse another character that you consider relevant in this regard.

	Hamlet	Claudius	Gertrude	
moral/ immoral behaviour				
reasons for revenge				
examples of betrayal and deception				
moral principles/ attitude towards morality				

b) Rank the different characters according to a scale ranging from 1 (morally good) to 6 (morally bad) and explain your decisions.

c) Explain the functions of these characters and their moral attitudes for the play.

d) Compare Hamlet, Laertes and Fortinbras in terms of the ways they deal with their desire for revenge.

e) EXTRA **Group work (5)** Host a talk show. Each of you plays a character you have analysed in a) and b) and one of you acts as the talk show host. The host and the other students from your class as the audience can ask the characters questions about their moral principles.

5

Thinking hats discussion Imagine: shortly before the fencing match is arranged, Hamlet contemplates his options. Discuss the following question: should Hamlet take revenge?

a) **Group work (3-5): Think-pair-share** Form 6 groups. Each group considers the problem from a different point of view.

white 🎩	yellow 🎩	black 🎩	red 🎩	green 🎩	blue 🎩
neutral What are the facts and figures?	**optimist** What are positive aspects?	**pessimist** What is wrong with the idea?	**emotional** How do I feel about this?	**creative** What alternatives do I have?	**organizing** What steps must I take?

1 Think: On your own, consider the problem and take some notes.
2 Pair: Exchange your ideas and prepare a short presentation to give to the group.
3 Share: Share your ideas within your group.

b) Stage the thinking hats discussion.

6

Write an essay on one of these topics. Refer to extracts from the play where appropriate.
- How does Shakespeare point out the ethical implications of taking revenge in *Hamlet*?
- When trying to find out the truth about a crime, does this end justify all means?
- Does revenge pay?
- Can betrayal or deception ever be justified?
- Is Hamlet too good to live in this world? Do his noble qualities and his sensitivity lead to his downfall?

Copyrights

TEXTQUELLEN

20 "A Horror Story [..] creator", The Editors of Encyclopaedia Britannica. https://www.britannica.com/art/horror-story, 30.03.2020.

21 "The role of ethics in science [...]" by Anthony Carpi, Anne E. Egger, Vision learning. https://www.visionlearning.com/en/library/Process-of-Science/49/Scientific-Ethics/161, 30.03.2020.

22 f. "Pro und Contra von 'Frankenfood'" by Volkart Wildermuth, Deutschlandfunk, https://www.deutschlandfunk.de/pro-und-contra-von-frankenfood.676 de.html?dram:article_id=23464, 30.03.2020.

24 ff. "'Frankenstein' Reflects the Hopes and Fears of Every Scientific Era" by Philip Ball, The Atlantic, 20.04.2017. From The Atlantic. © 2020 The Atlantic Monthly Group, LLC. All rights reserved. Used under license.

28 "Romanticism", 4thestate.co.uk. https://britannica.com/art/Romanticism, 30.03.2020.

30 f. "The theme of isolation ...", San Francisco: Fandom.com, https://mary-shelly.fandom.com/wiki/Isolation_and_Community, 30.03.2020.

34 f. "Burmese days" by George Orwell. London: Penguin Classics, 2001.

35 ff. "Immigration to Britain" by The National Archives, Richmond: The National Archives. http://www.nationalarchives.gov.uk/pathways/citizenship/brave_new_world/immigration.htm, 30.03.2020.

39 ff. "The Third and Final Continent" by Jhumpa Lahiri, The interpreter of maladies. London: Fourth Estate, 2014.

48 "Arranged marriage", Luxembourg: Erycia, http://www.youthinformation.com/Templates/Internal.asp?NodeID=90221, 30.03.2020

50 f. "It almost passes belief ...", The Telegraph, 1968. https://www.telegraph.co.uk/comment/3643823/Enoch-Powells-Rivers-of-Blood-speech.html.

52 ff. "The escape" by Quaisra Shaharaz, London: HopeRoad Publishing.

63 ff. "Loose Change" by Andrea Levy, in: Barbara Korte & Eva Ulrike Pirker (eds.): Britain Rewritten: Stories of a Multi-Ethnic Nation (pp. 42-53), Stuttgart: Reclam Fremdsprachentexte.

71 ff. "The Rain Missed My Face and Fell Straight to My Shoes" by Saeed Taji Farouky, in: Barbara Korte & Eva Ulrike Pirker (eds.): Britain Rewritten: Stories of a Multi-Ethnic Nation (pp. 128-146), Stuttgart: Reclam Fremdsprachentexte.

79 ff. "She Shall Not Be Moved" by Shereen Pandit, in: Barbara Korte & Eva Ulrike Pirker (eds.): Britain Rewritten: Stories of a Multi-Ethnic Nation (pp. 128-146), Stuttgart: Reclam Fremdsprachentexte.

85 "First they came for the Communists ..." by Martin Niemoller, England: Holocaust Memorial Trust. https://www.hmd.org.uk/resource/first-they-came-by-pastor-martin-niemoller/, 22.03.2020.

86 f. "Our Grandmothers" by Maya Angelou, in: I shall not be moved, London: Random House, 1990.

88 "What is Zivilcourage? Definition, Explication and Classification of a Complex Construct" by Silvia Osswald, Tobias Greitemeyer, Peter Fischer, Dieter Fre, in: Cindy Pure & Shane Lopez (eds.): Psychology of Courage (pp. 149-164). Washington: American Psychological Association, 2010.

89 "Zivilcourage: Einschreiten – oder nicht?" by Vivian Alterauge, DER SPIEGEL (online). https://www.spiegel.de/panorama/gesellschaft/zivilcourage-so-sollten-sie-reagieren-das-sollten-sie-vermeiden-a-1007508.html, 11.12.2014.

92 "Post-colonial literature" by Christopher O'Reilly, Cambridge University Press, 2001.

92 "The study of the cultures of countries", Oxford University Press. https://www.oxfordreference.com/view/10.1093/acref/9780199587261.001.0001/acref-9780199587261-e-0543, 25.03.2020.

92 "Postcolonialism also often involves ..." by Prof. Ato Quayson, The British Academy, 2001.

92 "In many works of literature" by Gianna Wilkerson, Study.com. https://study.com/academy/lesson/post-colonialism-in-literature-definition-theory-examples.html, 30.03.2020.

93 f. "My family moved from Pakistan to the UK 40 years ago – how far we've come" by Sarfraz Manzoora, The Guardian © Guardian News & Media Ltd 2021.

96 "How is it possible ..." by Abdelrahman Munif, San Francisco: Goodreads. www.goodreads.com/quotes/tag/displacement, 30.03.2020.

96 "Mingling with the remains of the plane" by Salman Rushdie, The Satanic Verses, Viking, 1989.

96 "The fish ..." by Mourid Barghouti, San Francisco: Goodreads. www.goodreads.com/quotes/tag/displacement, 30.03.2020.

96 "In Sri Lanka ..." by Nayomi Munaweera, San Francisco: Goodreads. www.goodreads.com/quotes/tag/displacement, 30.03.2020.

96 f. "Home" by Warsan Shire, Brookline: Facing History. https://www.facinghistory.org/standing-up-hatred-intolerance/warsan-shire-home, 30.03.2020.

98 "In an interview after she won ...", Brookline: Facing History. https://www.facinghistory.org/standing-up-hatred-intolerance/warsan-shire-home, 30.03.2020.

105 "A "culture clash" is a conflict ...", Oakland: Ask Media Group. https://www.reference.com/world-view/culture-clash-9e8e1d8ba1b567b9, 30.03.2020.

105 "Culture and Culture Clash: What is Culture?" by Nihal Adler, in: Zeitschrift Praxis English (pp. 6-8), Westermann Gruppe, 2007.

106 f. "Detroit, Michigan", World Population Review. http://worldpopulationreview.com/us-cities/detroit-population/.

109 "Some examples of genres", in: Klein, U. & Gabriele Kugler-Euerle (eds.): Einfach Englisch: Gran Torino verstehen (p. 7f.), Braunschweig: Schöningh/Westermann, 2019.

117 f. "Movie script Gran Torino: Scene: Sue invites Walt to their barbacue" by Nick Schenk, The Internet Movie Script Database (eds.): Gran Torino (min. 40:40-52:10), Warner Bros, 2008.

119 "Gran Torino" Text, (OT) Cullum, James / Eastwood, Clint / Eastwood, Kyle / Stevens, Michael Christopher Copyright Cibie Music / EMI Music Publishing Ltd / Robie Springs Music / Upward and onward / Wallet Music / Warner Olive Music LLC / Warner-Barham Music LLC Neue Welt Musikverlag GmbH, Hamburg / EMI Music Publishing Germany GmbH, Berlin / Universal Music Publishing GmbH, Berlin

119 "In the closing scenes of Clint Eastwood's ..." by John Heitmann, The Gran Torino, Warner Bros, 2008. https://automobileandamericanlife.blogspot.com/2011/12/clint-eastwoods-gran-torino-its-meaning.html, 30.03.2020.

120 f. "Movie script Gran Torino: Scene: Walt and Sue in the car on their way home" by Nick Schenk, The Internet Movie Script Database (eds.: Gran Torino (min. 36:16-38:23), Warner Bros, 2008.

121 "Overcome culture shock in a foreign country", wikiHow, 2019. https://www.wikihow.com/Overcome-Culture-Shock-in-a-Foreign-Country, 30.03.2020.

123 "Racism Without Racists" by Eduardo Bonvilla-Silva, Lanham: Rowman & Littlefield, 2003.

124 "Movie script Gran Torino: Scene: Patio scene" by Nick Schenk, The Internet Movie Script Database (eds.): Gran Torino (min. 36:16-38:23), Warner Bros, 2008.

127 "Violence and Truth in Clint Eastwood's Gran Torino" by Antonio Machuco, in: Anthropoetics XVI, no. 2 Spring 2011, Universidade do Porto, Portugal.

131 f. "Die Gang als Familienersatz" by Matthias Korfmann, in: Westdeutsche Allgemeine Zeitung, 2013.

132 "Gun Policy", Quote by Clint Eastwood, https://www.reddit.com/r/funny/comments/178bpp/clint_eastwood_and_i_have_similar_views_on_gun/, 27.01.2020.

133 f. "In der Schule, an der Uni, 21 Tote in 45 Tagen" by Silke Fokken, DER SPIEGEL, 15.02.2018. https://www.spiegel.de/panorama/justiz/usa-traurige-statistik-zu-waffengewalt-an-schulen-a-1193644.html.

135 "Bandenkrieg im Kölner Rockermilieu", in: Märkische Allgemeine Zeitung, 09.01.2019. © dpa

137 "Movie script Gran Torino: Scene: Sue and her boyfriend Trey meet members of the black gang" by Nick Schenk, The Internet Movie Script Database (eds.): Gran Torino (min. 40:40-52:10), Warner Bros, 2008.

168 "Problem of moral responsibility" by Peter Singer & Maya Eddon, Encyclopaedia Britannica, London: Britannica Group.

174 "Audience and social attitudes: Women", London: BBC.

174 "Shakespeare's Presentation of Women" by Lee Jamieson, Roles of Women in Shakespeare's Plays, New York. Dotdash, 2019.

BILDQUELLEN